Welcome to the fifth edition of the

Cheltenham Festival Stallion Guide

Introduction from the Author – James Iddiols

When it comes to the Cheltenham Festival, there is compelling evidence that a horse's breeding is a critical factor when it comes to picking winners. This Guide delivers fascinating observations through analysis of each stallion's festival record based upon the performance and results of that sire's offspring over previous festivals, culminating in an intelligent assessment of the progeny's chances of success at the forthcoming Cheltenham Festival. History has shown us that the progeny of some stallions perform creditably at the festival time and time again, whereas others consistently struggle. Here are some examples:

- Backing **Shantou**'s progeny blind at level stakes has resulted in a profit for the past six festivals.
- Backing every horse by **Saddler Maker** in a 2½m festival race has delivered a top three finish on 7 out of 8 occasions.
- Two thirds of **Germany**'s offspring that have gone to Cheltenham have been festival winners.
- One in every three bets on **Milan**'s festival runners will provide a win or a place.
- 10 of 11 festival runners by **Network** priced at 16/1 or shorter have finished in the first six positions.
- There has been a festival winner sired by **Robin Des Champs** at the past 10 Festivals.
- 21 of the last 25 festival runners by **Definite Article** have finished outside of the top ten places.

The Guide's central theme is how the offspring of particular stallions perform at Cheltenham Festivals, but the book delivers so much more, including the low-down on some of the festival's leading contenders, emotional memories of previous meetings, and recommendations on betting strategies.

As it rained and snowed in the build-up to last year's Cheltenham Festival, I must admit that I was rather concerned how results would be affected. This Guide is all about the trends of a stallion's offspring when racing in early spring, on a left-handed, galloping, undulating and testing track, where the atmosphere is electric and where the going is typically 'good' or 'good to soft', and not where the going reads as 'soft' or 'heavy'. My overall summation is that results were impacted by the going, although only marginally. Without doubt, some horses perform better in certain conditions than others, but nevertheless, if a high quality racehorse has been trained to its peak condition and is better than its rivals, then there is a strong possibility that the horse will always take the beating whatever the ground conditions.

With the going at last year's meeting being highly uncommon, I looked back to see what was the official going for every festival race going back to the meeting of 2000 onwards. I also carried out an analysis to see whether any of the stallions within the Guide showed a trend of improved performances when conditions were soft or heavy. The data confirms that anything other than 'good' or 'good to soft' going for a festival race is infrequent. Preceding last year's meeting, inclusive of all 17 festivals between 2000 and 2017, there had been 420 races of which just 24 (5.7%) had been run on going officially described as soft. Nine races had taken place on going described as good to firm, and zero had been run on firm or heavy.

With just 24 previous races to look at, it was largely inconclusive as to whether any of the stallions featured in the Guide would have benefitted from the going conditions at the 2018 Cheltenham Festival, although with **Oscar**, there was a hint that softer ground may have helped the offspring. The other stallion whose stock have shown a distinct preference for soft ground (or perhaps it is torrential rain) is **Beneficial**, but this information has been provided in every Cheltenham Festival Stallion Guide going back to 2015.

Despite the highly unusual ground conditions, I was pleased that for the most part, the analysis and advice provided in last year's Guide continued to confirm that a horse's breeding is highly influential in determining trends on how that horse is likely to perform in festival races. The results from last year supported my positive views about runners sired by **Germany, Kalanisi, Milan, Network, Oscar, Robin Des Champs, Saddler Maker, Shantou** and **Vinnie Roe** as well as my negative opinion about the chances of those entries sired by **Al Namix, Definite Article, Kayf Tara** and **Montjeu.**

The 2019 Cheltenham Festival Stallion Guide features three "new entries", generally younger stallions whose offspring have started to provide some early positive or negative festival trends. The sires making their debut appearance in this year's Guide are **Dubai Destination, Great Pretender** and **Yeats.** I have also dropped eight stallions from the Guide, either because the sire is not producing the quality of offspring rated high enough to get a run at the festival or simply due to the fact that the stallion's progeny are now too old to race. The eight who have appeared in previous Stallion Guides, but are not featured in 2019 are **Astarabad, Califet, Cape Cross, Dom Alco, Dr Massini, Shirocco, Sinndar** and **Turgeon.**

463 horses took part at the 2018 Cheltenham Festival, of which 53%, or 244 runners, were sired by stallions featured in this year's Guide. For the record, a total of 699 stallions have been responsible for the 4,817 entries to have run at the festival in the past decade, and of those, 16.6% have had ten or more festival runners.

I hope you enjoy reading this year's Stallion Guide and if you have any views or comments, please feel free to contact me on Twitter @festivalsires. I wish you all an enjoyable and rewarding 2019 Cheltenham Festival.

Finally, I would like to offer a genuine and heartfelt thank you to my wife, Katherine, for her unwavering support and patience in allowing me the space and time required to write this Guide.

James Iddiols @festivalsires

Highlights from the 2018 Cheltenham Festival Stallion Guide

Quotes from the 2018 Cheltenham Festival Stallion Guide	What happened at the 2018 Cheltenham Festival?
"A **Germany** sired runner will win at this year's festival, just not *Faugheen* . No prizes for guessing my nap of the festival. It is *Samcro* "	*Samcro* won the *Ballymore Novices' Hurdle* and *Faugheen* was unplaced in *Unibet Champion Hurdle*
"With **Kalanisi**, your best chance of making money is by supporting the progeny in the festival's six contests within the 2m hurdle category"	*Kalashnikov* by **Kalanisi** finished as the runner-up in the *Sky Bet Supreme Novices' Hurdle*
"**Milan** bred runners are averaging a win or place from close to one in every three festival runs"	4 of the 13 of **Milan**'s offspring that took part at the festival were placed.
"If an **Oscar** bred is to bag a winner at the 2018 Cheltenham Festival, the trends suggest that the victory will come in one of the festival's non-handicap races"	*Kilbricken Storm* by **Oscar** won the *Albert Bartlett Novices' Hurdle* at 33/1
"Will there be a **Robin Des Champs** bred victor at the 2018 meeting, making it 10 years on the trot for the progeny to register a Cheltenham Festival winner? I wouldn't bet against it."	The **Robin Des Champs** bred *Blow By Blow* won the *Martin Pipe Conditional Jockeys' Handicap Hurdle*
"**Saddler Maker**'s progeny have so far managed to achieve five top three finishes in six festival events over a distance of 2½ miles, making the middle distance by far the most profitable for punters to follow."	Two horses by **Saddler Maker** ran in races over a distance of two and a half miles. Both horses secured a top three finish.
"**Shantou** is a classic example of a stallion whose offspring perform at Cheltenham Festivals year after year."	Blindly backing every **Shantou** bred runner at level stakes resulted in a profit yet again - for the sixth year in a row
"An each-way bet on **Vinnie Roe** sired runners towards the front of the market may well produce a pay-out"	The **Vinnie Roe** bred *Barney Dwan* (15/2) was placed in the *Close Brothers Novices' Handicap Chase*

Cheltenham Festival 2019 – Race Schedule *(as of 21st January 2019)*

Tuesday 12th March 2019	Hurdles			Chases				Bumper
	2m	2½m	3m	2m	2½m	3m	4m	2m
1.30pm The Sky Bet Supreme Novices' Hurdle Race	✓							
2.10pm The Racing Post Arkle Challenge Trophy Steeple Chase				✓				
2.50pm The Ultima Handicap Steeple Chase						✓		
3.30pm The Unibet Champion Hurdle Challenge Trophy	✓							
4.10pm The OLBG Mares' Hurdle Race		✓						
4.50pm The National Hunt (Amateur Riders' Novices' Steeple Chase) Challenge Cup							✓	
5.30pm The Close Brothers Novices' Handicap Chase					✓			

Wednesday 13th March 2019	Hurdles			Chases				Bumper
	2m	2½m	3m	2m	2½m	3m	4m	2m
1.30pm The Ballymore Novices' Hurdle Race		✓						
2.10pm The RSA Steeple Chase						✓		
2.50pm The Coral Cup Hurdle (A Handicap Hurdle Race)		✓						
3.30pm The Betway Queen Mother Champion Steeple Chase				✓				
4.10pm The Glenfarclas Cross Country Steeple Chase							✓	
4.50pm The Boodles Fred Winter Juvenile Handicap Hurdle Race	✓							
5.30pm The Weatherbys Champion Bumper (A Standard Open NH Flat Race)								✓

Thursday 14th March 2019	Hurdles			Chases				Bumper
	2m	2½m	3m	2m	2½m	3m	4m	2m
1.30pm The JLT Novices' Chase					✓			
2.10pm The Pertemps Network Final (A Handicap Hurdle Race)			✓					
2.50pm The Ryanair Steeple Chase					✓			
3.30pm The Sun Racing Stayers' Hurdle			✓					
4.10pm The Brown Advisory & Merriebelle Stable Plate (A Handicap Steeple Chase)					✓			
4.50pm The Trull House Stud Mares Novices' Hurdle	✓							
5.30pm The Fulke Walwyn Kim Muir Challenge Cup Handicap Steeple Chase						✓		

Friday 15th March 2019	Hurdles			Chases				Bumper
	2m	2½m	3m	2m	2½m	3m	4m	2m
1.30pm The JCB Triumph Hurdle	✓							
2.10pm The Randox Health County Handicap Hurdle Race	✓							
2.50pm The Albert Bartlett Novices' Hurdle Race			✓					
3.30pm The Magners Cheltenham Gold Cup						✓		
4.10pm The St. James's Place Foxhunter Steeple Chase Challenge Cup						✓		
4.50pm The Martin Pipe Conditional Jockeys' Handicap Hurdle Race		✓						
5.30pm The Johnny Henderson Grand Annual Handicap Steeple Chase Challenge Cup				✓				

Right hand columns show race categories (by race format and nearest distance to a half mile)

Contents

Introduction..1
Highlights from the 2018 Cheltenham Festival Stallion Guide 3
Cheltenham Festival 2019 – Race Schedule 4

Stallions

Al Namix 6
Authorized 9
Ballingarry 12
Beneficial 14
Definite Article..19
Dubai Destination 20
Flemensfirth 23
Galileo 27
Germany..30
Gold Well...33
Great Pretender..35
High Chaparral..38
Kalanisi 41
Kapgarde..44
Kayf Tara 48
King's Theatre..51
Martaline...58
Midnight Legend 60
Milan 62
Montjeu..66
Network 69
Old Vic 73
Oscar 77
Poliglote...82
Presenting 85
Robin Des Champs...89
Saddler Maker 92
Saint Des Saints 95
Shantou 98
Stowaway 101
Vinnie Roe 104
Voix Du Nord 106
Westerner...108
Winged Love 111
Yeats 113

Index Table by Stallion..116

Al Namix (FR)

Quote from the 2018 Cheltenham Festival Stallion Guide - "With zero wins and just three places from 23 festival appearances, it seems unlikely that **Al Namix** will go down in the record books as a stallion prolific in producing festival winners."

Al Namix (22-y-o)							
Race Format	_Miles_	_Won_	_Placed_	_Unplaced_	_Total_	_Win %_	_Place %_
	About 2m	0	2	8	10	0%	20%
Hurdles	About 2m 4f	0	0	6	6	0%	0%
	About 3m	0	1	2	3	0%	33%
	About 2m	0	0	2	2	0%	0%
Chases	About 2m 4f	0	0	2	2	0%	0%
	About 3m	0	0	3	3	0%	0%
	About 4m	0	0	2	2	0%	0%
Bumper	About 2m	0	0	0	0	-	-
Total	2009-2018	**0**	**3**	**25**	**28**	**0%**	**11%**

Fourteen horses by **Al Namix** have raced on 28 occasions at Cheltenham Festivals of which just three have achieved a place dividend. In my judgement, an 11% place strike rate is a very poor return, especially when in 10 of those 28 starts, the horses representing **Al Namix** lined up at single figure odds.

Five of the offspring competed in races at the 2018 Cheltenham Festival, none of whom delivered a return on any wagers placed upon them. _Petit Mouchoir_, making his third festival appearance, came closest when he was placed third in the _Racing Post Arkle Challenge Trophy Novices' Chase_. At festival meetings, a third place is usually good enough to pick up a dividend, but only five runners ran in last year's contest, and **Petit Mouchoir** just missed out on 2nd place when he was unable to keep at bay the staying on _Brain Power_ who secured the runner-up spot close to the finishing line. The winner, meanwhile, was miles away. _Footpad_, the 5/6 favourite won easily by 14 lengths.

It was the second time that **Petit Mouchoir** had finished in third position at a festival, as 12 months previous to his _Arkle_ appearance he had secured one of three place positions, recorded by **Al Namix**'s stock, when his bold front-running tactics were enough to take 3rd place in the 2017 _Stan James Champion Hurdle Challenge Trophy_.

The second of **Al Namix**'s representatives at last year's festival would appear in Tuesday's last race, the _Close Brothers Novices' Handicap Chase_. **Ballyhill** was considered a no-hoper when making his festival debut a year earlier in the 2017 _Martin Pipe Conditional Jockeys' Handicap Hurdle_. He lined up at a price of 80/1 and performed accordingly, always towards the rear and finishing in 19th place. Having won for the first time at _Prestbury Park_ on New Year's Day 2018, in the _BetBright Best For Festival Betting Handicap Chase_, he lined up in his second festival event at 25/1. There was to be no repeat of New Year's Day. **Ballyhill** tracked the leaders for the first part of this competitive handicap chase for novices before making a blunder at the 12th fence and then weakening to finish in 9th position.

In Thursday's penultimate event, the *Trull House Stud Mares' Novices' Hurdle*, *Willie Mullins* had four entries, one of whom was the **Al Namix** sired *Cut The Mustard* (20/1) who bowled along in front of the field for most of the race alongside second favourite *Maria's Benefit*. As expected, both runners came back to the field two hurdles from home and the 4/7 favourite, a stablemate of *Cut The Mustard*, hurtled past the pair between the last two, and won effortlessly by 18 lengths. *Cut The Mustard* (excuse the pun) couldn't cut the mustard, and finished in 6th place.

There were no surprises from the other two **Al Namix** representatives at the 2018 Cheltenham Festival, who lined up in their respective races at huge prices. *Belamix Dor* (100/1) was pulled up in the *Glenfarclas Chase* having jumped 19 of the 30 fences and *Saphir Du Rheu* (66/1) jumped 17 of 22 before he too was pulled up in the *Timico Cheltenham Gold Cup Chase*.

It was *Saphir Du Rheu*'s fifth visit to *Prestbury Park* in mid-March and the first time that he had not completed the course. His starting price was over ten times lower when he made his festival debut as the 6/1 joint favourite for the 2013 *Fred Winter Juvenile Handicap Hurdle*. Unfortunately, his performance did not match what the market expected of him, as he trailed home in 20th place out of the 24 that set off. Having missed the 2014 Cheltenham Festival, he returned two years later, this time as the outright 5/1 favourite, in the 2015 *Ladbrokes World Hurdle*. It was a good performance to finish runner-up, but unfortunately on that day, he came up against a rival, *Cole Harden*, who was having one of his best ever race days. *Saphir du Rheu* would attempt the *World Hurdle* for a second time in 2016 but could not match the previous year's effort and he ended up in sixth place some 40 lengths behind the very impressive winner, *Thistlecrack*. Two appearances in the *Gold Cup* would follow, last year's effort at 66/1 as highlighted above, being preceded by a respectable 5th placing at half those odds in 2017. After five runs at the Cheltenham Festival, *Saphir Du Rheu* can console himself that he has recorded the highest ever finishing position at a festival of all of **Al Namix**'s offspring.

Saphir Du Rheu's best ever Official Rating of 165 was over hurdles in the early part of 2015, a rating that is one below the highest ever rated horse by **Al Namix**, *Grandouet*, who is the 3rd of **Al Namix**'s stock to have achieved a festival placing. Trained by *Nicky Henderson*, *Grandouet* secured his 3rd place dividend on his festival debut in the 2011 *JCB Triumph Hurdle*. He would make two more festival appearances, falling when travelling well in the 2013 *Stan James Champion Hurdle Challenge Trophy* and twelve months later, registering a 6th place finish in the *Racing Post Arkle Challenge Trophy Chase*.

As every year passes, very little seems to change with the stock of **Al Namix**. Performances at Cheltenham never exceed expectations. Whenever the market has deemed that the horse by **Al Namix** has a reasonable chance of winning, that is, single figure odds which has been the case for 10 of the 28 festival runners to date, invariably 1/3rd of the runners will finish in the 4-5 place positions outside of the first three places; a 1/3rd will secure a place; and another 1/3rd will finish well down the field. As for the bigger priced festival runners, not one of **Al Namix**'s progeny who has lined up at 10/1 or greater has finished in the first four place positions.

If an **Al Namix** sired horse is to register a first festival winner (or another place position), then although it is marginal, the trends would suggest that it will most likely occur in a two mile hurdle race, where so far, the progeny have registered four top six finishes, including two place positions. Two horses by **Al Namix** that may have the career profile to perhaps secure a place position in a two mile hurdle event at the festival are *Elixir De Nutz* and *Al Dancer*.

The five year-old, *Elixir De Nutz*, is trained by *Colin Tizzard* and has won his last three novice hurdles, including the Grade 2 *Sharp Novices' Hurdle* at Cheltenham's November meeting and the *Unibet*

Tolworth Novices' Hurdle at *Sandown* on 5th January. Historically both these races have been a relatively poor guide to picking the winner of the Cheltenham Festival's opener, the *Sky Bet Supreme Novices' Hurdle*, but last year's winner, *Summerville Boy* contested both events, winning the *Tolworth* and finishing 2nd in the *Sharp Novices'* contest. At the time of writing, **Elixir De Nutz** can be backed for the *Supreme* at around the 12/1 mark.

Al Dancer is a year older than **Elixir De Nutz** and trained by *Nigel Twiston-Davies*. The grey gelding has had three hurdle starts and won all three of them, the most valuable being an 11 length victory at Cheltenham in the *Catesby Handicap Hurdle*. **Al Dancer** is due to race in the *Betfair Handicap Hurdle* at *Newbury* on 9th February after this Guide has gone to press. He also holds an entry in the festival's *Supreme Novices' Hurdle* and like **Elixir De Nutz** is a general 12/1 chance.

Should either **Elixir De Nutz** or **Al Dancer** run at the festival, perhaps they can help to bring about an improvement in the festival results of **Al Namix**'s progeny. However, I would suggest that both runners are more likely to fall in line with the profile of most of the other **Al Namix** bred festival contenders, and finish just outside the places. On the basis that betting £1.00 each way blind to level stakes on all 28 festival appearances from **Al Namix**'s offspring to date would have resulted in losses of £49.50, there can be only one recommendation. Ignore runners by **Al Namix** at the 2019 Cheltenham Festival.

Authorized (IRE)

Quote from the 2018 Cheltenham Festival Stallion Guide - "Had one backed just **Tiger Roll** and **Nichols Canyon** at previous festivals, the profit to a £1.00 each-way stake would be £41.40. Backing every other **Authorized** sired festival runner, without **Tiger Roll** and **Nichols Canyon** to the same stake would result in a loss of £18.75."

Race Format	*Miles*	*Won*	*Placed*	*Unplaced*	*Total*	*Win %*	*Place %*
Hurdles	About 2m	1	2	10	13	8%	23%
	About 2m 4f	0	1	2	3	0%	33%
	About 3m	1	0	2	3	33%	33%
Chases	About 2m	0	0	0	0	-	-
	About 2m 4f	0	0	1	1	0%	0%
	About 3m	0	0	0	0	-	-
	About 4m	2	0	0	2	100%	100%
Bumper	About 2m	0	0	1	1	0%	0%
Total	2009-2018	**4**	**3**	**16**	**23**	**17%**	**30%**

Table title: Authorized (15-y-o)

I'm a little concerned that at next year's Cheltenham Festival, there will be a scarcity of **Authorized** sired entries. There may be a couple of older horses by **Authorized** entered in a handicap event, but I can't see any of them troubling the judge. And it may be the case that **Authorized** is represented by one or two juveniles in either the *Triumph Hurdle* or the *Fred Winter*, but unless any of these youngsters make a mark after this Guide has gone to print, I don't believe we will have any winning 4 year-olds from this stallion either. I guess supporters of this stallion have one consolation. **Tiger Roll**.

To me, before his victory in the 2017 *JT McNamara National Hunt Challenge Cup Amateur Riders' Novices' Chase*, **Tiger Roll** was the only one of **Authorized**'s offspring who had won a Cheltenham Festival race, this being the 2014 *JCB Triumph Hurdle*. To jump racing fanatics, his name may also have been recognised as one of four horses who won at the 2014 Cheltenham Festival that delivered an incredible 82,653/1 four-timer for horses owned by *Gigginstown Stud*.

Today, the name of **Tiger Roll** is known the whole world over. Why? Because on 14th April 2018, this small bay gelding, who measures just 15.2 hands, jumped 30 of the biggest fences in National Hunt Racing to win the *Randox Health Grand National Handicap Chase* at *Aintree* and in front of an estimated television audience of 500 to 600 million people in over 140 countries.

Not only has this versatile little horse won the *Grand National*, he has also won three very different Cheltenham Festival races, starting with his 10/1 success in the *JCB Triumph Hurdle* over two miles in 2014. Having finished down the field at 50/1 in the 2015 *Ladbrokes World Hurdle* and then being absent at the 2016 meeting, **Tiger Roll** returned to the festival in 2017 to participate in the *JT McNamara National Hunt Challenge Cup Amateur Riders' Novices' Chase* over a distance of four miles. Under a positive ride by *Lisa O'Neill*, **Tiger Roll** went clear at the last and stayed on up the hill to win by three lengths and give his amateur jockey her first festival victory.

Last year, **Tiger Roll** was one of three horses by **Authorized** to make it to the Cheltenham Festival, and as it turned out, he was the only one that mattered. The other two **Authorized** sired horses disappointed with **Boite** finishing in 20th of 23 runners in the *Pertemps Network Final Handicap Hurdle* and **Sternrubin** taking 10th place in the *Randox Health County Handicap Hurdle*.

Having raced in hurdle races of two miles and three miles before trying a 4m chase, connections decided to go for something different again, this time the *Glenfarclas Cross-Country Chase* over 3m6f. With **Tiger Roll**, at Cheltenham, he doesn't seem to care about the race conditions or distance. He puts his heart and soul into the race and invariably wins; as he did in this race to secure his third festival triumph. Lining up at a price of 7/1, he took up the running before the runners entered the racecourse proper, and although there was a strong challenge by *Urgent De Gregaine*, **Tiger Roll** held him off to win by two lengths. Just over four weeks later and **Tiger Roll** won the *Grand National*; and stardom.

It is really difficult to win a *Grand National* for two years in succession. It has happened twice in the last 100 years. *Reynoldstown* managed it in 1935 and 1936 followed by *Red Rum* in the early seventies. What about **Tiger Roll**? Can he achieve it? Doubtful maybe, but I think he has a better chance than most. An easier 'double' would be the 2019 *Glenfarclas Chase* for which **Tiger Roll** is the current favourite at 5/2. That said, in 14 renewals of this race, only *Garde Champetre* has managed to retain his title the following season. *Balthazar King* has also won the prize twice, but not in successive years. I think **Tiger Roll** has a great chance of making it four festival wins this spring, that's for sure.

As each year passes and I carry out my festival analysis of **Authorized**'s offspring, I am beginning to reach the conclusion that **Authorized** has sired two exceptional horses for National Hunt Racing whilst the rest of his progeny have been largely ineffective. **Tiger Roll** has won three races out of his four festival appearances and the other **Authorized** sired horse to deliver festival success is **Nichols Canyon**. Trained by *Willie Mullins*, **Nichols Canyon** secured 3rd place finishes on his first two festival appearances, the first in the 2015 renewal of the *Neptune Investment Management Novices' Hurdle*, and on the second occasion when a 15/2 chance in the 2016 *Stan James Champion Hurdle Challenge Trophy*. The third Cheltenham Festival contest for **Nichols Canyon** turned out to be his best performance as he came from off the pace to win the 2017 *Sun Bets Stayers' Hurdle* at 10/1. Tragically, later in that year, on 28th December, **Nichols Canyon** suffered a fatal fall in what was his 20th race over hurdles whilst racing in the *Squared Financial Christmas Hurdle* at *Leopardstown*. It was the third time in seven runs at *Leopardstown* where he had parted company with his jockey. In his other seventeen races, **Nichols Canyon** had never finished outside the front three.

The table at the top of this chapter reads well showing a win strike rate of 17% and a win/place strike rate of 30%. But let's take out the two exceptional horses by **Authorized** that are **Tiger Roll** and **Nichols Canyon**, and see what remains.

Authorized (15-y-o)							
Race Format	Miles	*Won*	*Placed*	*Unplaced*	*Total*	*Win %*	*Place %*
Total	2009-2018	**0**	**1**	**15**	**16**	**0%**	**6%**

Not much is the answer. Twelve horses by **Authorized** are responsible for the 16 festival outings as shown in the above table. The one placed position was achieved by **Sternrubin** who finished 3rd at 33/1 in the 2016 *Vincent O'Brien County Handicap Hurdle*. And he is quite an exception, because the vast majority of the other runs resulted in the horse by **Authorized** finishing towards the back of the field. Here are those 16 finishing places in chronological order: 5 12 18 15 14 6 13 13 3 18 10 12 10 19 20 10.

As implied right at the start of this chapter, I am not overly enamoured by the current crop of **Authorized**'s progeny. I can't see any of the older horses hitting a top ten position, let alone a win or place, and as for the juveniles by **Authorized**, they need to achieve something during February. To that end, keep an eye out for any February victories from the likes of *Authorizo*, *Maze Runner*, *Runrized* and *Surin*.

It is worth noting that after this Guide has gone to print, *Surin* is scheduled to run in the *Tattersalls Ireland Spring Juvenile Hurdle* at *Leopardstown* which historically has been an excellent Guide for picking out the winner of the *JCB Triumph Hurdle*. Five of the last seven winners of the *Triumph* had finished in the first 4 places of the *Leopardstown Spring Hurdle* and last year the *Spring Hurdle*'s first two home also finished 1-2 in the *Triumph*, albeit in reverse order.

In conclusion, as of today, the only one of **Authorized**'s offspring that gets me buzzing is *Tiger Roll*.

Ballingarry (IRE)

Quote from the 2018 Cheltenham Festival Stallion Guide - "With a disappointing turn-out of only two **Ballingarry** bred runners at last year's meeting and a total of just fourteen appearances on which to build any sort of analysis, I recommend a watching brief on the offspring until some meaningful trends emerge."

Ballingarry (20-y-o)

Race Format	Miles	Won	Placed	Unplaced	Total	Win %	Place %
Hurdles	About 2m	1	1	1	3	33%	67%
	About 2m 4f	0	0	6	6	0%	0%
	About 3m	0	0	2	2	0%	0%
Chases	About 2m	0	0	0	0	-	-
	About 2m 4f	0	1	1	2	0%	50%
	About 3m	0	0	3	3	0%	0%
	About 4m	0	0	0	0	-	-
Bumper	About 2m	0	0	0	0	-	-
Total	2009-2018	**1**	**2**	**13**	**16**	**6%**	**19%**

It's all quiet on the **Ballingarry** front. For the second year in succession, only two of this stallion's progeny would make it to the Cheltenham Festival, neither of whom made any impact. The same result as in 2017. Despite rather limited data upon which to determine any significant recommendations, I included **Ballingarry** in the Stallion Guide in 2017 as a result of a victory, a place dividend and a 33/1 fifth placing from four **Ballingarry** sired runners at the 2016 Cheltenham Festival. If the trend of the past two festivals continues, that is, just a couple of 'also-ran' entries make it to the festival, than this sire, unfortunately, won't make it into next year's Guide.

The two horses by **Ballingarry** to appear at the 2018 Cheltenham Festival were *Aubusson* and *Ahead Of The Curve*. The latter is trained by *Susan Corbett* in Northumberland and her 200/1 chance made the journey down south to clear four flights in the *Ballymore Novices' Hurdle* before being pulled up. *Aubusson* lined up in the *Fulke Walwyn Kim Muir Challenge Cup Amateur Riders' Handicap Chase* at the much shorter price of 12/1, but failed to sparkle, making some headway just after half-way before weakening in the second half of the race and eventually recording a 10th place finish.

The primary reason why I have kept **Ballingarry** in this year's Guide is in the hope that the stallion produces one or more four year-old juveniles. This is on the basis that the sole festival winner of **Ballingarry**'s stock is *Diego Du Charmil*, who at 13/2, just held on by a head from *Romain De Senam* in the 2016 *Fred Winter Juvenile Handicap Hurdle*. It was the second time that trainer *Paul Nicholls* was represented by a **Ballingarry** sired runner in this event for four year olds, as two years previously, he had entered the *Graham Wylie* owned, *Katgary*, who put in a gallant effort to finish runner-up behind 33/1 outsider *Hawk High*.

With the exception of the *Fred Winter Juvenile Handicap Hurdle* event, the only other race to note is the 2016 *Brown Advisory & Merriebelle Stable Plate*, as it is the only other event in which **Ballingarry**'s progeny has recorded a place dividend, courtesy of *Full Shift* who stayed on from the last to earn a 4th place dividend at a price of 7/1.

In early to mid-January, it is hugely difficult to have a clear picture as to which horses are going to make it to Cheltenham in March, especially in the lower grade handicaps, but the early signs aren't encouraging for festival entries by **Ballingarry**'s offspring. There are a handful of runners who could be possible entries in the Grade 1 races, but they are all big outsiders that in early January can be backed at 50/1 or more. If they line up in these events, they will almost certainly have no part to play in the finishes. A couple could be diverted into lower grade races, and there could be other entries as we approach the festival, but none of the **Ballingarry** sired horses are jumping out at me as potential festival winners.

All of which brings me back to the hope that a couple of **Ballingarry** bred juveniles come out of nowhere to make an appearance in the *Fred Winter*, a race in which the offspring have so far delivered a winner and a runner-up. Admittedly, with just two runs in this race, it is clutching at straws and wishful thinking to believe that this is 'The Race' for **Ballingarry** bred horses. Nevertheless, I will be fascinated to see what happens if this stallion can provide us with a third entry in the event. Especially, if the trainer of the **Ballingarry** bred juvenile is trained by *Paul Nicholls*. Here's hoping.

Beneficial (GB)

Quote from the 2018 Cheltenham Festival Stallion Guide - "If there is torrential rain at the festival that causes the going to be changed to soft or worse, punters should be very interested in the offspring's runners and each-way bets on them may well produce profitable rewards."

Beneficial (Died as a 23-y-o in 2013)							
Race Format	*Miles*	*Won*	*Placed*	*Unplaced*	*Total*	*Win %*	*Place %*
	About 2m	0	0	9	9	0%	0%
Hurdles	About 2m 4f	1	3	15	19	5%	21%
	About 3m	1	0	7	8	13%	13%
	About 2m	0	4	14	18	0%	22%
Chases	About 2m 4f	1	1	12	14	7%	14%
	About 3m	3	3	21	27	11%	22%
	About 4m	0	1	7	8	0%	13%
Bumper	About 2m	0	0	3	3	0%	0%
Total	2009-2018	**6**	**12**	**88**	**106**	**6%**	**17%**

In all previous editions of this Guide, **Beneficial** is the only stallion where I have highlighted that soft ground at the Cheltenham Festival will probably have a positive bearing on the performance of his offspring. So, it was hardly surprising that in the week leading up to last year's meeting, and the likelihood that the opening race at Cheltenham would most likely be heavy or soft for the first time since anyone could remember, that I received numerous correspondences referencing **Beneficial**. "Here's looking forward to a 'BENEFICIAL' festival" and "I can't wait to lump on BENEFICIAL's runners" are just two of the tweets I received in early March. The predictions about the going turned out to be correct as they set off in ground officially described as Heavy in Tuesday's opening race, the *Sky Bet Supreme Novices' Hurdle*.

For new readers to this Guide, I should provide some background as to why I have previously concluded that **Beneficial**'s progeny like soft ground. In short, I remember two very wet Friday's in fairly recent Cheltenham Festivals where there had been torrential downpours either overnight or on the Friday morning. The two Friday's in question were the 15th March 2013 and the 13th March 2015, and in analysing the results, it didn't take a rocket scientist to figure out that horses sired by **Beneficial** had performed well. In the races that took place on those two Gold Cup Fridays, a total of eleven runners by **Beneficial** lined up in miserable weather to take their chance on soft going, the ground conditions having changed considerably from the previous three days of the meeting. Had one backed all eleven of **Beneficial**'s offspring that raced over those two days, one would have made a profit of £26.40 to a £1.00 each-way stake, cheering home two winners and four others who were placed. Compare this profit with the 89 of **Beneficial** bred contenders that between 2008 and 2017 had competed in races without the benefit of heavy rain. Of these 89 festival runners, just four won and eight were placed and staking a £1.00 each-way bet on all of them blind would have delivered a rather painful £91.10 loss.

So, we return to March 2018, where **Beneficial**'s supporters were eagerly awaiting the opening day's last race, the *Close Brothers Novices' Handicap Chase*, where competing amongst the 19 runners, would be two horses by **Beneficial**, the first of the offspring to appear at the 2018 Cheltenham Festival. Looking at the connections of both runners, I was quite optimistic. *Gordon Elliott* was the trainer of the *Davy Russell* ridden, **De Plotting Shed**, who looked appropriately named, having been backed into 11/2 from an opening price of 8/1. The second of **Beneficial**'s representatives was a 10/1 chance, **Livelovelaugh**, trained by *Willie Mullins*, ridden by *Ruby Walsh* and owned by *Susannah Ricci*. Optimism turned to disappointment quite quickly as at the 6th fence, **Livelovelaugh** fell. As for **De Plotting Shed**, he was still in the race with four fences to go, but soon afterwards he was ridden, weakened quickly before being pulled up. There was always tomorrow.

Tomorrow came and went. Just the one horse by Beneficial was due to appear, the 33/1 outsider, **Abbyssial**, trained by *Willie Mullins*, and he struggled towards the business end of the race in the *Coral Cup Handicap Hurdle* and was pulled up before the last. My friend said to me, "That's three **Beneficials** so far, none of whom have crossed the finishing line!" That all changed on the Thursday, as supporters of **Beneficial** cheered on two encouraging performances. In the opening event of the day, the *JLT Novices' Chase*, sixth in the market of 9 runners at a price of 10/1, was the *Gary Moore* trained, **Benatar**. The six-year-old had won all three of his Novice Chases including the Grade 2 *Mitie Noel Novices' Chase* at *Ascot* preceding this race. Unfortunately, the occasion seemed to get to **Benatar** a little, and he pulled hard in the early stages, refusing to settle. Nevertheless, he was still in with a chance at the end of the race, disputing 2nd place approaching two out, before making a mistake at the last and not having the pace of the front two to cause them any concern. He rewarded his backers by finishing third, a very credible performance, albeit some 12 lengths behind the winner, *Shattered Love*.

Later in the day, in the third running of the *Trull House Stud Novices' Hurdle*, the odds on 4/7 favourite, *Laurina*, won incredibly easily to make it 3-3 in this race for trainer *Willie Mullins*. **Beneficial** was represented by **Maria's Benefit**, trained in Buckinghamshire by *Stuart Edmunds*. **Maria's Benefit** was a 9/2 chance, having won her previous five hurdle races, and she went for it, making all and leading alongside fellow front runner *Cut the Mustard* until two hurdles from home, after which she weakened quickly, hanging left and right before finishing outside the places in fourth.

On the final day of the meeting, three more runners by **Beneficial** took their chance and all three disappointed. **Ben Dundee** at 12/1 finished 11th in the *Randox Health County Handicap Hurdle*; **Mr Whipped** at 16/1 was pulled up in the *Albert Bartlett Novices' Hurdle*; and **Eastlake**, aged 12, and who was having his fifth run in this particular contest, finished 15th at 33/1 in the *Johnny Henderson Grand Annual Challenge Cup Handicap Chase*. **Eastlake** had finished a gallant runner-up in this race three years earlier, a race that was remembered for being *Tony McCoy*'s last festival ride.

In total, 75 of **Beneficial**'s offspring have registered 123 festival appearances, of which 106 have taken place within the past ten years. In analysing all of those 123 runs, it is very difficult to pick out any positive trends within a given race category, although the progeny of this stallion do appear to have a better record over fences. Over hurdles, the statistics show the vast majority of the progeny finishing towards the tail end of their respective races, within which there are hidden a small number of win and place positions. Take, for example, the 44 of **Beneficial**'s progeny that have appeared in the festival's hurdle events, where the vast majority have finished outside of the top ten places. Only nine of the 44 managed a top six placing, made up of two wins, a 2nd, a 3rd and five 4th place finishes, two of which were in big field handicaps providing each-way backers with a 4th place dividend.

Although the percentage strike-rate for wins, places and top 6 finishes for **Beneficial**'s stock are superior in the festival's chasing events compared to hurdles, the losses incurred if betting blind at level stakes are greater. If one had placed a £1.00 each-way bet on all 123 of **Beneficial** bred festival entries, one would have lost £27.90 in the 44 hurdle race appearances and £61.70 in the 71 chase events. To complete the picture, a loss of £13.60 would have resulted in placing the same wager on the eight horses by **Beneficial** who competed in the *Cheltenham Festival Bumper*.

From the above figures, it is clearly evident that supporting **Beneficial**'s offspring at Cheltenham Festivals is a largely unrewarding experience. Every so often, a runner by **Beneficial** will be up with the leaders as they approach the Cheltenham Hill, but it doesn't happen that often, and if it does, it is more likely to occur in the festival's chases. If we total up all the chase categories in **Beneficial**'s table of statistics, the combined win & place strike rate, which has delivered those previously highlighted losses of £61.70, is 18.3%. The strike rate for a top six finish in chase contests in which **Beneficial** has been represented is 32.4%. With regard to the smaller obstacles, the combined win & place strike rate across all hurdle distances is 13.6% and for a top six finish, 20.5%. Incidentally, if you are keen on amusing (or boring!) your friends with Cheltenham Festival trivia, here are a couple of quirky facts. In 71 festival chase events, horses by **Beneficial** have never finished in 4th place. And in 44 festival hurdle appearances, **Beneficial**'s offspring have never occupied 5th and 6th finishing positions! Fascinating – not!

It is very unlikely that anyone could persuade me to place my hard-earned cash on a **Beneficial** bred festival runner, but if a gun was put to my head, the following considerations would be at the forefront of my thinking. The starting point is to look at **Beneficial**'s current stock of horses and determine which ones, if any, have the necessary quality and class to make an impact at Cheltenham, provided that the race conditions are suitable. In looking at the current crop of **Beneficial** sired horses, my list of potential candidates and their Official Rating at the time of going to print, are *Benatar* (149), *Lady Buttons* (149), *Wenyerreadyfreddie* (148), Knocknannuss (148), *Forge Meadow* (146), *Maria's Benefit* (143) and *De Plotting Shed* (142).

My second consideration is to study the trends of the progeny's previous festival runs to see if there are any specific races or race categories, where a case could be made that runners by **Beneficial** have performed well, or at least, recorded better results than in other race categories. In all honesty, having analysed the results of **Beneficial**'s 123 festival representatives, I'm not sure that there is any evidence that this stallion's offspring have performed well in any specific race, so I am clutching at straws in advising that, potentially, punters may wish to focus their attention on three of the festival's Novice Chases. The races in question are the *JLT Novices' Chase*; the *RSA Novices' Chase*; and the *National Hunt Chase*.

In the *JLT Novices' Chase*, horses by **Beneficial** have never finished out of the first five places! Sounds great, until I advise that there have only been three appearances from the offspring! *Benefficient* won the contest at 20/1 in 2013, *Kilcrea Vale* (22/1) was 5th of six finishers in a field of 8 in 2017 and *Benatar* (10/1) claimed 3rd place in last year's race as highlighted earlier. Hardly concrete evidence! The suggestion of the *RSA Novices' Chase* is also based on flimsy evidence. Like the *JLT*, **Beneficial**'s progeny have appeared in the *RSA Novices' Chase* on three occasions, and two of the runners went off as the favourite. *Cooldine* (9/4F) won the race in 2009 and seven years later, *More Of That* (6/4F) took 3rd place. The other runner, *Annacotty* at 20/1, finished a long way back in 8th place in the 2014 renewal. As for the *National Hunt Chase* run over 4m, **Beneficial** has been represented on eight occasions, recording 5th position on three occasions and in the 2007 renewal of the race, having two runners part with their jockeys when well in contention. In that 2007 race, the *Paul Nicholls* trained *Gungadu* was the 2/1 favourite for the race and was still a narrow leader when falling two fences from home. At the other end of the market at 50/1, another runner by **Beneficial**, *Bengo I*, was prominent and still there three out, when jockey *Felix De Giles* was unseated having been hampered. The three **Beneficial** bred fifth place finishers in this race for amateur riders, were *Living Next Door* at 33/1 in 2014, *Sego Success* at 9/2 in 2015 and *A Genie In Abottle* at 4/1F in 2017.

So we now need to see if any of **Beneficial** sired horses as listed above are potential candidates for the three potential races. There have only been eight renewals of the *JLT Novices' Chase* where seven of the eight winners have been won by Irish based trainers. Every race has been won by a six or seven-year-old, rated between 144 and 155. One horse that meets two of the criteria is the *Jessica Harrington* trained **Forge Meadow**, being a seven-year-old and trained in Ireland. Her 146 rating, however, is based on her hurdles performances. She has started at shorter than 9/4 on all three of her novice chases to date but so far has failed to record a victory, which doesn't bode well for winning this particular race. Three other potential candidates are trained in Britain, **Maria's Benefit**, **Wenyerreadyfreddie** and **Knocknanuss**. At the time of writing, **Maria's Benefit** is currently entered in the *Racing Post Arkle Challenge Trophy Novices' Chase* and the *OLBG Mares' Hurdle*, so it doesn't look as if she will run in this race. Like **Forge Meadow**, she is a seven-year-old mare, so will need to match the success of *Shattered Love* in last year's running of the JLT. *Shattered Love* was the first of her sex to win a novice chase at the festival since 1995. The *Nicky Henderson* trained, **Wenyerreadyfreddie**, was pulled up in his one Novice Chase in the 2017-18 season and finished 2nd in his next chase event at *Uttoxeter* on 7th October 2018. Two victories at *Ascot* followed in November last year, so he appears to be on the right path, albeit he disappointed at Newbury in December. If he does enter the *JLT Novices' Chase*, he will be attempting to be the first 8-year-old to win the race. And if trainer *Gary Moore* decides to enter **Knocknanuss** in this event, then the **Beneficial** bred gelding will need to overcome the fact that he is even older, at nine years old. That said, like **Wenyerreadyfreddie**, he has also been putting in some encouraging performances of late. Having fallen on his debut chase, he has gone on to win both his next two outings at *Fakenham* and *Newbury*.

It is possible that one or more of the four horses highlighted above could be entered in the *RSA Novices' Chase*, where the last six winners have ran off official marks of between 144 and 158. It is also a good race for seven year old runners, as evidenced by 14 of the last 18 winners being of this age. Nevertheless, I'm not convinced that any of the four will take their chance in this event. This race requires tough horses with stamina, and at the time of writing, none of the four have so far raced as far as three miles under rules, although both **Maria's Benefit** and **Knocknanuss** won their first ever races over three miles in Maiden Point-to-Point events.

It is pointed out within the name, crystal clear, that the *National Hunt Challenge Cup Amateur Riders' Novices' Chase* is also a race for Novice Chasers! Hence, the four potential candidates by **Beneficial** for this prize have already been highlighted above. However, I very much doubt that any of them will be entered in this event. There is one other horse by **Beneficial** that could be a surprise entry, although it has to be said that I have no links whatsoever with the connections of **De Plotting Shed**, added to the fact that, at the time of writing, he isn't listed in the ante post list of runners on Oddschecker. That said, I have a respect for **De Plotting Shed**, despite the fact that he last tasted victory in a hurdle race at *Naas* on 6th November 2016. Indeed, if he turns up at the festival in whatever race, I, for one, will check him out. No doubt, many experts will be curious why I am paying **De Plotting Shed** so much respect, especially as he is by **Beneficial**. Perhaps I have lost my marbles! So what is it about **De Plotting Shed** that intrigues me?

First, he has been beaten by some very good horses. In April 2016, at *Punchestown*, he was beaten some 16 lengths in the Grade B *Coral Handicap Hurdle* by *Anibale Fly*, 3rd in last year's *Timico Cheltenham Gold Cup Chase*. Nine months later, and **De Plotting Shed** finished 5 lengths behind *Shaneshill* at *Gowran Park*, the same *Shaneshill* that has three successive Cheltenham Festival runner-up results against his name, achieved between 2014 and 2016. Then, in October 2017, **De Plotting Shed** found just one too good for him when he finished second to *Presenting Percy* in the *W.B. Gavin & Co. Irish EBF Beginners Chase* at *Galway*. For those who aren't aware, *Presenting Percy* has been to the Cheltenham Festival twice and has won on both occasions. He won the 2017

Pertemps Network Final Handicap Hurdle at 11/1, and at last year's meeting, he was the 5/2 favourite and outstanding in his victory over *Monalee* in the *RSA Insurance Novices' Chase*. Come the spring of 2019, *Presenting Percy* will almost certainly be going for a hat-trick of festival wins in the *Magners Cheltenham Gold Cup Chase*, for which, at the time of writing, he is a narrow favourite.

As well as being beaten by some very good horses over the past two years, there are some other factors that, in my mind, make ***De Plotting Shed*** an attractive betting proposition. First, despite being nine years old, he is still a novice chaser having yet to record a victory in nine races over fences, which means he is very experienced for the rough and tumble of Cheltenham. Secondly, although he disappointed in last year's *Close Brothers Novices' Handicap Chase*, it was clearly apparent from the betting before the race, that a number of punters and commentators believed that he had a good chance of victory. And although he has been disappointing over the past couple of years, his last three performances, all of which have been in 2½m hurdle events, have provided some green shoots that there may be better things to come. Last but not least, he is in the right hands. If anyone is able to get a tune out of this nine-year-old at the right time, then *Gordon Elliott* is no doubt a trainer who can succeed. It is still early days to figure out if he will appear at the 2019 Cheltenham Festival and indeed in which race, but I will keep my eye on him for sure.

We started this chapter discussing how important rain has been to this sire's offspring, and despite just one placing to show from the eight runners by **Beneficial** at last year's soft ground festival, I still consider soft going to be advantageous to the progeny. The evidence is compelling. If we divide up the 123 festival runs in which **Beneficial**'s offspring have competed, 23 of those appearances took place on soft going, in which the representatives recorded two wins and five places, which equates to a 30% win & place strike rate. Had one placed a £1.00 each-way bet on all 23 runners, a profit of £5.40 would be the result. The remaining 100 runners by **Beneficial** raced on ground that was officially declared as either good or good to soft. The losses incurred had one placed a £1.00 each-way bet on all one hundred runners would be £108.60 and a win & place strike rate of just 13%.

In summary, I am very unlikely to be supporting any runners by **Beneficial** at the 2019 Cheltenham Festival. However, if there is rain and one or more of **Beneficial**'s novice chasers impress me over the winter months, then perhaps I will put my hand in my pocket and place a bet on one of them. And I will keep a beady eye on ***De Plotting Shed***. There is something about this horse that has got under my skin. If he turns up at Cheltenham, I will just have to place a bet on him. Imagine if I don't back him and he wins!!

Definite Article (GB)

Quote from the 2018 Cheltenham Festival Stallion Guide - "In your 2018 Festival calculations, discount all entries sired by **Definite Article**."

Race Format	Miles	Won	Placed	Unplaced	Total	Win %	Place %
			Definite Article (27-y-o)				
Hurdles	About 2m	0	0	1	1	0%	0%
	About 2m 4f	0	0	2	2	0%	0%
	About 3m	0	0	5	5	0%	0%
Chases	About 2m	0	0	2	2	0%	0%
	About 2m 4f	0	0	1	1	0%	0%
	About 3m	0	0	4	4	0%	0%
	About 4m	0	0	1	1	0%	0%
Bumper	About 2m	0	0	4	4	0%	0%
Total	2009-2018	**0**	**0**	**20**	**20**	**0%**	**0%**

This chapter will be brief.

In total, there have been 34 festival appearances from **Definite Article**'s offspring, of which 20 have taken place within the past ten years. The record of **Definite Article** sired runners within the first five festivals in which they competed was very good. Out of a total of nine runs between 2002 and 2006, the progeny recorded two wins, one place, a 5th, 6th and 8th.

Since then, results have been truly abysmal. In the twelve Cheltenham Festivals from 2007 onwards, only four of the 25 **Definite Article** bred runners have registered a top ten finish; *Definity* (3/1 favourite) finished 5th in the 2011 *Centenary Novices' Handicap Chase*; *Virginia Ash* was 7th in the 2013 *Albert Bartlett Novices' Hurdle*; *Definitly Red* finished 7th in the 2014 *Weatherbys Champion Bumper*; And *Definitly Red* returned at last year's festival to finish 6th in the *Timico Cheltenham Gold Cup Chase*.

Of all the *Gold Cup* runners last year, the first horse that I struck off my list of potential winners was *Definitly Red*. I was surprised how short he was in the betting at just 8/1. It looks as if connections are going to return to Cheltenham to run him again in the 2019 *Gold Cup*. At the time of writing, if you wish, you can throw away your money by backing the horse at 25/1.

I have read that the 10 year-old's owner, *Phil Martin*, believes that *Definitly Red* is overpriced for the Festival's showpiece event. I have a message for *Phil Martin*. Forget Cheltenham and keep your horse fresh for the *Grand National* at *Aintree*, where your star chaser may have a chance.

For those who haven't got the message – forget about backing any horse by **Definite Article** at the 2019 Cheltenham Festival.

Dubai Destination (USA)

Dubai Destination was not featured in the 2018 Cheltenham Festival Stallion Guide.

Race Format	Miles	Won	Placed	Unplaced	Total	Win %	Place %
				Dubai Destination (20-y-o)			
Hurdles	About 2m	0	0	2	2	0%	0%
	About 2m 4f	0	1	4	5	0%	20%
	About 3m	0	0	1	1	0%	0%
Chases	About 2m	0	0	1	1	0%	0%
	About 2m 4f	0	0	0	0	-	-
	About 3m	0	1	0	1	0%	100%
	About 4m	0	0	0	0	-	-
Bumper	About 2m	0	0	1	1	0%	0%
Total	2009-2018	**0**	**2**	**9**	**11**	**0%**	**18%**

Dubai Destination makes it into the 2019 Cheltenham Festival Stallion Guide for the first time as a result of a couple of encouraging place performances from two of his progeny at last year's festival. The two horses in question both recorded third place finishes in Wednesday's opening two races. First up was **Next Destination** in the *Ballymore Novices' Hurdle* followed by **Elegant Escape** in the *RSA Insurance Novices' Chase*. Both horses were having their second festival outings, and arguably had provided a clue in their previous visit to Prestbury Park that better things were to come in 2018.

Next Destination, trained by *Willie Mullins*, made his festival debut in the 2017 *Weatherbys Champion Bumper*, where he stayed on well to finish in 4th place, just a neck behind the third placed horse, *Claimantakinforgan*. On the back of this encouraging performance, the horse lined up as the odds on favourite for the *Kildare Post Flat Race* at *Punchestown* towards the end of April, but was no match for the winner, *Dead Right*, and had to settle for second place. By the time **Next Destination** arrived at Cheltenham for his second festival appearance last season, he had won all three of his hurdle starts with connections hoping that the winning run would continue in the Grade 1 *Ballymore Novices' Hurdle*. To be victorious in the race would require him to overcome many people's festival banker, the *Gordon Elliott* trained and unbeaten odds-on favourite for the race, *Samcro*.

Based upon the starting prices, *Samcro*'s biggest danger was **Next Destination** who was priced up as the 4/1 second favourite, and the market wasn't too far out, with **Next Destination** finishing in 3rd place behind the 3rd favourite in the race, *Black Op* who took the runner-up spot. As for *Samcro*, he justified the pre-match hype and won quite comfortably. After the race, a few commentators suggested that **Next Destination** may have been better off contesting the 3m *Albert Bartlett Novices' Hurdle* instead, as in the *Ballymore*, he had become outpaced towards the business end of the race before staying on really well after the last and then passing three of his rivals to be rewarded with a place position.

It was hoped that **Next Destination**'s third festival appearance would be in the 2019 *RSA Novices' Chase* over three miles but sadly the *Malcolm Denmark* owned horse suffered a setback and so will miss the 2019 festival and the rest of the season. *Willie Mullins* has advised that the problem isn't serious and will be treated after which **Next Destination** will go novice chasing for the 2019-2020 National Hunt season. So, fingers crossed that we will see this talented horse at the 2020 festival.

One horse by **Dubai Destination** that we hope to see at this year's meeting is *Elegant Escape*, who at the time of writing, is priced at around 20/1 for the big one, the *Magners Cheltenham Gold Cup Chase*. There is a possibility that due to his victory in late December, in the *Coral Welsh Grand National Handicap Chase* at *Chepstow*, that connections will be tempted to forget about the festival and target all their efforts instead at *Aintree*'s 2019 *Randox Health Grand National*, for which their seven year-old is one of the leading fancies. I sincerely hope they dismiss this idea. Perhaps it will help if I advise trainer *Colin Tizzard* and connections that the last seven year-old to win the *Grand National* was *Bogskar* in 1940.

Elegant Escape has been beaten in both of his festival contests in which the victors have turned out to be two-time festival winners. In the 2017 Cheltenham Festival, *Elegant Escape* was one of four 100/1 outsiders for the *Albert Bartlett Novices' Hurdle*, and he performed best of the four anticipated no-hopers finishing in 7th position and some 26 lengths behind the 16/1 winner, *Penhill*, who picked up his second festival win in the 2018 *Sun Bets Stayers' Hurdle*.

In October 2017, *Elegant Escape* started his career as a chaser and as he lined up for the *RSA Insurance Novices' Chase* at last year's festival meeting, he had already competed in five events over the bigger obstacles, and had finished either 1st or 2nd on all occasions. In the *RSA*, he competed well although did not have the pace of the two in front of him and eventually took 3rd place having stayed on well after the last. The winner, *Presenting Percy*, was enjoying his second festival success, having won the *Pertemps Network Final Handicap Hurdle* the previous season. Provided *Elegant Escape* does appear in the *Magners Cheltenham Gold Cup Chase*, he will almost certainly be lining up with his *RSA Chase* conqueror, *Presenting Percy*, the current 3/1 favourite for the race.

If we turn to the other seven of **Dubai Destination**'s offspring that have been to the Cheltenham Festival, they have each made one appearance, and all of them disappointed with *Mischievious Max* (25/1) recording the highest placing of the septet last season when finishing in 9th place in the *Coral Cup Handicap Hurdle*. Limited data, clearly, but punters may wish to consider that the only two horses by **Dubai Destination** that put in a respectable performance on their festival debut, represented their stallion at the following year's meeting with success by claiming a place position. Remember that both *Next Destination* and *Elegant Escape* recorded a top 8 finish on their festival debuts.

An important factor to note within the analysis of races, within which horses by **Dubai Destination** are represented, is that the progeny appear to have stamina reserves enabling them to be staying on at the end of their races. Bearing this in mind, there are three horses by **Dubai Destination** that may be of interest should they make the trip to Cheltenham this coming March, these being *Kildisart*, *Roksana* and *Coole Cody*.

The last one in the list, *Coole Cody* is a relatively experienced 8-year-old who, at the time of writing, has had 13 career races under rules, of which all bar two have been over hurdles. He has won four of his eleven starts over the smaller obstacles, and his last victory in the *Martin & Co Jewellers Intermediate Handicap Hurdle* on 18th November 2017, which was his handicap debut, attracted my attention as it is the one and only time that he has raced at Cheltenham. The first two to finish in the race were both sired by **Dubai Destination**, with *Coole Cody* who jumped very well throughout the contest beating *Mischievious Max* by three lengths. Both horses stayed on up the Cheltenham Hill to reward any **Dubai Destination** Exacta backers with a dividend of £526.40 to a £1.00 stake.

This season, trainer *Michael Blake* decided to put *Coole Cody* over fences, but it didn't appear to work out, so on Boxing Day, the horse reappeared over hurdles at *Wincanton* where he finished in

6th place and some 30 lengths or more behind the winner. *Coole Cody's* next appearance will hopefully be in the *888Sport Heroes Handicap Hurdle* which is run at *Sandown* just after this publication has gone to press. This event, over a distance of almost three miles, used to be a good trial for the festival's *Pertemps Network Final Handicap Hurdle*, although in more recent years there has been less of a connection between the two. Should *Coole Cody* line up at *Sandown* and dependent upon his performance, if connections do decide to enter him in the *Pertemps Final*, then a small each-way bet on him at a big price may pay dividends. Three winners of the *Pertemps Final* in the past 18 years had previously contested the *Sandown 'Heroes'* contest, these being *Rubhahunish* who won both contests in 2000; *Oscar Park* (*Pertemps* winner 2007) finished 13th in the *'Heroes'*; and *Ballyfitz* (*Pertemps* winner 2008) finished 7th in the *'Heroes'*. Although no *Pertemps* winner has emerged from this Grade 3 *Sandown* contest over the past decade, it should be noted that the *Heroes Handicap Hurdle* was abandoned for three consecutive years between 2012 and 2014.

A year younger than *Coole Cody* is *Roksana*, an improving seven year-old mare who is trained by *Dan Skelton* in *Alcester*. It would appear that she has been kept under wraps having raced just twice last season, including a very satisfying 2nd placing behind *Santini* in the *Doom Bar Sefton Novices' Hurdle* at *Aintree's Grand National* meeting. At the time of writing, she has yet to race this year, but does hold an entry in the *888Sport Contenders Hurdle* at *Sandown* on 2nd February, a race that is at the minimum distance and almost certainly too short for her. *Roksana* is in the betting for two races at the 2019 Cheltenham Festival, the *OLBG Mares' Hurdle* (2m4f) and the *Sun Racing Stayers' Hurdle* (3m).

Also aged seven is *Kildisart*, who at the time of writing, has impressed in three chase starts and won the last two of them. As of mid-January, he is in the betting for two chases that take place on the festival's Thursday, these being the *JLT Novices' Chase* and the *Brown Advisory & Merriebelle Stable Plate*. As with the others of the progeny, he appears to be 'staying on' in his races, so I'm not sure he will have the necessary pace to trouble the leaders in either contest. Nevertheless, all three of his races to date have fallen between 2m3f and 2m5f, and the horse's trainer, the local to Cheltenham, *Ben Pauling*, will know his credentials far better than me.

In summary, 2019 is probably a year to watch horses by **Dubai Destination** rather than to bet on them, and as the common trait amongst the offspring appears to be staying power, I shall be especially interested in the performances of those competing in races of three miles and more.

Flemensfirth (USA)

Quote from the 2018 Cheltenham Festival Stallion Guide - "The last festival meeting in which supporting all of **Flemensfirth**'s stock blind would have been profitable, was the year in which *Paddy Brennan* rode **Imperial Commander** to victory over the *Paul Nicholls* trained pair of *Kauto Star* and *Denman* in what was a memorable *Totesport Cheltenham Gold Cup Chase*."

Flemensfirth (27-y-o)							
Race Format	*Miles*	*Won*	*Placed*	*Unplaced*	*Total*	*Win %*	*Place %*
Hurdles	About 2m	0	0	3	3	0%	0%
	About 2m 4f	0	4	18	22	0%	18%
	About 3m	0	2	11	13	0%	15%
Chases	About 2m	0	0	2	2	0%	0%
	About 2m 4f	1	3	11	15	7%	27%
	About 3m	1	2	22	25	4%	12%
	About 4m	0	2	12	14	0%	14%
Bumper	About 2m	1	1	8	10	10%	20%
Total	2009-2018	**3**	**14**	**87**	**104**	**3%**	**16%**

In the quote at the top of this page, I highlight that had one placed a £1.00 each-way bet on all of **Flemensfirth**'s festival runners from 2011 onwards, one would have made a loss every year. That changed at the 2018 Cheltenham Festival as a £1.00 each-way wager on all 19 of **Flemensfirth**'s representatives, would have resulted in a small profit of £2.60. The major contribution to earnings came from **Relegate**'s 25/1 success in the *Weatherbys Champion Bumper*. It was the first time that a horse by **Flemensfirth** had won a festival event since *Imperial Commander*'s *Gold Cup* success in 2010.

At the 2017 Cheltenham Festival, there were some small signals that perhaps a turnaround in performances was just around the corner. At that meeting, there were two 3rd place dividends and a 5th placing from just nine **Flemensfirth** bred runners, which although unprofitable, was certainly an improvement on the previous three years of 2014 through to 2016. In those three years, there was a total of 35 appearances from the progeny which was rewarded by just two runner-up spots and a further 30 horses that were unable to finish higher than 8th.

There was a large turnout of horses by **Flemensfirth** at last year's festival, over double the number of runners who appeared for this stallion at the 2017 meeting. Having achieved three place positions and, at long last, a festival victory from the 19 **Flemensfirth** bred runners, the record books will show that the 2018 Cheltenham Festival for **Flemensfirth** represented a 5% win rate and a 21% win & place strike rate, which is better than the strike rates achieved over the past decade. We should also note, however, that 5 of the 19 runners were pulled up in their races and a further seven finished in 10th place or worse, figures that are more in keeping with the also-rans of 2014 to 2016.

In last year's Guide, I highlighted that my favourite race of the 2017 Cheltenham Festival was the *Weatherbys Champion Bumper*, primarily because the mare *Fayonagh* was right at the back of the field and behind a wall of horses coming into the home straight, before coming from the clouds and sprinting past all her rivals to win. Somewhat bizarrely, the victory reminded me so much of how *Dancing Brave* won the 1986 *Prix de l'Arc de Triomphe*. To a degree, the style of **Relegate**'s victory in the 2018 *Weatherbys Champion Bumper* was quite similar to how *Fayonagh* had taken the prize a year earlier. Ridden by *Katie Walsh*, *Relegate* was well down the field with just over a furlong to go, when she showed a terrific turn of pace and kept on well to beat stablemate *Carefully Selected* by a neck. *Willie Mullins* entered five in the race and they all finished in the first seven positions, including the front three. Despite the fact that *Relegate* was unbeaten having won her first two National Hunt Flat races, according to the betting ring, she went off the 4th best of the quintet at a price of 25/1. There were three more **Flemensfirth** bred runners who took part in this *Bumper*, and *Willie Mullins* trained three of them. In addition to *Relegate*, he also trained the third home, *Tornado Flyer* (14/1) and *Colreevy* (50/1) who finished in 7th. *David Pipe* trained the one other horse by **Flemensfirth** who finished 14th and well behind the *Mullins* trio at a price of 20/1.

Relegate is the second **Flemensfirth** bred mare to win the *Weatherbys Champion Bumper*. Her predecessor was *Total Enjoyment*, who alongside *Major Vernon*, were the first two of **Flemensfirth**'s offspring to appear at a Cheltenham Festival, when they competed in the 2004 renewal of the race. It turned out to be a debut victory for the progeny as the *Thomas Cooper* bay mare, *Total Enjoyment*, won comfortably at odds of 7/1, ahead of the only other **Flemensfirth** bred runner of that year, *Major Vernon*, who finished 13th. Adding *Fayonagh*'s 2017 victory to the wins of the two **Flemensfirth** bred mares, means that the female sex have won three *Champion Bumpers* this century. Punters may wish to take note.

Two other place positions were registered by **Flemensfirth** representatives at last year's meeting, at odds that were not as generous as the 25/1 and 14/1 that were returned in the *Bumper* for the victory and 3rd place of *Relegate* and *Tornado Flyer* respectively. *The Last Samuri*, who finished runner-up in the 2016 *Grand National* at Aintree, was to tackle Cheltenham's Cross-Country course for the very first time in the 3m6f *Glenfarclas Chase*. Trained by *Kim Bailey*, *The Last Samuri* was well supported in the market and lined up as the 11/4 favourite. He ran well but never threatened in the closing stages, finishing in 3rd place and thirteen lengths behind the impressive *Tiger Roll*, who a month after this success, went one better than *The Last Samuri* when winning the 2018 *Randox Health Grand National Handicap Chase*.

The *Paul Nicholls* trained, *Topofthegame*, lined up in last year's *Coral Cup Handicap Hurdle* in good form, having won his previous race, the *Betfred Heroes Handicap Hurdle* at Sandown. The **Flemensfirth** sired chestnut gelding was raised 8lb as a result of that success, but he was still relatively well fancied in the market, and went off the third favourite for the race at price of 9/1. As always, it was a highly competitive contest with less than 7½ lengths covering the first 8 home. *Topofthegame* led at the last, but was headed in the final 100yards, and despite keeping on up the Cheltenham Hill, he couldn't claw back the game winner, *Bleu Berry*, and was eventually beaten by a neck.

Flemensfirth's festival runners performed exceptionally well from 2004 through to 2010, after which the wheels came off. In those first seven years in which **Flemensfirth** was represented at the festival, this stallion's offspring registered 7 winners and 8 places from just 38 festival appearances, which would have yielded a profit of £71.20 to a £1.00 each-way stake wagered on all 38 runs. In the 89 appearances since then, from the 2011 festival onwards, *Relegate* is the progeny's sole winner and there have been 11 place dividends. Backing all 89 blind to a £1.00 each-way stake would have resulted in a £97.98 loss to a £1.00 each-way stake, easily wiping out the previous seven years' worth of profit.

I would advise punters not to get carried away by last year's £2.60 profit, the result of backing at £1.00 each way, all 19 of **Flemensfirth**'s 2018 festival representatives. It was *Relegate*'s 25/1 success that accounted for the bulk of winnings, and without the victory, it would have been yet another year of significant losses. So, I am far from convinced that the tide has changed and we should all now start supporting the progeny. In my view, it is far more preferable to delve deeper into all 127 runs by this sire's offspring and to see if there is any one race category or further still, any specific races where the trends suggest that **Flemensfirth**'s runners have a greater chance of success. To that end, and as a result of **Flemensfirth** having sired three of the first seven home in last year's *Weatherbys Champion Bumper*, I thought that this would be the first race in which to start my analysis.

As we all know, a big priced winner has a huge influence on whether or not a day at the races turns out to be profitable or not, and in analysing how horses by **Flemensfirth** have performed in the festival's *Bumper*, it is no surprise to see that *Relegate*'s 25/1 success means that the *Weatherbys Champion Bumper* has been a profitable event in which supporters of **Flemensfirth** would have made money. In a total of 17 runs, the offspring has registered two victories and two place positions, which would have yielded a profit of £14.20 had one placed a £1.00 each-way stake on all seventeen runners. There may well be an angle for punters to seek out **Flemensfirth** bred mares that compete in Cheltenham's Grade 1 *Bumper*. Of the 17 National Hunt Flat Race festival competitors bred by **Flemensfirth**, only three have been mares, of which two, *Total Enjoyment* and *Relegate* as highlighted earlier, have won. *Colreevy* is the other mare by **Flemensfirth** to have raced in the *Bumper*, finishing in 7th at 50/1 last year.

Another race where horses by **Flemensfirth** have achieved success is the *Coral Cup*. Once again, a big priced winner has ensured that betting blind to a £1.00 each-way stake on all ten of **Flemensfirth**'s bred runners to compete in this event, would have resulted in profits, on this occasion, a very rewarding £34.75. The sole winner from the progeny was *Idole First*, who won the 2005 renewal of this race at a price of 33/1. Of the other nine of the offspring to have lined up in the *Coral*, three of them have finished runner-up; *Kicks for Free* at 11/1 in 2008; *Meister Eckhart* at 14/1 in 2013; and *Topofthegame* at 9/1 in 2018 as advised earlier. Although six of the runners to have raced in the *Coral Cup* have finished outside the top ten places, the fact that 2 in every 5 **Flemensfirth** bred entries in the *Coral Cup* have finished either 1st or 2nd is a highly important statistic on which to take note.

There are two other contests at the festival, where although the offspring have yet to win either event, the **Flemensfirth** bred contenders do appear to have put in a number of reasonable performances. In the race preceding Friday's *Cheltenham Gold Cup*, the *Albert Bartlett Novices' Hurdle* takes place run over a distance of three miles. Seven horses by **Flemensfirth** have competed in this event and despite just one 3rd placing to show for those efforts, when *The Midnight Club* secured 3rd place in 2009, it would be fair to say that the progeny have been up with the leaders on more occasions than not. The six most recent finishing positions and starting prices for **Flemensfirth** representatives in this race have been 3rd @ 14/1, 4th @ 9/1, 5th @ 22/1, Pulled Up @ 20/1, 4th @ 20/1 and 10th @ 10/1. The first **Flemensfirth** bred competitor in this race was *Black Harry* (13/2) who fell at the last in 2007 having just been headed by eventual winner, *Wichita Lineman*, the 11/8 favourite. Had *Black Harry* stayed on his feet, he would have been a clear second.

In Tuesday's last race, the *Close Brothers Novices' Handicap Chase*, **Flemensfirth** has been represented on seven occasions, and three of the runners picked up a third place dividend, these being *Two Taffs* at 7/1 in the 2017 renewal and *The Midnight Club* (2010) and *Ohio Gold* (2013) who both returned a price of 16/1. None of the other four **Flemensfirth** bred runners in this 2m4½f Novices' Chase was able to finish higher than tenth.

Looking at the potential candidates by **Flemensfirth** who could take their chance in this contest come March, I have identified two seven-year-old novice chasers, these being the *Paul Nicholls* trained *Topofthegame*, and *Lostintranslation*, who hails from *Colin Tizzard*'s yard in Dorset. At the time of writing, however, both horses are most likely to appear in either the *JLT Novices' Chase* or the *RSA Insurance Novices' Chase*.

Flemensfirth sired runners have shown a slight improvement in performances over the past two festival meetings, and although I am convinced that performances will not return to pre-2011 levels, where for every five of the offspring that would line up in a festival event, we would witness a victory and a place position, I will concede that horses by **Flemensfirth** do have the potential to pick up a win at the 2019 Cheltenham Festival. For those punters who are keen on a particular **Flemensfirth** sired runner come the meeting in March, I would suggest that the probability of picking up any return for your bet is greater in Tuesday's *Close Brothers Novices' Handicap Chase*, Wednesday's *Coral Cup Handicap Hurdle* and Friday's *Albert Bartlett Novices' Hurdle*.

Finally, with the female sex of **Flemensfirth**'s offspring having already picked up a couple of victories in Cheltenham's *National Hunt Flat Race*, I shall have no alternative other than to place a large bet on any **Flemensfirth** bred mare that, unlikely though it is, happens to appear amongst the list of entrants for the 2019 *Weatherbys Champion Bumper*.

Galileo (IRE)

Quote from the 2018 Cheltenham Festival Stallion Guide - "If you are keen on a **Galileo** bred festival entry, for it to have any chance of winning, make sure your pick has either an Official Flat Rating of 100 plus, or that your selection's career began in National Hunt Flat races. **Galileo**'s offspring that meet neither criterion can be safely disregarded."

Galileo (21-y-o)							
Race Format	*Miles*	*Won*	*Placed*	*Unplaced*	*Total*	*Win %*	*Place %*
Hurdles	About 2m	0	1	16	17	0%	6%
	About 2m 4f	2	0	7	9	22%	22%
	About 3m	0	2	4	6	0%	33%
Chases	About 2m	0	0	0	0	-	-
	About 2m 4f	0	0	0	0	-	-
	About 3m	0	0	0	0	-	-
	About 4m	0	0	0	0	-	-
Bumper	About 2m	0	0	2	2	0%	0%
Total	**2009-2018**	**2**	**3**	**29**	**34**	**6%**	**15%**

The current champion sire of horses that race on the Flat in Great Britain and Ireland is **Galileo**. And this superlative stallion of top class flat racehorses has held the title since 2010. So **Galileo** is clearly a stallion to follow on the Flat, but this isn't the case when it comes to National Hunt racehorses, or specifically, the Cheltenham Festival.

The two biggest money earners for **Galileo**'s progeny over the jumps have acquired more than £500,000. The horses are ***Celestial Halo*** with prize-money of £651,417 and, as of early January, earnings of £531,866 for ***Supasundae***. The next in the list, ***Shelford***, is some way behind with £152,738. It is fascinating to compare these figures with the earnings of **Galileo**'s stock on the Flat, where at the time of writing, 57 of **Galileo**'s progeny had already earned over £500,000 each.

Only one of **Galileo**'s offspring appeared at the last year's Cheltenham Festival, and it wasn't a wasted journey for the *Jessica Harrington* trained ***Supasundae***, who claimed the runner-up position at a price of 6/1 in the *Sun Bets Stayers' Hurdle*. The previous year, ***Supasundae*** had claimed a rare festival victory for **Galileo** sired runners when he won, at 16/1, the 2017 *Coral Cup Handicap Hurdle* by two lengths from the veteran *Taquin Du Seuil*.

Following last year's 2nd place finish in the *Sun Bets Stayers' Hurdle*, ***Supasundae*** had two Grade 1 races in April 2018, finishing 2nd in the *Betway Aintree Hurdle* and then going one better to win the *Betdaq 2% Commission Punchestown Champion Hurdle*. Following a well-earned rest, he raced twice in December, finishing runner-up on both occasions, first in the *baronracing.com Hatton's Grace Hurdle* at *Fairyhouse* and then at *Leopardstown* in the *Ryanair Hurdle*. *Jessica Harrington* appears to have the nine-year-old in good form and although he has an entry in the *Unibet Champion Hurdle Challenge Trophy*, I expect ***Supasundae*** to have another tilt at the *Stayers' Hurdle*. As to his chances of going one better and winning the 2019 renewal, I have my doubts, albeit that ***Supasundae***'s current official rating of 164 is higher than five of the past six winners. My biggest concern is that ***Supasundae*** has yet to win a Grade 1 or Grade 2 hurdle event further than two miles. His two victories over further than two miles were in the 2m5f Grade 3 *Coral Cup Handicap Hurdle* and a

12,300 Euros 2m4f Hurdle at Punchestown on 31st December 2016. Admittedly, he has been knocking at the door in his 3 races at three miles, all of which were Grade 1s, finishing runner-up on every occasion.

In my view, there are a number of other negative factors that work against **Supasundae** winning the *Stayers' Hurdle*. To start with, the two lowest rated winners of the *Stayers'* this century were *Solwhit* (rated 154) in 2013 and last year, when *Penhill* won with an official rating of 153. So, taking last year's race first, **Supasundae**, off a mark of 164, has already been beaten by the lowest rated winner of a *Stayers'* this century. And in 2013, one could make the case that *Solwhit* was able to win as a nine-year-old because it was arguably a weak renewal of the race. Being a nine-year-old himself, **Supasundae** will be attempting to be the fourth horse of his age group to win the *Stayers' Hurdle* this century, and the other two older winners were rated far higher than *Solwhit*. *Inglis Drever* was winning this specific contest for the third time when he won in 2008 off a mark of 172 and then along came *Big Buck's* to win the next four renewals, the last of which, when aged nine, his official rating was 174.

Supasundae may clinch a place in the *Sun Racing Stayers' Hurdle*, but I believe he is up against too many negative trends for him to win the race. And if you think, at the age of nine, he has a better chance in the *Unibet Champion Hurdle Challenge Trophy*, I suggest you think again. Only two nine-year-olds have won the *Champion Hurdle* this century – *Rooster Booster* (rated 167) in 2003 and the superb *Hurricane Fly* in 2013 who won off a mark of 172, the highest rated winner this century. **Supasundae** is nowhere near that class. It is also worth noting that six of the last eight Champion Hurdle winners were rated above **Supasundae**'s current rating of 164.

Going back briefly to Cheltenham's *Stayers' Hurdle*, it is interesting to note that the most successful of **Galileo**'s offspring (we're talking National Hunt here!) is *Celestial Halo*, who ran in a handful of 3m hurdle races, winning one of them, the *bet365 Long Distance Hurdle* at *Newbury* in November 2013. That victory was sandwiched between his two attempts at winning the *Stayers' Hurdle* at Cheltenham, which was then named the *Ladbrokes World Hurdle*. He was 10 years old on his second attempt in 2014 when he finished last of ten, but as a nine-year-old, he ran a cracker in the 2013 renewal, securing the runner-up position to the previously mentioned *Solwhit*, and at the rewarding odds of 40/1.

24 horses by **Galileo** have made a total of 36 appearances at the Cheltenham Festival, 34 of which have taken place within the past decade. Nineteen of those 24 **Galileo** sired runners made one festival appearance only, which means that five horses have made multiple festival appearances, totalling 17 runs. We can forget three of the offspring - *Fiulin* (3 runs), **Ballyglasheen** (2 runs) and **Swing Bowler** (2 runs) all failed to trouble the judge. As for the other two of the progeny, they have been the most successful. **Supasundae** has appeared at the past four festivals and, as already highlighted, has achieved one win and one placing, both of which occurred in the *Stayers' Hurdle*. Outstripping **Supasundae** in festival appearances as well as prize-money is *Celestial Halo*, who made the spring trip to Cheltenham on six occasions. *Celestial Halo* rewarded punters with winnings in half of those runs. In addition to his runner-up performance, as noted above, in the 2013 *Ladbrokes World Hurdle*, he won the 2008 *JCB Triumph Hurdle* and took second place in the 2009 *Smurfit Kappa Champion Hurdle Challenge Trophy*.

Celestial Halo's 2008 Triumph win, as well as an "also ran" from 200/1 *Lord Adonis* in the 2007 *Triumph*, aren't included in the table detailing **Galileo**'s festival statistics, as they were contested over ten years ago. If we add in the victory from *Celestial Halo*, then it doesn't need a mathematical genius to calculate that 5/6^{ths} of the win and place positions achieved by **Galileo**'s offspring at Cheltenham Festivals is down to the aforementioned *Celestial Halo* and **Supasundae**. Nineteen horses by **Galileo** appeared at a festival just once, and 18 of them were unable to finish higher than

5th. The odd-ball was the *Dermot Weld* trained **Windsor Park** *(*9/2) who was victorious in the 2015 *Neptune Investment Management Novices' Hurdle.*

As highlighted in the 2018 Cheltenham Festival Stallion Guide, it is the Official Flat Rating of **Galileo**'s progeny that is the best pointer as to whether they will perform at a Cheltenham Festival. Of the 24 of the progeny to have raced at Cheltenham, 21 of them had an Official Flat Rating, courtesy of them running at least three times on the flat. All 16 of the offspring who could not manage to achieve a top rating of at least 100 during their flat career, have generally struggled at the festival with none of them able to register a top four finish. Of the five who did break the 100 barrier, two of them won at the festival. **Windsor Park** achieved a flat rating of 102 from his four runs on the flat, although he kicked off his career with five runs in National Hunt Flat races, and **Celestial Halo** had an Official Flat Rating of 110, a figure he obtained when as a three-year-old, he finished 7th in the 2007 *Ladbrokes St Leger Stakes* at *Doncaster*. The other three of the offspring who were rated above 100 failed to win or place, although all three did manage a placing of 7th or higher. Just three **Galileo** sired festival runners did not race on the flat, all starting their careers in National Hunt Flat Races, **Supasundae** being one of them.

Having had a brief look through **Galileo**'s current crop of youngsters, there are four horses that have an Official Flat Rating of around 100 who could, potentially, be entered for Cheltenham. Punters will need to judge for themselves whether they consider any of the quartet being good enough to match the exploits of **Windsor Park** or **Celestial Halo**. The gang of four with their Official Flat Ratings as of early January 2019 are **Astronomer** (109), **Triplicate** (101), **Carlo Biraghi** (99) and **City Hall** (98).

In summary, every now and again, a horse by **Galileo**, who holds an Official Flat Rating of over 100, will pop up at a festival meeting and reward backers with a win or place dividend. But it doesn't happen that often which is why supporting **Galileo**'s offspring at Cheltenham Festivals has historically been unprofitable, and where a £1.00 each-way bet on all 36 festival runners to date, would have resulted in a loss of £20.70. I guess one may wish to spend time second-guessing the festival potential of a **Galileo** bred 100+ Flat-Rated contender. Not me. Come the meeting this March, I will overlook **Galileo**'s progeny and search for winners elsewhere.

Germany (USA)

Quote from the 2018 Cheltenham Festival Stallion Guide - "A **Germany** sired runner will win at this year's festival, just not *Faugheen*. No prizes for guessing my nap of the festival. It is *Samcro*".

Germany (Died as a 22-y-o in 2013)							
Race Format	*Miles*	*Won*	*Placed*	*Unplaced*	*Total*	*Win %*	*Place %*
	About 2m	1	0	3	4	25%	25%
Hurdles	About 2m 4f	2	0	0	2	100%	100%
	About 3m	0	0	0	0	-	-
	About 2m	0	1	4	5	0%	20%
Chases	About 2m 4f	0	0	1	1	0%	0%
	About 3m	0	0	0	0	-	-
	About 4m	0	0	0	0	-	-
Bumper	About 2m	0	0	0	0	-	-
Total	2009-2018	**3**	**1**	**8**	**12**	**25%**	**33%**

Well, my nap for last year's festival didn't let me down. In the 2018 *Ballymore Novices' Hurdle*, *Samcro* travelled smoothly around the outside of the field, took up the lead on the bend before the home straight and then ran powerfully up the Cheltenham Hill to score from *Black Op* by 2½ lengths. It wasn't the most original selection as a festival banker, that's for sure, but you can only beat what's in front of you and *Samcro* rightly deserves his place on the front cover of the 2019 Cheltenham Festival Stallion Guide. The **Germany** sired *Samcro* was unbeaten going into last year's race having won a Point-to-Point, three National Hunt Flat Races and three novice hurdles. However, following that festival success, fortunes for the **Germany** sired eight times winner have gone about-face. *Samcro* hasn't won a race since.

His 9th career start was in the *Betdaq 2% Commission Punchestown Champion Hurdle* where he was once again the odds-on favourite, with his main rival being *Melon* at 11/4, who had lost out by a neck to *Buveur D'Air* in Cheltenham's Champion Hurdle. Bizarrely, both *Samcro* and *Melon* fell independently of each other at the third last flight leaving the race open for *Supasundae* to win at 7/1.

Next up for *Samcro* was another 2m contest, this time at *Down Royal* in the Grade 2 *WKD Hurdle*, where *Samcro* was the 4/9 favourite. There were only four runners in the race, one of whom was a 100/1 no-hoper. The race provided us with a hugely surprising result as *Samcro* looked out of sorts, putting in a performance that was miles away from what he had achieved at Cheltenham the previous season. He finished second to 12/1 chance *Bedrock*.

On 1st December 2018, *Samcro* jostled for favouritism with *Champion Hurdle* winner *Buveur D'Air* in the *BetVictor Fighting Fifth Hurdle* at *Newcastle*, eventually setting off as the 6/5 favourite with Buveur D'Air having the slightly more generous odds of 11/8. Although this was clearly a better run by *Samcro*, in the end, he was no match for *Buveur D'Air* who cruised past his rival to win by eight lengths. *Samcro*, in turn was another 13 or more lengths in front of the third placed horse, *Vision Des Flos*.

Samcro's connections persisted with a distance of two miles when the *Gordon Elliott* trained runner lined up in the Grade 1 *Ryanair Hurdle* at *Leopardstown* on 29th December. *Samcro* put in a tame effort especially in the closing stages when he weakened on the run-in to finish 5th of six runners. Connections have been scratching their heads as to why *Samcro*'s form has deteriorated since his festival win but nothing had come to light until early 2019, when it was discovered that the horse was suffering from a deep-seated lung infection. Even if antibiotics sort out the lung infection, it is going to take a humongous effort for *Gordon Elliott* and his team to get *Samcro* in peak physical fitness for the demands of a Cheltenham Festival. Speaking on behalf of owners *Gigginstown House Stud*, *Eddie O'Leary* advised that although *Samcro* had not been categorically ruled out of the 2019 Cheltenham Festival, it was very unlikely that the 2018 *Ballymore Novices'* winner would be competing. I hope that *Samcro* can return to somewhere near his best in the forthcoming months and that we will see him once again at the 2020 Cheltenham Festival. This March is almost certainly too soon for him.

As well as telling everybody that *Samcro* would win at the 2018 Cheltenham Festival, I was also adamant that another **Germany** sired star, *Faugheen*, would not. *Faugheen* has been a fantastic servant to *Susannah Ricci* and trainer *Willlie Mullins* and has already provided connections with two festival victories, the 2014 *Neptune Investment Management Novices' Hurdle* followed by the 2015 *Stan James Champion Hurdle Challenge Trophy*. In the lead up to the 2016 Cheltenham Festival, he was odds-on to retain his *Champion Hurdle* Crown to make it three festival victories in a row, when a few weeks before the festival, he was ruled out with a suspensory ligament injury. I'm sure he would have secured a festival hat-trick if he had been fit. The next time he was able to compete at a Cheltenham Festival was at last year's meeting, but *Faugheen* was now a veteran, aged ten.

At the 2018 Cheltenham Festival, *Faugheen* was entered in both the *Sun Bets Stayers' Hurdle* and the *Unibet Champion Hurdle Challenge Trophy* and connections eventually opted for him to run in the latter event. I didn't think he would win either race. As I stated in last year's Guide, the last horse older than nine years old to win the *Champion Hurdle* was *Sea Pigeon*, who was aged 11, back in 1981. He also won the race in 1980 as a ten-year-old. Only five horses over the age of eight have won the *Champion Hurdle* prize since 1951, the most recent being 2013 winner, *Hurricane Fly*, aged nine. In the 2018 renewal of the *Champion Hurdle*, I thought that *Faugheen*'s starting price of 4/1 was frankly ridiculous, but that's sentimentality for you. For a ten-year-old, he ran as well as could be expected in my view, registering a 6th place finish, some 22 lengths behind the winner, *Buveur D'Air*.

Looking forward to the 2019 Cheltenham Festival, at the time of writing, **Faugheen** is around 10/1 to win the *Sun Racing Stayers' Hurdle*. I've bad news for *Faugheen* supporters. The last horse older than nine years old to win this event was *Crimson Embers* in 1986. Even though he won't win, he will receive a grand reception from the Cheltenham crowd. We love our champions.

Sometimes, I have questioned myself why **Germany** is included in the Stallion Guide. Only six of this sire's progeny have competed at the Cheltenham Festival to run in a grand total of just 15 festival races spread out over thirteen years, twelve within the past decade. So why include **Germany** and leave out other stallions who have also amassed a similar amount of festival appearances? The reason is that when it comes to success at the Cheltenham Festival, **Germany** is a freak.

If we take the six horses by **Germany** that have appeared at Cheltenham Festivals, four of them are festival winners. Interestingly, the four winners have all hailed from Irish yards; *Edward P Harty* with **Captain Cee Bee**; *Arthur Moore* with **Tiger Cry**; *Willie Mullins* with **Faugheen**; and *Gordon Elliott* with **Samcro**. Combined, the above four horses have competed in eleven festival races, the record of which is won 5, placed 2, unplaced 4. These are amazing statistics.

Most punters will look at the table at the top of the page that show the festival runs of **Germany**'s stock over the past decade and think they are rather good. And indeed they are, but if we include the three runs pre-2009, which include two wins and one runner-up, the stats are even better:

Germany (Died as a 22-y-o in 2013)							
Race Format	*Miles*	*Won*	*Placed*	*Unplaced*	*Total*	*Win %*	*Place %*
Total	2009-2018	**5**	**2**	**8**	**15**	**33%**	**47%**

Incidentally, if one decided to exclude the four unsuccessful runs from the two British based runners of *Fighting Chance* and *Germany Calling*, the win strike rate would read as 45% and the win/place strike rate as 64%. This stallion's festival record is immense.

Due to **Germany**'s death in 2013, it is most likely that further festival success will be placed upon **Samcro**'s shoulders, so let us hope that he is fit and well for the 2020 Cheltenham Festival. Looking at the remaining progeny of **Germany**, there is a slim possibility that another **Germany** bred legend may materialise for the future, but we would need to see how some of the younger generation develop over the coming year or so. Four horses by **Germany** that may have what it takes to follow in the footsteps of their predecessors are:

Advantage Point, a 6-y-o gelding trained by *Edward P Harty*. 4 career starts to date (6th 1st 4th 3rd)
Frau Georgia, a 5-y-o mare, trained by *Neil Mulholland*. 1 career start to date (2nd)
Hell On Earth, a 5-y-o gelding trained by *Gordon Elliott*. 1 career start to date (3rd)
Iconic Lady, a 6-y-o mare, trained by *Robert Tyner*. 3 career starts to date (6th, 8th, 3rd)

By all accounts, it looks likely that *Faugheen* will be the sole representative of **Germany**'s offspring at the 2019 Cheltenham Festival. Irrespective of his placing in the *Sun Racing Stayers' Hurdle*, my friends and I will raise a glass to this celebrated Irish hurdler. Appropriately, the drink will be Guinness.

Gold Well (GB)

Quote from the 2018 Cheltenham Festival Stallion Guide - "Between 2013 and 2016, supporting all of **Gold Well**'s representatives blind to level stakes, would have resulted in a profit at three of the four meetings, the exception being in 2015 where backing all five runners at £1.00 each way would have resulted in a small loss of £2.75. Against the above backdrop, for fans of this stallion, the 2017 Cheltenham Festival turned out to be rather wretched, as none of the eight **Gold Well** sired runners that took part, could manage a place position; let alone win."

Gold Well (18-y-o)

Race Format	Miles	Won	Placed	Unplaced	Total	Win %	Place %
	About 2m	0	0	1	1	0%	0%
Hurdles	About 2m 4f	0	1	1	2	0%	50%
	About 3m	1	0	4	5	20%	20%
	About 2m	0	0	0	0	-	-
Chases	About 2m 4f	0	1	3	4	0%	25%
	About 3m	1	2	4	7	14%	43%
	About 4m	0	0	5	5	0%	0%
Bumper	About 2m	0	0	2	2	0%	0%
Total	2009-2018	**2**	**4**	**20**	**26**	**8%**	**23%**

As far as **Gold Well**'s progeny are concerned, we can skip over the 2018 Cheltenham Festival rather quickly. Just three horses by **Gold Well** would race at Prestbury Park last March and none of them passed the finishing line. *Shoal Bay* (80/1) was pulled up in the *Sky Bet Supreme Novices' Hurdle*; *Clondaw Cian* (66/1) was pulled up in the *National Hunt Challenge Cup Amateur Riders' Novices' Chase*; and *Arctic Gold* (25/1) was a faller in the *Fulke Walwyn Kim Muir Challenge Cup Amateur Riders' Handicap Chase.*

Last year's three representatives were all big outsiders so it would have been quite a surprise had any of them managed to reward the likely very few bets that were placed on them. Nevertheless, following on from the 'also-ran' performances from the eight horses by **Gold Well** that raced at the 2017 festival, the past couple of years has resulted in a rapid decline in this stallion's win and place strike rates.

If we go back to the 2016 Cheltenham Festival, there were four **Gold Well** sired runners at that meeting, three of whom finished in the first five positions, including two place dividends that consisted of a 40/1 3rd placing from *Legacy Gold* in the *OLBG Mares' Hurdle* and an 8/1 runner-up finish by *Holywell* in the *Ultima Handicap Chase*. At that meeting's close, **Gold Well** had been represented at Cheltenham Festivals on 15 occasions boasting strike rates of 13% for a win and 40% for a win/place. Two years later, and the strike rates have almost halved. A deeper analysis of the 14 **Gold Well** runners that make up those 28 festival appearances offers some appreciation as to why results have deteriorated, and in particular, how influential *Holywell* has been to this stallion's festival record.

If we look at the results of the **Gold Well** sired horses that have raced at the festival, ten of them have failed to provide a win or place, although three of them were thereabouts with the leading bunch in their races, registering 5th and 6th place finishing positions. Of the four horses by **Gold Well** that did provide some winnings for their supporters, three of them secured place positions on a single occasion; *Johns Spirit* (9/1) 4th place in the 2014 *Byrne Group Plate*; *Grand Jesture* (25/1) 2nd in the *Ultima Business Solutions Handicap Chase*; and as already mentioned, *Legacy Gold* (40/1) in the 2016 *OLBG Mares' Hurdle*. That leaves *Holywell*, who in his five festival appearances, provided trainer *Jonjo O'Neill* with a runner-up place and two victories.

Holywell's debut at the Festival resulted in him being victorious at 25/1 in the 2013 *Pertemps Final*, where his trainer had applied blinkers for the first time. The following season he won again at 10/1 in the *Baylis & Harding Affordable Luxury Handicap Chase*, beating *Ma Filleule* by 1¾ lengths. In 2015, *Holywell* took a major step up in class in an attempt to win the big one, the *Betfred Cheltenham Gold Cup Chase*. He finished just outside the place positions with a sound performance to finish in 4th place. The following season, he was once again entered for the renewal of the race that he won in 2014, now named the *Ultima Handicap Chase*. This time he had to settle for the runner-up spot at odds of 8/1, as *Un Temps Pour Tout* won readily by 7 lengths. In the 2017 running of the *Ultima*, *Holywell* was to take on *Un Temps Pour Tout* once again, but their performances could not have been wider apart. *Un Temps Pour Tout* went on to win the contest for a second time, whereas, *Holywell*, now a 10-year-old, jumped with no fluency whatsoever and was pulled up half way round.

The prices returned on all of **Gold Well**'s festival winning and placed wagers have been highly rewarding, ranging from 8/1 to 40/1. Taken overall, had one placed a £1.00 each-way wager on all 26 of **Gold Well**'s festival runners to date, a profit of £18.25 would be the outcome. If we ignore *Holywell*'s five performances, that £18.25 profit turns into a loss of £22.50 which demonstrates *Holywell*'s significant contribution to the numbers.

As we approach the 2019 Cheltenham Festival, my recommendation to punters is to leave **Gold Well**'s offspring out of your calculations. I have had a brief look at the current crop of horses by **Gold Well** and I can't see a future '*Holywell*' amongst them and overall, they don't appear to have the necessary class to have a major impact at the festival. That may well change for future festivals as **Gold Well**, at 18 years of age, is a very young stallion. For the 2019 meeting, I suggest we just watch and learn.

Great Pretender (IRE)

Great Pretender was not featured in the 2018 Cheltenham Festival Stallion Guide.

Race Format	Miles	Won	Placed	Unplaced	Total	Win %	Place %
	About 2m	0	1	6	7	0%	14%
Hurdles	About 2m 4f	1	0	2	3	33%	33%
	About 3m	0	0	2	2	0%	0%
	About 2m	0	0	2	2	0%	0%
Chases	About 2m 4f	0	0	1	1	0%	0%
	About 3m	0	0	0	0	-	-
	About 4m	0	0	1	1	0%	0%
Bumper	About 2m	0	1	0	1	0%	100%
Total		**1**	**2**	**14**	**17**	**6%**	**18%**

Title row: Great Pretender (20-y-o)

Twelve horses by **Great Pretender** have competed in 17 festival races, and with a couple of early trends to focus upon, this stallion enters the Cheltenham Festival Stallion Guide for the first time.

In looking at the race categories in which runners by **Great Pretender** have raced, at this juncture, there doesn't appear to be any significant trend suggesting that, for betting purposes, a specific race category is more preferable than any other. To provide an overview of the category of race that the progeny have appeared in, twelve of the seventeen outings from the offspring have taken place over hurdles and all bar three runs have been over a distance within the 2m and 2½m categories.

The figures in the table that provide a summary of festival results from **Great Pretender**'s stock aren't especially exciting but with so few runs on board, strike rates can alter significantly with a couple of wins or places to add. And from a betting and financial perspective, had one placed a £1.00 each-way bet on all 17 runners to date, the result would be a loss of £14.70.

All of the above doesn't tell us much, other than perhaps to wait until this stallion's offspring have had a few more festival runs before making any judgements. That said, I have analysed the results in more detail and there is an area which punters may find insightful, albeit the analysis is based on limited data. Take a look at the two sets of seven finishing positions below:

A. 1st 5th 7th 8th PU Fell 11th
B. 3rd 3rd 6th 12th PU 5th 11th

The first set of results (A) relate to the seven horses by **Great Pretender** that have raced at the festival where their starting prices have ranged between 9/2 and 8/1 (shortest price shown first). In my opinion, these results are disappointing and tell us that overall, horses by **Great Pretender** towards the front of the market have under-performed. The one exception is the sole winner from the progeny who was successful at a price of 9/2, the shortest returned price of all 17 festival runners to date.

The second string of results (B) relate to the seven horses by **Great Pretender** that have raced at the festival where their starting prices have ranged from 22/1 to 200/1 (again shortest price shown first). Although there is no winner amongst the seven, four of them attained a top six finish, two of whom were placed. My view is that the outsiders from this sire's stock are over-performing, and from a betting perspective, a £1.00 each-way stake on all seven (including a 200/1 no-hoper!) is close to break-even, coming in as a loss of £2.10. With regard to the same staking plan on the seven more fancied festival contenders, where the sole return came from the 9/2 shot, the losses would amount to £6.60. For the mathematicians and 'completer-finishers' among us, I will advise that the three missing results are 8th at 12/1, 5th at 16/1 and 17th at 16/1.

There were five horses by **Great Pretender** that competed at the 2018 Cheltenham Festival, and one of them, **Benie Des Dieux**, provided the first win for this stallion's stock when winning the *OLBG Mares' Hurdle* at a price of 9/2. The *Willie Mullins* trained mare wasn't expected to win the race because there was a 1/2 odds-on runner in the contest and almost everyone expected the favourite to win. But *Apple's Jade* finished in 3rd place having suffered an off-day, which enabled **Benie Des Dieux** to benefit, getting her head in front of the 33/1 outsider, *Midnight Tour*, in the final 120 yards.

In the opening event of the 2019 festival, the *Sky Bet Supreme Novices' Hurdle*, I was interested how the course commentator would cope with the pronunciation of the **Great Pretender** bred **Claimantakinforgan**. I think he was probably relieved that the *Nicky Henderson* trained horse was behind the leaders for the almost the entirety of the race, only staying on at the end when all the action would have been on the battle for victory between *Summerville Boy*, who eventually prevailed to win, and *Kalashnikov*. As for **Claimantakinforgan**, he stayed on to finish in 5th place (16/1) and just over five lengths behind the winner. To be fair, it was another very good festival run by **Claimantakinforgan**, who in his previous festival appearance had secured 3rd place at 22/1 in the 2017 *Weatherbys Champion Bumper*.

The other three runners representing **Great Pretender** at the 2018 Cheltenham Festival could be labelled as 'also-rans'. **Dortmund Park** (12/1) finished 8th in the *Albert Bartlett Novices' Hurdle*; **Pravalaguna** (50/1) was pulled up in the same race that was won by **Benie Des Dieux**, the *OLBG Mares' Hurdle*; and **Diablo De Rouhet** (200/1) finished 11th in the *Ballymore Novices' Hurdle* won by my nap of last year, *Samcro*.

From previous Cheltenham Festivals, the one horse by **Great Pretender** that is worth mentioning is **Ptit Zig**, who put in some good performances in his three festival appearances. He made his festival debut just six weeks after switching stables and countries, from *Yannick Fouin* in France to *Paul Nicholls*' yard in Somerset. Within a week of his arrival in Britain, *Paul Nicholls* ran him in a class 4 maiden hurdle event at *Ludlow*, and at odds of 11/2 he hacked up, beating the 2/7 favourite, *New Year's Eve*, who previously had finished runner-up in the 2012 Cheltenham Festival *Bumper*. **Ptit Zig** put in another good performance on his festival debut, finishing in 3rd place at 22/1, in the 2013 *Fred Winter Juvenile Handicap Hurdle*.

The following year, **Ptit Zig** ran in the *Stan James Champion Hurdle Challenge Trophy*. He was almost certainly biting off more than he could chew in this event, but nevertheless, finishing less than 15 lengths behind the winner in 6th place at a price of 28/1 is a very reasonable effort. Soon afterwards, **Ptit Zig** was put over fences, and he made his third festival appearance in the 2015 *JLT Novices Chase*, a race in which I remember *Vautour* demolishing his rivals with a superb round of jumping to win by a wide margin of 15 lengths. The next four to finish in that race were separated by 3½ lengths, with **Ptit Zig** the last of the quartet, finishing in 5th place at 11/2.

For the 2019 Cheltenham Festival, we are in the midst of an unfortunate time for this stallion's offspring in my opinion. Quite a few of the higher rated horses by **Great Pretender** are either injured, haven't run for quite a while or appear out of form. The horse with the highest rating of the progeny is **Great Field**, who has won 6 out of 9 runs since being under the tutelage of trainer *Willie Mullins* and owner *John P McManus*. He looks to have a lot of class, but he has fallen on his last two outings, the last tumble of which has apparently put him out for the season. I also liked **Claimantakinforgan** after his two previous festival runs, but apparently he is also out of the 2019 festival having injured a leg.

Gordon Elliott has a couple of outsiders who could be entered for the *Sun Racing Stayers Hurdle*. The seven year-old **Cracking Smart** flopped on his first outing for almost a year at *Leopardstown* on 28th December and so I am not keen on his chances. Nor **Dortmund Park** for that matter, even though he put in an excellent performance at *Punchestown* when winning the Grade 1 *Profile Systems Champion Novice Hurdle* six weeks after his Cheltenham defeat in the *Albert Bartlett Novices' Hurdle*. This season, at the time of writing, **Dortmund Park** has struggled to put together any semblance as to what he achieved at *Punchestown* last April.

The likeliest shortest priced runner of **Great Pretender**'s progeny for the festival is **Benie Des Dieux** who at the time of writing is 5/2 for the *OLBG Mares' Hurdle* and about double that for the *Stayers' event*. A lot depends on who runs in which race, but I am never comfortable when a horse goes almost a whole year without a prep run before appearing at a Cheltenham Festival (unless your name is *Quevega*!) **Benie Des Dieux** had her last run at *Punchestown* on 28th April and appears to be going straight to Cheltenham. *Willie Mullins* recently stated, "She's in good form and we're aiming for the *Mares' Hurdle*. The only reason she hasn't run this season is the ground". At last year's festival, **Benie Des Dieux** got the better of *Apple's Jade* because the latter was off colour. I don't believe history will repeat itself at the 2019 Cheltenham Festival if the two girls meet again.

Going back to my earlier theme of the outsiders sired by **Great Pretender** over-performing, one runner that takes my fancy is the *David Cottin* trained nine year-old, **Amazing Comedy**. In the 2017 *Glenfarclas Cross Country Chase*, **Amazing Comedy** finished in 5th position at a price of 50/1. He ran really well that day and was leading towards the end of the race before his stamina gave way. He returned to compete over the same course and distance for just the second time on 14th December 2018. This December event is not at level weights but a handicap, so **Amazing Comedy** was racing off a light weight of 10-3, which may have nudged the French raider towards being the 7/2 joint favourite. Once again, the horse ran well and perhaps the mistakes he made at the last two fences cost him the race, but he finished in 4th place and 2¼ lengths away from the winner, *Fact Of The Matter*. I've no idea whether *David Cottin* will send **Amazing Comedy** over for a third attempt at winning over this course and distance on the 13th March, but I hope he does, as I fancy a little each-way bet on him. *Tiger Roll* is a problem of course. I believe he has a great chance of regaining the prize he won last year and his current odds of 9/4 is probably an accurate reflection of his chances. As for **Amazing Comedy**, at the time of writing, he can be supported at around 33/1.

To summarise, it is very early days to make any wild judgements about how well **Great Pretender**'s offspring will perform at the forthcoming 2019 Cheltenham Festival, but based on my very early analysis, if you like one of the progeny's outsiders, then back your judgement with a small each-way bet. As for the more fancied runners, I'm not convinced. The betting market, for whatever reason, may be over-enthusiastic about their chances. We will soon find out.

High Chaparral (IRE)

Quote from the 2018 Cheltenham Festival Stallion Guide - "Of the 16 **High Chaparral** sired horses to have appeared at a Cheltenham Festival, one stands out above all others, the *Nicky Henderson* trained **Altior**."

	High Chaparral (Died as a 15-y-o in 2014)						
Race Format	*Miles*	*Won*	*Placed*	*Unplaced*	*Total*	*Win %*	*Place %*
	About 2m	2	0	13	15	13%	13%
Hurdles	About 2m 4f	0	0	1	1	0%	0%
	About 3m	0	0	2	2	0%	0%
	About 2m	2	0	0	2	100%	100%
Chases	About 2m 4f	0	0	0	0	-	-
	About 3m	0	1	2	3	0%	33%
	About 4m	0	0	0	0	-	-
Bumper	About 2m	0	0	1	1	0%	0%
Total	2009-2018	**4**	**1**	**19**	**24**	**17%**	**21%**

When we look at **High Chaparral**'s progeny that have gone on to race over the Jumps, one horse is far superior to any other national hunt racehorse sired by this stallion, the *Nicky Henderson* trained **Altior**. At the time of writing, **Altior** has been engaged in five hurdle races and twelve chases. He has won all of them. His only defeats were in two National Hunt Flat Races during the first four months of 2015. His first festival appearance was in the 2016 *Sky Bet Supreme Novices' Hurdle*, where **Altior** (4/1) was particularly impressive, quickening clear after the last, to win by seven lengths ahead of the 15/8 favourite, *Min*. That was his last appearance over hurdles as *Nicky Henderson* started the process to campaign **Altior** over fences. Following four runs over fences, all of which he won starting as the odds-on favourite, he returned to the Cheltenham Festival in 2017 to line up in the meeting's second event, the *Racing Post Arkle Challenge Trophy Novices' Chase*. There was no great depth to the race as the *Patricia Pugh* owned star had almost certainly scared off a number of other potential entries. Although taking a little while to engage top gear, **Altior** stormed up the Cheltenham run-in to beat *Cloudy Dream* by six lengths. He returned the 1/4 odds-on favourite.

Towards the end of 2017, **Altior** was found to be making a whistling noise which required a wind operation and so following a 287 day break, perhaps there were a few nerves as he lined up in February 2018 for the *Betfair Exchange Chase*. He would be in a field of just three with his main competitor being *Politologue*, trained by *Paul Nicholls*. It was a satisfactory return and it wasn't hard to see the significant gap in class between the two horses. **Altior** was on course for the forthcoming *Betway Queen Mother Champion Chase* at the 2018 Cheltenham Festival.

With the *Willie Mullins* trained pair of *Min* and *Douvan* in the field, most commentators were predicting a highly competitive and intriguing renewal of this Grade 1 two mile chase, and the highlight of the festival's second day. **Altior** lined up as the Evens favourite with his main rivals not too far away in the betting with *Min* at 5/2 and *Douvan* at 9/2. As it turned out, although it was clearly a more challenging race for the favourite than the previous year's *Arkle*, when the excitement started to build as they turned into the straight, **Altior** still looked head and shoulders above his rivals. *Min* finished as the runner-up, seven lengths behind the Champion, and *Douvan* fell mid-race.

Since his third Cheltenham Festival victory last year, **Altior** has won four more 2m chases, three of them Grade 1s. In all four races, the starting prices for this Champion 9-year-old, who holds an Official Rating of 175, is a reflection of his class, quality and superiority:

28th April 2018 – *Sandown* Grade 1 *Bet365 Celebration Chase* (2/11F)
8th December 2018 – *Sandown* Grade 1 *Betfair Tingle Creek Chase* (8/13F)
27th December 2018 – *Kempton* Grade 2 *Unibet Desert Orchid Chase* (1/8F)
19th January 2019 – *Ascot* Grade 1 *Matchbook Clarence House Chase* (1/10F)

At the time of writing, **Altior** is 4/7 for the *Champion Chase*. *Min* who was 5/2 for the 2018 renewal can be backed at 12/1. These prices say everything about **Altior**'s continued dominance. Just in case anyone out there are concerned about **Altior**'s age having a negative impact on his speed over the minimum distance of two miles, seven *Champion Chase* winners this century have been nine years old or more. They include, *Moscow Flyer* who won twice aged 9 and 11; *Big Zeb, Sizing Europe, Finian's Rainbow* (all aged 9); and two more recent 10-year-old winners - *Sprinter Sacre* and *Special Tiara*.

Whilst writing about **Altior**, I was intrigued how he compares with more recent *Champion Chase* winners, and specifically those who many commentators would consider top class or "one of the great two-milers". Names that come to mind this century are *Moscow Flyer, Master Minded* and *Sprinter Sacre*. The easiest place to find expert opinion is in the Official Ratings, so I looked at these ratings for this century's *Champion Chase* winners. Based on Official Ratings, (and note that no Official Rating was provided for *Moscow Flyer*'s two wins), two winners this century had an Official Rating higher than **Altior**'s which stands at 175. *Sprinter Sacre* was rated 179 when winning in the 2013 renewal and surprisingly to me, *Master Minded* had an Official Rating of 186 when he won in 2009. In an attempt to have some comparison with *Moscow Flyer*, I noted that the Racing Post Rating (RPR), for when he won in 2005, was 182. **Altior**'s RPR when he won in 2018 was 183. **Altior** is up there with the best, that's for sure.

Altior was one of only two **High Chaparral**'s representatives at last year's festival, the other being **Tower Bridge** (33/1) who put in a very reasonable performance to finish in 5th place in the *Albert Bartlett Novices' Hurdle*. I can't see too many horses by *High Chaparral* making it to the 2019 Cheltenham Festival either, as there is a dearth of quality amongst the sire's jumps progeny. **Altior** aside, only two of **High Chaparral**'s stock hold an Official Rating above 140. Both horses, neither of whom has set the world alight in recent performances, are owned by *John P McManus* and trained by *Joseph Patrick O'Brien*. **Landofhopeandglory**, rated 142, has visited the festival once before when he was placed in fifth position in the 2017 *JCB Triumph Hurdle*. **Tower Bridge**, who like **Landofhopeandglory** is a six year-old, was also placed in 5th place on his sole visit, the race already highlighted above.

It is rather fascinating that of the 24 festival appearances of **High Chaparral**'s offspring, 17 of them have come in the festival's juvenile and novice races. Intriguingly, only three horses secured a top three finish on their debuts in these events, the three being **Altior, Hawk High** and **Hadrian's Approach**. Having performed successfully on their festival debuts, all three of them returned to race again at more Cheltenham Festivals. What about those juveniles and novices who failed to achieve a top three finish on their festival debuts? They never appeared at a festival again. It follows, therefore, that it is most unlikely that **Tower Bridge**, 5th in the 2018 *Albert Bartlett Novices' Hurdle* and **Landofhopeandglory**, 5th in the 2017 JCB Triumph Hurdle, will ever again set hoof at a Cheltenham Festival!

There is a slim possibility that one or two of the more youthful members of **High Chaparral**'s stock make an appearance this March in one of the meeting's juvenile or novice events. However, should this scenario come about, punters should bear in mind the information provided above, in that the chances of a runner by **High Chaparral** attaining a top three finish is approximately one in five.

The advice to readers of this Guide is straightforward. If you are one of those punters who are comfortable betting on sure things at odds-on, then help yourself to the odds on offer for **Altior** to win the *Betway Queen Mother Champion Chase*. And, if a **High Chaparral** sired juvenile or novice should make it to the 2019 Cheltenham Festival, then don't clutch at straws thinking that it may turn out to be another *'Altior'*. It won't be. Back something else.

Kalanisi (IRE)

Quote from the 2018 Cheltenham Festival Stallion Guide - "If you are going to support one of **Kalanisi**'s stock at the 2018 Cheltenham Festival, then based upon the statistical trends to date, it would appear that your best chance of making money is by supporting the progeny in the festival's six contests within the 2m hurdle category."

Race Format	Miles	Won	Placed	Unplaced	Total	Win %	Place %
				Kalanisi (23-y-o)			
Hurdles	About 2m	0	3	7	10	0%	30%
	About 2m 4f	0	0	5	5	0%	0%
	About 3m	0	0	2	2	0%	0%
Chases	About 2m	0	1	0	1	0%	100%
	About 2m 4f	0	0	2	2	0%	0%
	About 3m	0	0	2	2	0%	0%
	About 4m	0	0	0	0	-	-
Bumper	About 2m	1	0	4	5	20%	20%
Total	2009-2018	**1**	**4**	**22**	**27**	**4%**	**19%**

The majority of my family and closest friends don't have a clue what I am talking about when I tell them about the incredible experience of being in the stands at Prestbury Park at around 13:27 on a Tuesday afternoon in mid-March for what is the opening day of a Cheltenham Festival. However cold the weather might be, you are as warm as toast, squashed up against numerous other human beings who are feeling just as excited as you are about the start of the festival. You stretch your neck to the left, looking down the course as the runners for the *Supreme Novices' Hurdle* go round in circles preparing for the contest ahead of them. Then you hear the racecourse commentator announce, "They are about to come into line". Your sense of anticipation grows and you shiver with excitement. Tens of thousands of Cheltenham Festival devotees are completely covered in goose bumps. "And they're off!" shouts the racecourse commentator. A huge roar from the stands is heard for miles around. Wow!

As the roar from the crowd started to fade away, and the runners for the *Sky Bet Supreme Novices' Hurdle* went past the stands for the first time in last year's opening contest, my eyes skimmed across the 19 runners in an attempt to find the yellow and purple silks of my selection for the race, **Kalashnikov**. As they came round the second time and started to race up the hill to the finish, it was very easy to spot the **Kalanisi** bred **Kalashnikov**. He was leading. He started tiring just as they approached the last, but he kept on. My 5/1 selection was game, very game, but as he and his rider *Jack Quinlan* got closer and closer to the line, *Summerville Boy* was gaining. With yards to go, **Kalashnikov** could give no more. He had run his heart out. But *Summerville Boy* was stronger and his stamina reserves kicked in just in time, as he won by a neck.

At my hotel whilst having breakfast the following morning, I looked up at the TV that was showing not only a replay of the race, but also, so it appeared, a camera that was fixed upon **Kalashnikov**'s trainer *Amy Murphy* as she watched the closing stages of the race. With a big floppy hat, she was running up and down at the side of the track, willing **Kalashnikov** forward, waving her arms and cheering and shouting. As *Summerville Boy* gained ground, excitement turned to despair. And then, once the reality had sunk in that **Kalashnikov** had been beaten, it was all smiles again. She knew that her runner had given his all. Watching the emotions of *Amy Murphy* says everything about why so many racegoers, me included, absolutely worship the Cheltenham Festival.

Kalashnikov was the first of three horses by **Kalanisi** that would compete in races at the 2018 Cheltenham Festival, and we only had to wait about half an hour before the next representative would appear, the race in question being the *Racing Post Arkle Challenge Trophy Novices' Chase*. Surprisingly, only five runners were entered for this event, and the *Nicky Henderson* trained **Brain Power** lined up at a price of 14/1. Only *Robinshill* at 66/1 was a bigger price. My view of the race is that the **Kalanisi** sired **Brain Power** was very fortunate in that the race was run to suit him. *Petit Mouchoir* and *Saint Calvados* led from the off, locked in a duel and ultimately it couldn't last. First *Saint Calvados* and then *Petit Mouchoir* started to fade, and by the time they reached the final bend before the home straight, the 5/6 favourite, *Footpad*, had eased past both of them and stayed on strongly up the hill to win by 14 lengths. It seemed like an eternity before the next two horses passed the post, but **Brain Power** finally mustered up enough stamina to wear down the legless *Petit Mouchoir* in the dying yards to secure the runner-up spot.

With two places from the first two races, it was clear that the 2018 Cheltenham Festival would be a profitable one for anyone backing **Kalanisi**'s offspring blind at level stakes. We had to wait for the last race on Thursday to see what would transpire with the third of **Kalanisi**'s festival entries. Not much was the answer, as **Millanisi Boy** (16/1) was pulled up in the *Fulke Walwyn Kim Muir Challenge Cup Amateur Riders' Handicap Chase*.

Anyone looking at the table at the top of this chapter which gives an overview of how **Kalanisi**'s offspring have performed at Cheltenham Festivals may decide to give this sire's runners the cold shoulder with just one win in 27 appearances. However, to put it bluntly, the table is massively understating **Kalanisi**'s record as a festival stallion, as only results from 2009 onwards are included. There were just two festival appearances from **Kalanisi**'s stock that pre-date 2009, these being *Katchit*'s victory at 11/2 in the 2007 *JCB Triumph Hurdle*, followed up by the same horse's second festival win, at 10/1, in the *Smurfit Kappa Champion Hurdle Challenge Trophy* twelve months later. The strike rates look rather different when we add in the achievements of *Katchit* as can be seen from the table below showing an update in the 2m hurdles category and its impact on the strike rates as a whole:

Kalanisi (23-y-o)								
Race Format	*Miles*		*Won*	*Placed*	*Unplaced*	*Total*	*Win %*	*Place %*
Hurdles	About 2m		2	3	7	12	17%	42%
Total	**2009-2018**		**3**	**4**	**22**	**29**	**10%**	**24%**

In analysing the 29 festival performances from Kalanisi's progeny, the results clearly indicate that this stallion's runners are far more successful in two mile hurdle races than in any other race category. In twelve 2m hurdle appearances, horses by **Kalanisi** are very close to picking up a win or place position for one in every two festival appearances. Contrast this with the 11 unplaced runs (chases or hurdles) over distances above two miles, where on only one occasion has a **Kalanisi** bred runner secured a top six finish.

There isn't enough data to make any firm conclusions as to how successful the progeny are in the other contests at the minimum distance, which incorporates three chases and the *Bumper*, although the early signs are positive. In five appearances in the *Weatherbys Champion Bumper*, **Kalanisi**'s offspring have been successful once, courtesy of the mare, **Fayonagh**, who won at 7/1 in 2017. The style of **Fayonagh**'s victory as she swept past almost the entire field with a devastating burst of speed made this race one of my favourites of the 2017 festival. As an aside, the other **Kalanisi** bred runners to appear in the *Bumper* have all been unfancied lining up at prices of 25/1, 40/1, and 100/1 twice. As for two mile chase events, this has already been covered. ***Brain Power***'s second placing in last year's *Arkle* is the only time that **Kalanisi** has had a runner within the category.

In looking a little deeper into the progeny's 2m hurdle results, if we ignore the three outsiders who returned prices of 40/1 and 50/1 twice, then the nine remaining finishing positions in chronological order read as 1 1 6 2 3 6 9 8 2. Backing all nine blind to a £1.00 each-way stake would have provided a profit of £12.30. Punters should definitely be interested in any horse by **Kalanisi** that is entered in the festival's two mile hurdle events, and pay extra special attention should any 4-year-old make an appearance. **Kalanisi** has been represented in the *Triumph Hurdle* on 4 occasions; ***Katchit*** (11/2) won in 2007; ***Simarian*** (40/1) finished 7th in 2009; and ***Barizan*** (14/1) and ***Alaivan*** (9/2) finished 2nd and 3rd respectively in the 2010 renewal.

I'm not expecting that many horses by **Kalanisi** to be entered at the 2019 Cheltenham Festival, but for punters the advice is dead easy. Rule 1: Think seriously about placing an each-way bet on any **Kalanisi** bred horse that lines up in a two mile hurdle race. Rule 2: Albeit the data is so far inconclusive, one may also find reward in following the progeny in the *Weatherbys Champion Bumper* or in one of the festival's two mile chases. Rule 3: Strike a line through any horse by **Kalanisi** that has a race entry where it is expected to travel further than 2m1f.

Finally, it may well happen that once again we will see ***Kalashnikov*** and ***Brain Power*** compete on the first day of the 2019 Cheltenham Festival. At the time of writing, ***Brain Power*** is a 16/1 chance in the *Unibet Champion Hurdle Challenge Trophy* and ***Kalashnikov*** is a 7/1 chance in the *Racing Post Arkle Challenge Trophy Novices' Chase*. It will be great to see ***Kalashnikov***'s highly likeable trainer in the Winners Enclosure. Good Luck Amy!

Kapgarde (FR)

Quote from the 2018 Cheltenham Festival Stallion Guide - "With a 7% place strike rate and having yet to provide a winner from 27 festival runs, a £38.75 loss would have been the result if one had placed a £1.00 each-way bet on all of **Kapgarde**'s festival representatives to date."

Race Format	Miles	Won	Placed	Unplaced	Total	Win %	Place %
	About 2m	0	3	8	11	0%	27%
Hurdles	About 2m 4f	0	1	4	5	0%	20%
	About 3m	0	0	2	2	0%	0%
	About 2m	0	0	4	4	0%	0%
Chases	About 2m 4f	0	0	7	7	0%	0%
	About 3m	0	0	2	2	0%	0%
	About 4m	0	0	1	1	0%	0%
Bumper	About 2m	0	0	1	1	0%	0%
Total	2009-2018	**0**	**4**	**29**	**33**	**0%**	**12%**

Table title: Kapgarde (20-y-o)

One may read the quote from last year's Guide, glance at the table that summarises the festival results of **Kapgarde**'s stock and decide to skip this section. But wait a second! A horse by **Kapgarde** won the 2018 *32Red King George VI Chase* at *Kempton Park* and (as of early January) is now in the region of 8/1 to win the *Magners Cheltenham Gold Cup*! Stick around and read all about *Clan Des Obeaux*.

When *Clan Des Obeaux* won the King George, my immediate reaction was "Who?" He does appear to have arrived at the *Cheltenham Gold Cup* party late in the day. The horse is owned by three chaps who have all done rather well in their respective fields; Morson Group CEO *Ged Mason*; ex-Manchester United football manager, *Alex Ferguson*; and *Paul Barber* whose family firm have been making cheddar cheese for almost 200 years. The trainer of their *King George* winner hasn't done too badly either, as *Clan Des Obeaux* provided *Paul Nicholls* with his 10th win in the race. There was drama halfway through the race when *Bristol De Mai* fell at the fence in front of the stands and badly hampered *Waiting Patiently*, who unseated jockey *Brian Hughes*. Towards the end of the race, it was a battle between *Clan Des Obeaux* and the 10-year-old *Thistlecrack*, who won this prestigious prize two years previously. Youth won out in the end, as *Clan Des Obeaux*'s jockey *Harry Cobden*, pulled alongside *Thistlecrack* in the closing stages, before a fine leap at the last sealed victory. Preceding the race, *Clan Des Obeaux* had been 50/1 to win the *Cheltenham Gold Cup*. Afterwards, he was in single figures. Can he win the 2019 *Magners Cheltenham Gold Cup*?

Let's start with some positives. *Clan Des Obeaux* has had 12 chase starts so clearly is an experienced chaser, yet he has only just turned seven, so one would expect him to keep improving. And when it comes to winning the big one at Cheltenham, the most significant race from which the winner can materialise is the *King George VI Chase* at *Kempton*. This century, of the 14 *King George* winners who went on to contest that season's Cheltenham *Gold Cup*, five did the double and three finished 2nd or 3rd. The five who won both contests were *Best Mate* (2002/3), *Kicking King* (2004/5), *Kauto Star* (2006/7), *Kauto Star* (2008/9) and *Long Run* in 2011 *(Due to Kempton's Boxing Day meeting being abandoned, both races took place in the same calendar year).* Based on this trend alone *Clan Des Obeaux* has a 57% chance of finishing in the first three of the *Gold Cup* and a 35% chance of winning.

At the time of writing (early January), provided the horse doesn't have two more races before appearing in the *Gold Cup* and punters are still backing him so that his starting price on the day is 8/1 or shorter, then there are a couple of other positive trends for **Clan Des Obeaux**. 17 of the past 18 winners have been priced at no bigger than 8/1 (*Lord Windermere* at 20/1 being the exception in 2014). And 10 of the past 11 winners had raced no more than three times in their *Gold Cup* winning season. The *King George* was **Clan Des Obeaux**'s second race of the season.

To provide more encouragement to the horse's wealthy owners, it clearly helps that the trainer knows what it takes to win a *Gold Cup*. Not only has *Paul Nicholls* trained the winner of the *King George* on 10 occasions, he also has four *Gold Cup* successes to his name with *See More Business* (1999), *Kauto Star* in 2007 and 2009, and *Denman* in 2008.

Before anyone decides to put their mortgage on **Clan Des Obeaux** for the *Gold Cup*, let's look at some of the negative trends. In the past 18 years, twelve of the winners have been Irish bred, three French, two GB and one German. As the name suggests, **Clan Des Obeaux** is French-bred, and so he will need to up there with *Long Run* (FR) and *Kauto Star* (FR) to be the 3rd French-bred to win the *Gold Cup* this century. And I'm far from convinced that he is as good as *Long Run* and *Kauto Star*. *Kauto Star* was truly an exceptional horse. He won the *King George* on five occasions from six appearances and in 2009 he became the first horse to regain the *Gold Cup* in the event's history, having previously won the race in 2007 and then finishing runner-up to *Denman* in 2008. The one time when *Kauto Star* didn't win the *King George*, he finished 3rd. In that same season of 2010/2011, he also finished 3rd in the *Cheltenham Gold Cup*. The horse that beat him on both occasions was *Long Run*, who must have been quite a horse to topple *Kauto Star* twice in one season. It was also a big achievement for the *Nicky Henderson* trained *Long Run* to win the *Gold Cup* as a six-year-old. The last time a six-year-old had won the Blue Riband prize was when *Mill Reef* was victorious back in 1963. Punters should think about whether they believe **Clan Des Obeaux** to be in the same league as these two French-Bred Greats that were *Kauto Star* and *Long Run*.

It may be an encouragement to **Clan Des Obeaux** supporters to know that 17 of the past 18 *Gold Cup* winners had raced at a previous Cheltenham festival. **Clan Des Obeaux** qualifies as his very last hurdles appearance was in the 2016 *JCB Triumph Hurdle* when he finished in 6th position at a price of 12/1. But 2016 is going back three years and is sixth position in a novice hurdle in the same bracket as the other seventeen winners who had previously raced at a festival? The analysis suggests not. Indeed, 15 of the 17 winners had last appeared at the festival in a chase event and most of them had finished quite a bit higher than 6th place. In the year before their *Gold Cup* win:

- 5 had contested the *RSA Chase*, 4 winning the event and one other finishing 3rd
- 4 had ran in the previous year's *Gold Cup*; *Best Mate* regained his *Gold Cup* crown twice in 2003 and 2004, *Kauto Star* finished second to *Denman* in 2009 and *Native River* won last season having finished in 3rd place in 2017
- 3 had contested the *Arkle*, two being runner-up and another finishing in 7th place
- 2 had contested the *Ryanair Steeple Chase* (1st and 3rd)
- 1 had fallen in the *Queen Mother Chase*

The two *Gold Cup* winners who had previously contested a festival hurdle event were *Best Mate* and *Synchronised*. *Best Mate* was runner-up in the 2000 *Capel Cure Sharp Supreme Novices' Hurdle*, two years before his first *Gold Cup* win in 2002. He almost certainly would have been at the festival in 2001 had the meeting not been cancelled due to the foot and mouth crisis. All of which leaves us with *Synchronised*, the one horse that didn't set the world alight with a hurdle performance three years preceding his 2012 *Gold Cup* win. *Synchronised* fell in the *Pertemps Hurdle Final* in 2009.

Should **Clan Des Obeaux** win the *Gold Cup* this March, his profile (in terms of previously competed at a festival) most closely matches *Synchronised*.

The task now is to weigh up all the pros and cons highlighted above and make a judgement as to whether or not **Clan Des Obeaux** will win the *Magners Cheltenham Gold Cup*. However, there is one more compelling factor to consider. This book is about a horse's breeding being a critical factor in picking Cheltenham Festival winners. And as it states in my introduction, the progeny of some stallions perform creditably at the festival time and time again, whereas others consistently struggle. So, let's go back to the top of this chapter and look again at the table that summarises the festival results of **Kapgarde**'s stock.

The table makes dismal reading. **Kapgarde**'s offspring have achieved just four place positions in 33 festival outings. To date, backing horses by **Kapgarde** has resulted in picking up the place part of an each-way bet for one in eight runs. It is hard to believe but the ratio for recording a place position was far worse twelve months previously when it stood at 1 in 14 races. The ratio has improved as a result of two of last year's six **Kapgarde** representatives securing runner-up spots in their respective two mile hurdle events. In the 2018 *Boodles Fred Winter Juvenile Handicap Hurdle*, **Style De Garde** was no threat to the winner, but it was still a pleasing performance to record 2nd position at a price of 12/1. The following day, the *Willie Mullins* trained *Laurina* annihilated the opposition in the third running of the *Trull House Stud Mares' Novices Hurdle*. The closest horse to get to her, some 18 lengths behind, was the **Kapgarde** sired *Cap Soleil*, who returned a price of 10/1.

The four festival places achieved by **Kapgarde**'s progeny have come in hurdle events, three of them at the minimum distance. Of the four runs to date where a horse by **Kapgarde** has travelled over three miles, 9th is the highest position achieved. We can't read anything into this as the numbers are so small and the starting price of the four were 66/1, 33/1 and 25/1 twice. With little festival data to go on, and knowing that **Kapgarde**'s offspring had so far failed to win a festival race, I decided to find out how many winners had **Kapgarde** sired horses achieved at Cheltenham outside of the festival.

As of early January, in over 1400 National Hunt Rules Races, **Kapgarde**'s offspring had registered over 200 wins, of which around 46% were achieved in chase events, 41% over hurdles and 13% in National Hunt Flat races. If anything, these figures are marginally encouraging for fans of **Clan Des Obeaux**. But, how many of those 200-odd wins were achieved at Prestbury Park? The answer is just five, which in my view doesn't bode well for the chances of **Clan des Obeaux**. Worse still, only one of those five victories was over a distance of greater than 2m½f and only one of the wins was over the Cheltenham Fences. **Garde La Victoire** was responsible for both, winning the 2m4½f *Citipost Novices' Hurdle* (13/8 favourite) in 2014 and the *Racing Post Arkle Trophy Trial Novices' Chase* (2m) in November 2015 when the odds on 8/15 favourite.

In conclusion, there is a weight of evidence to suggest that **Kapgarde**'s progeny find it very difficult to win at Cheltenham. And on the few occasions where horses by **Kapgarde** have been victorious at Prestbury Park, it has largely been in hurdle events at the minimum distance. In line with that, the four places that have been achieved at a Cheltenham Festival meeting have all occurred in hurdle contests, three of them over a distance of two miles. All of which tells me that the first festival victory for **Kapgarde**'s offspring will not happen in a competitive chase event over a distance of 3m2½f. Supporters of **Clan Des Obeaux** may well argue that the horse has been knocking at the door at Cheltenham, having been runner-up on 3 of the 4 occasions in which he has been to the course. But I would counter that on the basis that one of the three events was a hurdle event at the minimum distance and the two chase events were over 2m5f. Also, all three contests were Grade 2 or Grade 3 contests.

Forget **Clan Des Obeaux**. If you are interested in finding the first festival winner to be sired by **Kapgarde**, then look into the two mile hurdle contests. It will happen sooner or later.

Kayf Tara (GB)

Quote from the 2018 Cheltenham Festival Stallion Guide - "Perhaps one of the offspring will win at the 2018 Cheltenham Festival, but my advice to punters is not to waste your time trying to work out which one it will be from the likely 15-25 **Kayf Tara** bred entries. Focus your efforts to pick winners elsewhere."

Kayf Tara (25-y-o)							
Race Format	*Miles*	*Won*	*Placed*	*Unplaced*	*Total*	*Win %*	*Place %*
Hurdles	About 2m	0	0	13	13	0%	0%
	About 2m 4f	0	1	19	20	0%	5%
	About 3m	2	2	16	20	10%	20%
Chases	About 2m	1	3	11	15	7%	27%
	About 2m 4f	0	0	13	13	0%	0%
	About 3m	3	6	18	27	11%	33%
	About 4m	0	1	8	9	0%	11%
Bumper	About 2m	1	0	4	5	20%	20%
Total	2009-2018	**7**	**13**	**102**	**122**	**6%**	**16%**

Seventy-four horses sired by **Kayf Tara** have registered 126 festival appearances between them, of which 122 runs have occurred in the past decade. Just under 10% of the progeny have passed the post in first place and all seven have succeeded once only, which translates into a win strike percentage of a mere 6%, or one win for the offspring for every 16 appearances. All of which explains the quote at the top of the page, advising punters not to waste time trying to find **Kayf Tara** bred festival winners.

For anyone who ignored the advice, they ended up out of pocket. Fifteen horses by **Kayf Tara** lined up at the 2018 Cheltenham Festival and all 15 were beaten. Supporters of **Kayf Tara** may look for excuses and perhaps suggest that the soft going was the culprit, an argument with which I disagree. Preceding last year's meeting, in eleven previous runs on soft ground at the festival, the highest finishing position from **Kayf Tara**'s stock was 5th with the next best placing being 8th. That record was bettered in 2018, where in 15 soft-ground appearances, horses sired by **Kayf Tara** registered finishing places of second, third and fourth, rewarding each-way backers with two place dividends.

I've already said that it is unproductive trying to find **Kayf Tara** sired winners at Cheltenham. And it is also a worthless exercise to procrastinate about the state of the going or indeed inventing any other negligible rationale as to why **Kayf Tara**'s offspring don't perform at the festival. Put simply, horses by **Kayf Tara** aren't at their best in early spring, racing on a left-handed course with undulations, where the atmosphere is electric. And there are 13 years of overwhelming evidence, going back to the first of the progeny's 126 festival appearances in 2006, to support my assertion.

If you are a huge fan of **Kayf Tara**'s stock but only gamble on the offspring when you attend the Cheltenham Festival in person, then you will be extremely lucky if you have only been to the festival twice in the past 13 years, in 2009 and 2012. For these are the only two years in which betting on **Kayf Tara**'s offspring blind to level stakes would have made a profit. To a £1.00 each-way stake, backing all of **Kayf Tara**'s runners would have resulted in profits of £11.00 in 2009 and £9.25 in 2012.

At this juncture, I am guessing that a number of **Kayf Tara** supporters are reading this, thinking that I haven't done my homework. I can hear the cries of "What about 2016?" Undoubtedly, 2016 was **Kayf Tara**'s year. The offspring had managed just three victories (all in handicap events) from 70 appearances preceding the 2016 Cheltenham Festival. This all changed at the 2016 festival, where we witnessed not only a doubling of wins, but all three of them were Group 1 victories. No other stallion achieved three wins at that festival. So, what would have been the profits for any punter who had backed all 25 horses sired by **Kayf Tara** at that meeting? To a £1.00 each-way stake, the answer was a loss of £23.00.

With just two profitable festival meetings, and a loss-making 2016 when the **Kayf Tara** sired trio of **Thistlecrack**, **Blaklion** and **Ballyandy** claimed Group 1 crowns, punters may be interested to know the total scale of losses had one backed all 126 of the offspring at the past 13 festivals. The answer is a loss of £99.36 to a £1.00 each-way stake. The losses aren't defendable by the idea that perhaps the majority of **Kayf Tara**'s 126 festival representatives were outsiders. The reality is that 54% of the offspring lined up at odds of 20/1 or shorter, and 9 of the 126 entrants were sent off as favourite, of which only **Thistlecrack**, at evens, was successful in the 2016 *Ryanair World Hurdle*.

Two of those nine favourites raced at last year's festival with wildly different outcomes. In the *Pertemps Network Final Handicap Hurdle*, two horses trained by *Gordon Elliott* fought out a hugely exciting finish, with the **Kayf Tara** sired 9/2 favourite, **Glenloe**, just failing to take the prize by a nose. **Glenloe**, who was having just his ninth race under rules, would probably have won the race had he not blundered at the last hurdle. Despite rallying after the last, the *John P McManus* owned 7-year-old was unable to get past the game winner, *Delta Work* (6/1) who being owned by *Gigginstown House Stud*, also benefitted from powerful connections.

Another **Kayf Tara** bred seven year-old, **North Hill Harvey**, was the 7/1 favourite in a field of 22 runners for the last race of the festival, the *Johnny Henderson Grand Annual Challenge Cup Handicap Chase*. Tragically, the race was marred by the death of three of the runners, one of whom was **North Hill Harvey** who was still travelling well, disputing 2nd place, when he fell three fences from home. In total, there were six deaths at the festival meeting, and in the immediate aftermath, the *British Horseracing Authority* announced that they would carry out a detailed review of the equine fatalities and long-term injuries that occurred at the 2018 Cheltenham Festival. In late October 2018, *Robin Mounsey*, the BHA's media manager, announced that the review was nearing its conclusion and that over the coming weeks, the recommendations would be discussed with stakeholders and welfare organisations ahead of the report being finalised and published.

It is worth noting two other encouraging performances from **Kayf Tara**'s progeny from last year's festival, the first of which was in the opening day's *Unibet Champion Hurdle Challenge Trophy*, where **Identity Thief** finished in 4th place. The gelding found the searching gallop rather difficult in the early stages of the race, making a couple of mistakes, before his stamina kept him going from three out enabling him to finish in fourth, albeit over 12 lengths away from the odds-on 4/6 winner, *Buveur D'Air*. At a price of 50/1, it was an encouraging effort in the heavy going, and as a result, trainer *Henry de Bromhead* and *the Gigginstown House Stud* owners decided to race him over three miles for the first time at *Aintree*, the following month. The decision clearly paid off as **Identity Thief** saw out the trip in the Grade 1 *Ryanair Stayers Hurdle* really well, winning the event by 5 lengths at a price of 14/1.

In last season's *St James's Place Foxhunter Challenge Cup Open Hunters' Chase*, a race that was run about 15 seconds slower than the immediate contest before it, the *Timico Cheltenham Gold Cup Chase*, a **Kayf Tara** bred horse finished in a dead heat for 3rd place at a price of 66/1. **Cousin Pete**, owned by *Mrs Scilla Phillips* and trained by Cirencester based, *Mrs Elizabeth Brown*, was enjoying only his third National Hunt race under Rules. Perhaps, connections should enter *Cousin Pete* in more Rules races. In his three runs as of early January, the 11-year-old has finished 1st, 2nd and 3rd.

In looking at the festival performance table of **Kayf Tara**'s stock over the past decade, three race categories have win & place strike rate percentages of 20% or greater, which may suggest that if one is so inclined to bet on a horse by **Kayf Tara**, it makes sense to focus efforts on any race within the 3m categories and two mile chases. I would agree with this strategy if one is very much taken by a particular runner sired by **Kayf Tara**, although a deeper analysis of the win and place positions suggests that one shouldn't be too hasty before placing any wagers.

In 15 festival chases over a distance of around two miles, **Kayf Tara**'s progeny have secured one victory and 3 place positions, boasting a 27% win & place strike rate. However, it is worth knowing that *Special Tiara* alone is responsible for the victory and two of the three 3 place positions, when taking 3rd place in both the 2015 and 2016 renewals of the *Queen Mother Champion Chase*, before winning the contest on his 4th attempt in 2017. When it comes to the 3m chase category, which shows an 11% winning percentage and a 33% win & place hit rate, two of **Kayf Tara**'s offspring have undoubtedly had a domineering impact on the numbers. In short, 66% of both the win positions and the place dividends have been achieved by two of **Kayf Tara**'s better offspring, these being The *Package* (1 win and 3 places) and *Alfie Sherrin* (1 win and 1 place).

If I was forced to place a bet on a **Kayf Tara** festival entry, then I would plump for one of the three long distance hurdle events, with my preference being the handicap contest, the *Pertemps Network Final*. In 12 appearances in this race, **Kayf Tara**'s offspring have secured a win with *Kayf Aramis* at 16/1 in 2009; a runner-up with *Glenloe* (9/2 fav) in 2018, and a third place with *Cantlow* at 33/1 in 2012. The progeny have contested the non-handicap 3m events on far fewer occasions. In six appearances in the *Spa Novices' Hurdle*, runners by **Kayf Tara** have so far failed to reward punters with a return on bets, although two of the entrants have finished just outside the places, registering 4th and 5th positions. As for the *Stayers Hurdle*, only two horses by **Kayf Tara** have appeared in this race, one of whom was *Lieutenant Colonel* who was largely disappointing in both his appearances in 2015 and 2016. In the latter race, when *Lieutenant Colonel* was pulled up, it was another of **Kayf Tara**'s offspring, and indeed the very best of them, who claimed the crown. After winning the 2106 *Stayers Hurdle*, **Thistlecrack**, owned by *John* and *Heather Snook*, was raised 6lb to an Official Rating of 174, the highest rating of any **Kayf Tara** bred racehorse. He has also amassed the most earnings of the progeny, at the time of writing, £657,986, a few thousand pounds ahead of *Special Tiara* and well over double the 3rd highest earner.

Come March, among the likely fifteen or more runners from this stallion's progeny to appear at Prestbury Park, although there could be an 8th **Kayf Tara** sired Cheltenham Festival winner, my belief is that it won't happen. And even if there is a win, or indeed a couple of place dividends, any loyal punter who is foolish enough to bet blind on all of this offspring's runners at level stakes, will undoubtedly make a loss.

Festival entries by **Kayf Tara** aren't for me.

King's Theatre (IRE)

Quote from the 2018 Cheltenham Festival Stallion Guide - "In total, there have been 19 **King's Theatre** sired runners who have taken part in festival hurdle races over a distance of three miles. Six of the twelve runners that were priced at 20/1 or less, have managed to register a win or 2nd placing. For the record, a £1.00 each-way bet on all twelve **King's Theatre** bred runners in the festival's three mile hurdle events, who had an SP of 20/1 or under, would have produced a profit of £10.58".

King's Theatre (Died as a 20-y-o in 2011)							
Race Format	*Miles*	*Won*	*Placed*	*Unplaced*	*Total*	*Win %*	*Place %*
	About 2m	1	4	12	17	6%	29%
Hurdles	About 2m 4f	3	3	24	30	10%	20%
	About 3m	2	3	14	19	11%	26%
	About 2m	1	2	7	10	10%	30%
Chases	About 2m 4f	2	3	16	21	10%	24%
	About 3m	2	3	34	39	5%	13%
	About 4m	2	0	8	10	20%	20%
Bumper	About 2m	1	2	6	9	11%	33%
Total	2009-2018	**14**	**20**	**121**	**155**	**9%**	**22%**

At the last 10 Cheltenham Festivals, 87 of **King's Theatre**'s progeny have registered 155 runs between them. Three of the offspring have won at the festival twice, these being *Balthazar King* and *Cue Card* within the past decade, and *Wichita Lineman*. *Cue Card* is the most renowned of **King's Theatre**'s stock and also the highest rated, having been given an official rating of 176 which he held throughout the whole of 2016, when competing in 6 events, five of them being Grade 1 Chases.

Last season, at twelve years old, *Cue Card* made his 7th Cheltenham Festival appearance in the *Ryanair Chase*. It was a small field of just six runners, with *Cue Card* being the 9/2 second favourite behind the 8/11 odds-on *Un De Sceaux*. As it turned out, the favourite was beaten unable to stay in front of the 8/1 impressive winner from *Henry De Bromhead*'s yard, *Balko Des Flos*, who drew clear between the last two fences to win by 4½ lengths. As for *Cue Card*, it was one race too far and he was pulled up for the only time in his career six fences from home. One month later and owner *Jean Bishop* decided that this wonderful servant to *Colin Tizzard*'s yard should be retired, a decision that for me, was wholeheartedly the correct one.

Cue Card, who played such a huge part in setting up *Colin Tizzard* to be such a prolific National Hunt training force, accumulated prize money of £1,447,454 in his 41-race career, winning 16 races, including two festival victories comprising of his shock 40-1 victory in the 2010 *Weatherbys Champion Bumper* and his win in the 2013 *Ryanair Chase* three years later. Considering that *Cue Card* was such a talent, it is rather surprising to realise that his success in the latter race was to be the last time in which he completed a Cheltenham Festival race. He missed the 2014 festival after pulling some muscles in his back and twelve months later, he missed the festival again due to a small wind problem. The following two years in 2016 and 2017, he suffered two heart-breaking falls in the *Timico Cheltenham Gold Cup Chase*, crashing out at the third from home in both renewals.

With **King's Theatre**'s offspring having amassed 14 festival victories in the past decade, *Cue Card* won't be the only familiar name amongst the winners, and many punters will have happy memories of collecting winnings from backing horses such as **Captain Chris, Menorah, Riverside Theatre, The New One, Wichita Lineman** and **Balthazar King**. There aren't too many stallions who can boast that their progeny have recorded more than ten Cheltenham Festival victories, and within this Guide, there are just four sires who have secured ten festival wins in the past decade, these being **King's Theatre** (14), *Robin Des Champs* (14), *Presenting* (11) and *Oscar* (10). That said, **King's Theatre** supporters have had a rather lean time of it recently, with just one victory to show for the 61 of the progeny who have lined up in festival races at the past three Cheltenham meetings.

Having been represented by 24 festival entries in both 2016 and 2017, there was quite a drop in runners sired by **King's Theatre** at last year's meeting, with just 13 appearances. The fall in numbers may be partly explained by some trainers deciding to withdraw their potential participants because of the soft ground, although this century, the record of **King's Theatre**'s stock in previous soft ground festival races is in line with this stallion's performances on better ground, with two place positions to show for the nine previous soft ground runs from the offspring this century. At the 2018 Meeting, despite the soft ground, just two of the 13 runners by **King's Theatre** failed to complete their races. **Dawn Shadow**, a 50/1 outsider, was a faller three out in the *Trull House Stud Mares' Novices' Hurdle*, and **Diamond King** at 33/1 was pulled up in the *Coral Cup Handicap Hurdle*. It was **Diamond King**'s second appearance in the *Coral Cup* and a very different outcome from his first run in 2016, where jockey *Davy Russell* registered his 16th Festival winner on board the 12/1 chance. **Diamond King** is the solitary **King's Theatre** bred winner out of the 61 appearances from this sire's progeny at the past three Cheltenham Festivals.

In addition to **Diamond King**, there were two more runners by **King's Theatre** in the 2018 *Coral Cup Handicap Hurdle*, one of whom was **William Henry**, the 8/1 joint favourite. Riding **William Henry**, just a couple of days after his 17th birthday, was *James Bowen*, who at *Chepstow* in January 2018, became the youngest jockey to win the *Coral Welsh Grand National Handicap Chase*, when securing the prize aboard the oldest horse in the race, the thirteen-year-old, *Raz De Maree*. In the *Coral Cup*, the conditional jockey gave **William Henry** a fine ride, but the 8-year-old didn't have the pace of his younger rivals, eventually picking up a place dividend for backers, when finishing in 4th and 2¾ lengths behind the winner, *Bleu Berry*. The other **King's Theatre** bred representative in the race was **Royal Vacation** (22/1) who completed the race to finish 18th.

The other performance of note for **King's Theatre** supporters at last year's meeting, was in the Grade 3 *Brown Advisory & Merriebelle Stable Plate Handicap Chase*, where once again, **King's Odyssey** (14/1) was in a good position and running well before his lack of a finishing kick played out once again and he was unable to keep pace with victor, *The Storyteller* and runner-up, *Splash Of Ginge*. Nevertheless, it was still a very satisfactory performance from **King's Odyssey**, who managed to keep going all the way up the famous Cheltenham Hill, to record a 3rd place finish for trainer *Evan Williams* and jockey *Adam Wedge*.

Despite the achievement of **King's Odyssey** to finish 3rd in the *Brown Advisory & Merriebelle Stable Plate Handicap Chase*, my rule for punters is to steer clear of runners by **King's Theatre** in the festival's two 2½m chase handicap events. In a total of 14 appearances within this category, comprising of 9 runs in the *Brown Advisory & Merriebelle Stable Plate Handicap Chase* and 5 runs in the *Close Brothers Novices' Handicap Chase,* the offspring have never finished 1st or 2nd. Three of the progeny managed a 3rd place finish; **King's Palace** (2016) and **King's Odyssey** (2018) in the *Brown Advisory & Merriebelle Stable Plate* and **Tumbling Dice** in the 2006 *Novices' Handicap Chase*, when the event was sponsored by *Jewson*. Of the remaining eleven runs by the representatives of **King's Theatre**, seven were pulled up, one fell, and three managed to complete their races, with finishing positions of 6th, 10th and 14th.

Within the races run over a distance of 2½ miles, a few years ago, I wasn't especially keen on supporting **King's Theatre** bred runners in the festivals 2½m handicap hurdles either, which consist of the *Coral Cup Handicap Hurdle* and the *Martin Pipe Conditional Jockeys' Handicap Hurdle*. As a result of **William Henry**'s 4th place finish in last year's *Coral Cup* following on from **Diamond King**'s 2016 victory in the same race, I am no longer so negative about the *Coral Cup*. In 10 appearances by **King's Theatre**'s stock in this contest, as well as the results from **Diamond King** and **William Henry** highlighted above, one can add **Tumbling Dice**'s third place finish at 16/1 in the 2005 running. The other 7 runs have been uninspiring, with results of 8th, 20th, 21st, 11th, 15th, 18th and PU. In the other 2½m handicap contest, the *Martin Pipe Conditional Jockeys' Handicap Hurdle*, the six runs by **King's Theatre** bred horses has resulted in just two top ten finishes of 6th and 9th.

Whilst on the topic of festival races over two and a half miles, if we analyse the four contests that are non-handicaps, I believe that the chances are remote for **King's Theatre**'s progeny to add to the victories secured by **The New One** (2013 *Neptune Investment Management Novices' Hurdle*), **Glen's Melody** (2015 *OLBG Mares' Hurdle*) and the successes of **Riverside Theatre** (2012) and **Cue Card** (2013) in the *Ryanair Chase*. There are a number of reasons why I am pessimistic, the most compelling being that with **King's Theatre** death in 2011, the majority of entries by **King's Theatre** at the 2019 Cheltenham Festival onwards will most likely be 8 years of age or older, perhaps with one or two runners being 7-year-olds. And it is highly unusual for older runners in these non-handicap 2½m events to win. Take, for example, the *Ballymore Novices' Hurdle*. Only twice in the 47 contests since the race was first established in 1971 has the winner been over six years old. *French Holly* claimed victory as a 7-year-old in 1998 and *Brown Lad* took the prize as an 8-year-old way back in 1974. All of which means that **King's Theatre**'s stock will, in all likelihood, forever have a 100% win record in the race, courtesy of **The New One**, who has been the one and only **King's Theatre** bred horse to be entered in the race. The horse, trained by *Nigel Twiston-Davies* and ridden by his son, *Sam*, ran on strongly to beat *Rule The World*, who himself went on to win the 2016 *Crabbie's Grand National Chase* at *Aintree*.

The other 2½m non-handicap hurdle at the Cheltenham Festival is restricted to mares, the *OLBG Mares' Hurdle*, where no less than seven of the 11 winners have been aged older than six. The statistics, however, are significantly influenced by the brilliant *Quevega* who won this race on six occasions, being a five-year-old on her debut in 2009 and winning on her 6th appearance as a 10-year-old in 2014. **King's Theatre**'s offspring have been represented in this race on no less than sixteen occasions. Only six of the runners lined up at odds of 25/1 or less and, in chronological order, the finishing positions and the starting prices were 5th (9/2), 3rd (9/4), 7th (8/1), 2nd (14/1), 1st (6/1) and 4th (25/1). If one had backed all six of the above to a £1.00 each-way stake, the result would be a profit of £2.45, although it should be noted that the positive figure is largely due to **Glens Melody** benefitting from *Annie Power*'s fall in the 2015 contest. **Glens Melody** was seven years old when she won that year and indeed three of the past four winners have been aged seven also. That said, looking through the current list of mares sired by **King's Theatre**, there are very few aged seven, let alone one who looks to have the class necessary to win the race. The four most recent winners all held an official rating of 147 or higher.

The two Grade 1 festival chases within the 2½m category are the *JLT Novices' Chase* and the *Ryanair Chase*. On the eight occasions in which the former race has been run, it has been won by either a six or seven-year-old rated between 144 and 155. That profile certainly limits the chance of a runner bred by **King's Theatre** winning this race, although I guess there is a chance that the connections of **Drinks Interval** may give some thought to entering their improving mare in the race. Trained in Dorset by *Colin Tizzard*, **Drinks Interval** was entered in her first Novice Chase at *Newton Abbot* in July 2018 with an official rating of 125. She caused an upset too, beating *The Unit*, who was the 140 rated 4/11 odds-on favourite. **Drinks Interval** won two of her next three races, her best performance being in the *Istadia Outdoor LED Screens Supports Racing Novices' Chase* at *Chepstow* over a distance of 2m7½f, where she won by 11 lengths at a price of 10/1. In her fifth novice chase on November 8th, and now off an official mark of 147, she was running well and looking the likely winner when she fell two from home in a Listed mares' race at *Market Rasen*. Following two mares' chases in December, it is still far too early to know whether **Drinks Interval** will travel to Cheltenham or more to the point, in which race she will be entered, especially given that four of her last five races have been at a distance of around three miles. That said, with a rating of 145 and being a seven-year-old, she does fall within the profile of the eight previous winners of the *JLT Novices Chase*. If she does run, connections will hope that a mare can win the race for the second consecutive year, following the success of *Shattered Love* in the 2018 running. It will be a tough ask. *Shattered Love* was the first of her sex to win a novice chase at the festival since 1995.

As for the *Ryanair Chase*, the first running of this contest took place in 2005, when the *Paul Nicholls* trained, *Thisthatandtother*, off a mark of 155, beat *Fondmort* by half a length. Back then, the race was a Grade 2, but was raised to Grade 1 status in 2008, a year when *Our Vic* won off an official rating of 165. Since then, in the past decade, seven more winners have been successful off official ratings of between 165 and 176. Although 9 of the 14 winners of this race have been aged eight or more, it will still take a very high quality **King's Theatre** bred horse to take this prize at the 2019 Cheltenham Festival. The only one of the progeny who could potentially fit the bill is **Bellshill**, who hails from *Willie Mullins'* yard and has an official rating of 168. However, following his *Punchestown* victory on 25th April 2018, in the Grade 1 *Coral Punchestown Gold Cup*, it would appear that he will be campaigned for a shot at the big one, the *Magners Cheltenham Gold Cup Steeple* Chase, a race that *Willie Mullins* is yet to win.

In looking at the table of festival statistics over the past decade for runners by **King's Theatre**, the top three strike rates for win & place positions are all in the two mile distance categories, with 2m hurdles showing 29%, 2m chases 30% and the National Hunt Flat percentage registering 33%. Unfortunately, as highlighted earlier, **King's Theatre**'s remaining progeny are now approaching their later years and as a result, festival entries for the offspring in the two mile events are going to be limited. For example, if we look at the six hurdle races, because of age, it can almost be guaranteed that **King's Theatre** will be unrepresented in the four 2m novice hurdle events. And for the *Champion Hurdle*, one almost certainly requires a horse that has an official mark in excess of 160. There have only been two *Champion Hurdle* winners in the past decade who have been older than seven years old. The exceptional *Hurricane Fly* was rated 172 and nine years old when taking the hurdling crown in 2013 and *Annie Power* was aged eight and rated 162 when winning in 2016. Perhaps we may see a **King's Theatre** bred runner in the *Randox Health County Handicap Hurdle*, but then again, older winners are rare, with just two winners aged older than six years old in the past decade. Both winners, *Alderwood* in 2012 and *Arctic Fire* in 2017, were eight years old and both, coincidentally, won at the rewarding odds of 20/1.

Of the remaining four festival events run over the shortest distance, because of the age range of **King's Theatre**'s remaining stock, we can discount the *Racing Post Arkle Challenge Trophy Novices' Chase* and the *Weatherbys Champion Bumper*, which leaves just two races remaining, both of which have had older horses win. In the past decade, there have been six winners aged eight or more in the *Grand Annual Chase Challenge Cup* and seven winners aged greater than seven, have won the *Queen Mother Champion Chase*, five of whom were aged nine or ten. In this contest, the evidence clearly suggests that a classy animal with the ability to jump at speed is far more important than age, as only the 10-year-old *Special Tiara*, with an official rating of 159, is the only winner in the past decade to have run off a mark below 160. In both of the above races, the offspring of **King's Theatre** have been represented on just five occasions, once in the *Queen Mother* and four times in the *Grand Annual*, the highest position registered being **Dick Dundee**'s 6th placing at 100/1 in the 2015 *A.P.*

McCoy Grand Annual Chase Challenge Cup, named in honour of the multiple champion jockey's last festival ride.

There have been 170 runners by **King's Theatre** who have lined up at the Cheltenham Festival, which all started with **Lord Joshua** being pulled up in the 2002 *JCB Triumph Hurdle*. Within those 170 runs, there have been 15 victories which is the reason why **King's Theatre** has so often been mentioned as a sire to follow at the Cheltenham. Seven of these 15 successes have come in races run over three miles or more, and due to this stallion's passing in 2011, it will be within the 3m and 4m distance categories where future **King's Theatre** bred winners are likely to come from. Fortunately, for **King's Theatre** supporters, there are ten races at the Cheltenham Festival that are run over these longer distances. Within these ten events, **King's Theatre**'s progeny have claimed victories in the four races listed below:

Spa Novices' Hurdle (3m) - **Wichita Lineman** (2007) and **Brindisi Breeze** (2012)
Pertemps Network Final (3m) – **Fingal Bay** (2014)
Ultima Handicap Chase (3m) – **Wichita Lineman** (2009) and **The Druids Nephew** (2015)
Glenfarclas Cross Country Chase (3m6f) – **Balthazar King** (2012 and 2014)

Despite the wins shown above, which shows a 10% win strike from the 70 appearances from the progeny in the 3m and 4m contests, it is apparent to me that over these longer distances, further success for **King's Theatre**'s offspring is by no means a foregone conclusion. The first insight is that four of the seven wins have been secured by just two of the 46 of **King's Theatre** bred horses that have been engaged in these 3m and 4m categories; **Wichita Lineman** and **Balthazar King**. In addition, two of the victories came in the *Spa Novices' Hurdle* which was first introduced to the Cheltenham Festival in 2005. In 13 of the 14 years in which this race has been run, the winner has been aged five, six or seven. Only once has the race gone to an eight-year-old, when *Unowhatimeanharry* took the prize in 2016.

As for the 3m event for novices over fences, it would appear that there is a strong advantage to being a seven year in the *RSA Novices' Chase*, as 14 of the last 18 winners were aged 7, which means that it could be an appropriate target for the **King's Theatre** bred 7yo **Drinks Interval**, who I covered earlier in this chapter when covering the *JLT Novices' Chase*. The last six winners of the *RSA Novices' Chase* ran off official ratings of between 144 and 158, so **Drinks Interval** is a possible entry with her official mark of 145. To close off on the *RSA Chase*, the two most recent 8yo winners were *Rule Supreme* in 2004 and *Might Bite* in 2017.

In analysing the remaining eight long distance festival contests, in the past decade, 53 of the 80 winners of these races have been aged eight or more, so it is in these races where one would expect to see more entries by **King's Theatre**, and hence some further winners. If we discount the *Spa Novices' Hurdle*, in the other two 3m hurdle events, **King's Theatre** has been represented on 13 occasions, managing a 20/1 runner-up finish with **Voler La Vedette** in the 2012 *Ladbrokes World Hurdle* and a 1-2 finish in the 2014 *Pertemps Network Final* when the **King's Theatre** bred duo of **Fingal Bay** (winner) and **Southfield Theatre** (runner-up), were separated by just a nose.

If we set aside the *RSA Novices' Chase* which has already been covered above, the remaining four 3m category contests over fences make interesting reading. Runners by **King's Theatre** have participated in thirty 3m chase events, of which exactly half have lined up in the *Ultima Handicap Chase* which has resulted in two victories, courtesy of the previously mentioned, **Wichita Lineman** and **The Druids Nephew**. In the other 13 appearances, only **King Fontaine** has managed to deliver a top six finish, when registering fifth position at 16/1 in 2011. The closest that a **King's Theatre** bred horse has come to winning any of the three other chases at three miles is almost certainly on the two occasions when **Cue Card** fell three from home in both the 2016 and 2017 *Timico Cheltenham Gold Cup Chase* contests. Indeed, even though the offspring have only had five appearances in the race, it is the *Cheltenham Gold Cup* where runners by **King's Theatre** probably have the best 3m chase record. In addition to **Cue Card**'s two departures from the race, **Captain Chris** managed a respectable 6th position in 2013 and **Carlingford Lough** was one outside the places, finishing 4th in 2016. *Willie Mullins* has never won the Cheltenham Gold Cup, but he may have a chance with the **King's Theatre** sired, **Bellshill**, who was victorious at odds of 4/1 when winning the Grade 1 *Coral Punchestown Gold Cup* back in April 2018. As for the *Foxhunters* (4 runs) and the *Fulke Walwyn Kim Muir Challenge Cup Handicap Chase* (6 runs), performances need to improve, as runners by **King's Theatre** have never finished higher than 8th.

As for the two races within the 4m category, producing any conclusions based on just a total of ten runs is inappropriate. The **King's Theatre** sired **Balthazar King** has taken part in the *Glenfarclas Cross Country Chase* on three occasions, winning twice in 2012 and 2014, and then falling in 2016. There has only been one other participant in this event, this being **Kingswell Theatre** who finished 10th in the 2017 running. As for the six runners by **King's Theatre** who have contested the *National Hunt Challenge Cup Amateur Riders' Novices' Chase*, four of them ran in the 2015 race, two of whom parted company with their jockeys. The other two horses ran respectable races, albeit they both weakened up the run-in. **Perfect Gentleman** led with a circuit to go but the 10-year-old's stamina emptied when headed at the last fence and he eventually finished in 4th, two places in front of the other **King's Theatre** representative, **Cogry**, who made up a lot of ground approaching the latter stages of the race, but couldn't maintain the momentum after jumping the last. There was a single runner by **King's Theatre** in the 2016 and 2017 *National Hunt Chase*; **Ballychorus** unseated jockey, *Mr S Clements* in 2016 and **Ballycross** finished 10th at odds of 100/1 in the 2017 contest.

Historically, there has been very little coverage given to the importance of breeding and stallion trends in the build-up to a Cheltenham Festival, hence my decision to write this Guide back in 2015. However, at that time, when something did appear in the media about the performance of certain stallions at the festival, invariably **King's Theatre** was the first sire to be mentioned. And to be truthful, rightly so, as very few stallions have amassed fifteen festival winners from their bloodlines. But we are now in 2019 and **King's Theatre** passed away in 2011, hence most of his offspring are now eight years old, with a couple of exceptions being aged seven, such as **Drinks Interval**. As a result, a large percentage of the 28 Cheltenham Festival races are now out of reach for **King's Theatre**'s offspring, and so, in my opinion, further winners by **King's Theatre** will be few and far between.

In the festival races where older horses do win, the trends for runners sired by **King's Theatre** are rather inconclusive, and so any advice to punters would be rather whimsical. Nevertheless, I will conclude with some observations. By the time this Guide is published, punters will hopefully have taken a view on the **Kings' Theatre** bred duo of **Bellshill** and **Drinks Interval**. Will either take part in the festival? And if so, which race will they contest? And do either have the necessary class to win?

At the time of writing, I'm undecided about both horses, but I can't see any other runner by **King's Theatre** troubling the judge in four of the festival's biggest races. If you are impressed with **Bellshill**, then look out for him in the *Ryanair Chase*, or more likely, the *Magners Cheltenham Gold Cup Steeple Chase*. And if you believe that **Drinks Interval** can be the second mare, since 1995, to win a novice chase at the festival, then the races to focus upon are the *JLT Novices' Chase* and the *RSA Novices' Chase*.

As for the remaining festival races, the three events where runners by **King's Theatre** have the best chance of securing a victory or placing are the *Sun Racing Stayers' Hurdle*, the *Pertemps Network Final* and the *Ultima Handicap Chase*.

Martaline (GB)

Quote from the 2018 Cheltenham Festival Stallion Guide - "Don't be surprised if a **Martaline** sired runner picks up a festival event in one of the other race categories (other than 2½m chases). Picking out any sort of trend for **Martaline**'s offspring based on previous festival appearances is rather difficult."

Race Format	Miles	Won	Placed	Unplaced	Total	Win %	Place %
	Martaline (20-y-o)						
	About 2m	0	0	3	3	0%	0%
Hurdles	About 2m 4f	0	0	5	5	0%	0%
	About 3m	1	0	5	6	17%	17%
	About 2m	0	0	1	1	0%	0%
Chases	About 2m 4f	1	3	2	6	17%	67%
	About 3m	0	1	4	5	0%	20%
	About 4m	0	0	1	1	0%	0%
Bumper	About 2m	0	1	4	5	0%	20%
Total	2009-2018	**2**	**5**	**25**	**32**	**6%**	**22%**

Martaline continues to challenge me. Of all the Stallions featured in this Guide, he is by far the most difficult in which to find any trends. Seven of the offspring raced at the 2018 Cheltenham Festival, delivering two place positions. Adding the seven runs to the 25 that went before hasn't shed any more light on being able to predict how his progeny will perform at this year's meeting.

The best that I could offer in the 2018 Cheltenham Festival Stallion Guide was a hunch that horses by **Martaline** may be most suited to chases within the 2½m category, and on the Thursday at last year's festival, we had the chance to watch two of the offspring in chases over this distance. In the opening event, the _JLT Novices' Chase_, **Martaline** was to be represented by _Terrefort_, trained by _Nicky Henderson_. Lining up as the 3/1 favourite, the market expected _Terrefort_ to run well, and he obliged, jumping well and travelling strongly. In the end, he was beaten by a top class mare in the shape of the _Gordon Elliott_ trained, _Shattered Love_. A month after this race, _Terrefort_ showed his potential at _Aintree_, winning the _Betway Mildmay Novices' Chase_.

Later that afternoon, the second 2½m chaser by **Martaline** would make an appearance in the _Brown Advisory & Merriebelle Stable Plate Handicap Chase_. In this race, the market took the view that _Viconte Du Noyer_ (33/1) would not be troubling the judge at the end of the race, and once again, the market was right. _Viconte Du Noyer_ struggled at the rear throughout the race and was pulled up with three fences still to jump.

A 3/1 favourite finishing 2nd and a 33/1 outsider being pulled up in 2½m chases doesn't tell us anything, but nevertheless, I should mention that in three appearances in the _JLT Novices' Chase_, runners by **Martaline** have a 100% record of being placed, again not especially unexpected as all three were short in the market. Before _Terrefort_, _Dynaste_ was the 11/8 favourite when runner-up in 2013 and _Disko_ was priced at 4/1 when finishing 3rd in the 2017 renewal. An acknowledgement of _Disko_'s achievements is appropriate here as sadly _Disko_ suffered a fatal injury when falling at the last fence in the _Savills Chase_ at _Leopardstown_ on December 28th 2018. _Disko_ was a dual Grade 1 winner, who, at just seven years of age, had many more races in him. He had 13 career starts, winning six of them.

The second of the place dividends registered by **Martaline**'s offspring at last year's festival was achieved by **Squouateur** in the *Fulke Walwyn Kim Muir Challenge Cup Amateur Riders' Handicap Chase*. My guess is that many punters lost quite a few bets on the *Gordon Elliott* trained **Squouateur** at the previous two Cheltenham Festivals. He was all the rage in the 2016 *Martin Pipe Conditional Jockeys' Handicap Hurdle* when backed into 9/4 favouritism, but couldn't ever get into the race and he eventually finished seventh. The following year, **Squouateur** was once again the favourite, this time at 5/1, in the 2017 renewal of the *Kim Muir*. Just as he was starting to make some steady progress into the race, he unseated his rider three fences from home. With the highly talented amateur jockey, *Jamie Codd*, in the saddle, I guess some punters may have believed that had he not unseated, the horse would have made further progress to win, but I don't believe so. He was still a long way back when he came down. **Squouateur** would finally provide some respite for backers when he finished third in the 2018 *Kim Muir*. He was the second favourite on this occasion at a price of 5/1. He was again held up towards the back of the field, made some steady progress and looked capable of winning as they turned for home, but ultimately couldn't go with the first two to finish and perhaps the trip in soft ground found him out.

The 2014 Cheltenham Festival was by far the best for **Martaline**'s offspring, as it resulted in two wins from two runners. The *David Pipe* trained **Dynaste** (3/1 favourite) won the *Ryanair Chase*, quickening two out and then staying on strongly after the last to win by 2¼ lengths from *Hidden Cyclone*. Twenty-Four hours later and **Very Wood** surprised everyone by winning the *Albert Bartlett Novices Hurdle* at a price of 33/1. A £1.00 win double on the two **Martaline** bred runners at that festival would have paid £136.00

To date, **Martaline**'s progeny have made 32 festival appearances, the 2019 Cheltenham Festival is just around the corner, and I have no real opinion on how entries by **Martaline** will perform at the meeting. The best I can offer is to repeat what I said twelve months ago, which is a belief (backed up by limited evidence) that **Martaline**'s offspring are best suited to 2½m chases. Until some trends start to appear as a result of more runs from this stallion's stock, the best advice is to maintain a watching brief.

Midnight Legend (GB)

Quote from the 2018 Cheltenham Festival Stallion Guide - "Considering that the festival win rate of **Midnight Legend** bred runners is once in every 16 plus appearances (6%), it is perhaps surprising that had one backed blind all 54 festival appearances of **Midnight Legend**'s offspring to a £1.00 each-way stake, the outcome would have been a profit of £39.35."

Race Format	Miles	Won	Placed	Unplaced	Total	Win %	Place %
	About 2m	0	3	3	6	0%	50%
Hurdles	About 2m 4f	0	3	14	17	0%	18%
	About 3m	0	0	4	4	0%	0%
	About 2m	0	1	4	5	0%	20%
Chases	About 2m 4f	1	1	12	14	7%	14%
	About 3m	1	1	7	9	11%	22%
	About 4m	1	0	4	5	20%	20%
Bumper	About 2m	0	1	1	2	0%	50%
Total	2009-2018	**3**	**10**	**49**	**62**	**5%**	**21%**

Midnight Legend (Died as a 25-y-o in 2016)

In total, 43 of **Midnight Legend**'s progeny have registered 66 festival appearances, 62 of which have taken place within the past decade. The highest ever rated of all National Hunt racehorses sired by **Midnight Legend** is *Sizing John*, who was raised to an Official Mark of 170 in December 2017 following a comprehensive victory in the *John Durkan Memorial Punchestown Chase*, beating *Djakadam* by seven lengths. Eighteen days later, and *Sizing John* was sent off as the 9/10 favourite for the *Leopardstown Christmas Chase*, but disaster struck for connections as the 2017 *Cheltenham Gold Cup* winner ran no race at all and trailed home in seventh. Following an immediate post-race examination, veterinary staff at the track found *Sizing John* to be clinically abnormal. During the rain and snow of early March, most of us were looking forward to *Sizing John* making his reappearance to defend his crown in the 2018 *Timico Cheltenham Gold Cup*. However, it wasn't to be. In the week before the blue riband event of the festival, *Sizing John* was withdrawn from the contest after suffering a hairline fracture to his pelvis. It was the 3rd year in succession where the defending *Gold Cup* winner missed the race twelve months later.

At the time of writing, *Sizing John* has still not seen a racecourse since that perplexing performance in the *Leopardstown Christmas Chase*, but his trainer, *Jessica Harrington*, seems unperturbed. She had planned to run *Sizing John* at *Leopardstown* over the Christmas period but decided to take him out of the meeting as the horse was reported to be some 15 kilograms above his ideal racing weight. Earlier reports had suggested that *Sizing John* could make his reappearance in the *Kinloch Brae Chase* at *Thurles* on January 20th but that also seems doubtful following the trainer's New Year's Day comments advising, "I'm not sure we'll have him ready for the *Kinloch Brae*. He's in absolutely fine form but the long dry spell we had meant that we've been a bit behind schedule with him." If anyone can have *Sizing John* racing fit for Cheltenham, it is *Jessica Harrington*. And if he isn't ready, rest assured that the trainer won't run him. Fingers crossed that he is ready to run!

History has told us that approximately 50% of Cheltenham entries sired by **Midnight Legend** achieve a top six placing in their festival races, and so 2018 has to be recorded as a bad year for the stallion. From twelve runners at last year's meeting, only two runners were able to finish in the first six positions of which one registered a place dividend. Although the performances were disappointing, I am very sympathetic to the argument that it would be unrealistic to expect anything else, considering that all twelve runners could be labelled as outsiders. The starting prices for those that lined up at 2018 Cheltenham Festival were 16/1, 20/1, 25/1, 4 horses at 33/1, 40/1, 50/1, two at 66/1 and a 100/1 chance. That said, in previous years, punters haven't needed to be too concerned about the odds offered on **Midnight Legend**'s progeny, as in the 54 festival appearances from the offspring preceding 2018, eight of the fourteen win and place positions have been at odds of 20/1, 25/1, 25/1, 25/1, 25/1, 50/1, 100/1, 100/1.

As a result of **Midnight Tour**'s run in last year's *OLBG Mares' Hurdle*, where she finished a gallant runner-up at 33/1, **Midnight Legend**'s stock have now recorded 15 win and place positions out of a total of 66 festival appearances, with 60% of those win and place successes courtesy of horses returning starting prices of 20/1 or greater. As a result of the rewarding odds returned, supporting the progeny at Cheltenham Festivals has been profitable. Had one backed blind all 66 festival appearances of **Midnight Legend**'s offspring to a £1.00 each-way stake, the outcome would have been a profit of £22.95. The profit could so easily have been £56.95 had the *Alan King* trained **Midnight Tour** held off the challenge of *Benie Des Dieux* in the final 120 yards of last year's *OLBG Mares' Hurdle*. It was a super run from the mare who just before the last hurdle accelerated past *Apple's Jade*, the 2017 winner of this race, and looked as if she would win the race before *Benie Des Dieux* got the better of the outsider by half a length at the winning line.

99% of people who go to the Cheltenham Festival in March have the most wonderful time, and I guess that the majority of them have decided to have a flutter on their festival fancies. Some punters like to back short-priced favourites and when their selections win, even if it delivers a negligible return, they contribute to a roar from the crowd that can be deafening. There are others who have a tendency to take a chance on some big priced outsiders, and when their horse wins, the cheers for the winner tend to be more muted! For this latter group, let me point you in the direction of horses by **Midnight Legend**. The win and place percentage strike rate across all 66 of **Midnight Legend**'s festival representatives is 23% which is pretty much a win or place for every 4th appearance from one of the sire's offspring. So far, only three of the 66 runners have won, whilst twelve have been placed, so it is imperative for punters to place each-way bets on this sire's festival entries. Of those 15 horses that have paid a return to punters, eight of the 12 placed horses were returned at odds of 20/1 or greater. The three winners have been at reasonable odds also - 25/1, 8/1 and 7/1. Last year's results of just one horse to be placed from 12 runners hasn't put me off this sire's festival representatives, and as always, I will be on the look-out for some big priced **Midnight Legend** bred outsiders.

At the 2019 Cheltenham Festival, if you are in the stands watching the tail-end of a race, and all appears a little muffled as the first three horses cross the line, it almost certainly means that those towards the front of the betting market have failed to finish amongst the placed horses. As they announce the result, take your race-card out of your pocket, and check on the runners that came home in front, and specifically the name of each horse's sire. Is **Midnight Legend** one of those sires? If he is, don't be surprised!

Milan (GB)

Quote from the 2018 Cheltenham Festival Stallion Guide - "In the past couple of Guides, I have highlighted that in recent seasons, **Milan** bred runners are averaging a win or place from close to one in every three festival runs, and at last year's meeting, it was déjà vu once again, as of the 13 of the offspring that took part at Cheltenham, four of them were placed."

Race Format	Miles	Won	Placed	Unplaced	Total	Win %	Place %
	About 2m	1	3	2	6	17%	67%
Hurdles	About 2m 4f	0	0	10	10	0%	0%
	About 3m	2	3	12	17	12%	29%
	About 2m	0	1	4	5	0%	20%
	About 2m 4f	0	4	3	7	0%	57%
Chases	About 3m	0	6	13	19	0%	32%
	About 4m	2	2	6	10	20%	40%
Bumper	About 2m	0	0	8	8	0%	0%
Total	2009-2018	**5**	**19**	**58**	**82**	**6%**	**29%**

*Table title: **Milan (21-y-o)***

I will start with the quote at the top of this page. In the Oxford English Dictionary, it advises that "déjà vu" means a feeling of having already experienced the present situation. So, at the 2017 Cheltenham Festival, 13 horses by **Milan** faced the starter of which four secured place positions, specifically two runners finished in 2nd place and two runners finished in 3rd place. At the 2018 Cheltenham Festival, 13 horses by **Milan** faced the starter of which four secured place positions, specifically two runners finished in 2nd place and two runners finished in 3rd place. No, there is no misprint above. The only difference in the above two sentences is the year! What was that film - Groundhog Day?

All joking aside, **Milan**'s offspring are highly consistent at the Cheltenham festival in averaging a win or place for close to one in every three runs. It has been pretty much the same ratio for the past six Cheltenham Festivals. 2 from 7 in 2013; 5 from 12 in 2014; 4 from 16 in 2015; 3 from 9 in 2016; and for the past two years, 4 from 13. That said, for the second year running, **Milan**'s progeny failed to provide us with a festival victory, which was not the case in the preceding four festivals, where supporters cheered home at least one festival winner. In addition, had one blindly backed at level stakes all 69 **Milan** bred festival runners from 2013 onwards, it would have resulted, to a £1.00 each-way stake, earnings of £18.40, and provided a profit for supporters at five of the past six Cheltenham Festivals.

Blindly backing to level stakes every **Milan** bred festival runner, a strategy which had worked so well for five consecutive years, came unstuck in 2018, where the losses incurred amounted to £16.98 to a £1.00 each-way stake. As they say, all good things must come to an end, but in **Milan**'s case, I am still very much convinced that punters should continue to follow this stallion at the 2019 Cheltenham Festival and beyond. Despite last year's losses, I would argue that overall, **Milan**'s representatives performed well. Of the 13 appearances from the offspring, there were eight top six finishes, half of them producing a place dividend.

Just like their sire, the four horses by **Milan** that were placed at last year's festival are a model of consistency when it comes to appearing at Cheltenham. Taking all four placed horses together, they have numbered a total of 13 appearances at Prestbury Park, where only once has a runner failed to finish in the top three places. Beginning with the lowest rated of the quartet, the 13-year-old *Barel Of Laughs* has appeared at Cheltenham on six occasions, and has never finished outside the front three. His first appearance at Cheltenham was when he finished in 3rd position in the *Irish Times Amateur Riders' Handicap Chase*, back in November 2011, when he was trained by *Jim Culloty*. His last run for the *Gold Cup* winning trainer was at *Ffos Las* in August 2013, after which he was off course for 888 days before switching to Point-to-Point and National Hunt races for *Bridgnorth* based trainer, *Philip Rowley*. Following four encouraging runs in the early part of 2016, **Barel Of Laughs** appeared at Cheltenham for the second time on 27th April 2016 where he finished runner-up to *Pearlysteps* in the *Champions Hunters' Chase* at a price of 16/1. Since that performance, **Barel Of Laughs** has raced on a further nine occasions at starting prices ranging from 30/100 favourite right through to 100/1, and only twice has he failed to finish either 1st or 2nd. Those two appearances were far from disappointing though as they happened in the last two renewals of the *St. James's Place Foxhunter Challenge Cup Open Hunters' Chase*, where **Barel Of Laughs** finished 3rd on both occasions, priced up at 100/1 in 2017, and 14/1 last year. If **Barel of Laughs** is amongst the runners for the 2019 *Foxhunters*, on the basis that there has only been one thirteen-year-old winner of this race going back to 1956, then I would anticipate *Philip Rowley*'s runner once again lining up at a big price. I will place a small each-way bet on the veteran if he takes his chance.

With a current mark of 161, **Monalee** is the highest rated of the four horses that secured a place dividend last year. Trained by *Henry de Bromhead*, **Monalee** has raced at Cheltenham just twice, both times finishing runner-up in Grade 1 festival races. He has been beaten by two very good horses. In 2017, **Monalee** was beaten by 3½ lengths in the *Albert Bartlett Novices' Hurdle* by the *Willie Mullins* trained *Penhill*, who at the time of writing, is favourite for the 2019 *Sun Racing Stayers' Hurdle*, the race in which he was victorious in 2018. The favourite (as of early January) for the 2019 *Magners Cheltenham Gold Cup* is *Presenting Percy*, who was seven lengths clear of **Monalee** when winning last season's *RSA Insurance Novices' Chase*. Twelve months previous to this success, *Presenting Percy* was the winner of the 2017 *Pertemps Network Final Handicap Hurdle*. **Monalee**, therefore, has been beaten in his two festival appearances by two dual festival winners who, as of early 2019, are both heading the 2019 festival market for two of the meeting's most prestigious races. Like **Barel Of Laughs**, I may have a small each-way wager on **Monalee**. He is currently priced up at 10/1 for the *Ryanair Chase* and 33/1 for the *Gold Cup*.

The early January festival markets highlight that the favourite for this year's *RSA Insurance Novices' Chase* is the **Milan** bred **Santini**, trained by *Nicky Henderson* and owned by *Mr and Mrs Kelvin Hughes*. Having had just the one run in a Point-to-Point event in March 2017 at *Didmarton* where he won by 15 lengths, **Santini** has since appeared in just six Rules Races. In his last four races, he has been the market leader, which followed on from only his second Rules race in January 2018, when at a price of 4/1, he was victorious in the *Ballymore Classic Novices' Hurdle* at Cheltenham Festival Trials Day. His second appearance at Cheltenham racecourse was in last season's *Albert Bartlett Novices' Hurdle*, his first run over three miles since his Point-to-Point success a year earlier. Starting as the 11/4 favourite, **Santini** stayed on well towards the end of the race but could get nowhere near the two in front of him and so had to settle for 3rd. In my opinion, to win an *RSA Insurance Novices' Chase*, stamina is a key ingredient and so "stayed on well", which has been written in the post-race analysis of **Santini**'s last three racecourse appearances, bodes well for the seven-year-old's race chances. The last six winners of the *RSA Chase* lined up off official marks of between 144 and 158 (**Santini**'s Official Rating as of January 2019 is 153). It is also a good race for seven-year-old runners, as evidenced by 14 of the last 18 winners being of this age. All of the factors above will have a bearing on *Santini*'s likely starting price and punters will need to make their own judgement as to whether the odds on offer represent value.

The last of the quartet of **Milan** bred placed horses at last year's festival was *Mall Dini*, who has appeared at the Cheltenham Festival for the past three years. On his first visit to the festival, *Mall Dini* rewarded trainer *Patrick Kelly*, who also has the aforementioned *Presenting Percy* in his yard, with his first Cheltenham Festival winner, when taking victory in the 2016 *Pertemps Network Final*, at the rewarding odds of 14/1. Returning to Cheltenham in 2017, *Mall Dini* was just outside the places when finishing in fifth place in the *Fulke Walwyn Kim Muir Challenge Cup Amateur Riders' Handicap Chase*. The trainer entered the horse in last year's renewal of this race, and *Mall Dini* was sent off the 4/1 favourite but just missed out on victory finishing runner-up to the game *Missed Approach* who stayed on to beat *Mall Dini* by half a length. Having finished 1st, 5th and 2nd in the past three Cheltenham Festivals, I must admit that I was quite surprised when looking through *Mall Dini*'s race history, to discover that the nine-year-old is yet to win a Chase under rules and remains a novice. Indeed, his last success was that 2016 victory in the 2016 *Pertemps Network Final*. The current debate is whether he will appear at Cheltenham in 2019 or have a crack at Aintree's *Grand National*.

In previous Guides, I have been at pains to point out that that there was enough evidence to suggest that **Milan** bred runners can and will perform equally as well across all race categories. Although I still believe that statement to be largely true, as the number of appearances from **Milan**'s offspring increases, there are the beginnings of a couple of trends with which we should keep an eye upon. The first is quite glaring. In just five appearances in the *Albert Bartlett Novices' Hurdle* (Registered as the *Spa Novices' Hurdle*), **Milan**'s representatives have an 80% win & place strike rate. In the 2015 renewal which was run on soft ground, *Martello Tower* (14/1) just got the better of *Milsean* (33/1) to provide forecast backers with an Exacta dividend of £635.60. Both horses were sired by **Milan**. None of **Milan**'s stock were entered in the 2016 running, but *Monalee* (8/1) and *Tommy Rapper* (33/1) lined up in the 2017 renewal, and as previously highlighted *Monalee* took the runner-up spot behind *Penhill*, with *Tommy Rapper* finishing 8th. Finally, as already advised, in last year's contest, *Santini* crossed the line to finish third. Undoubtedly, we should be very interested in any **Milan** bred runner that takes their chance in this three mile hurdle race which precedes the *Cheltenham Gold Cup*.

The second trend that is potentially emerging is far less obvious and is contained within the three mile chase category, within which **Milan**'s progeny have yet to provide a winner. In nineteen runs within this category, horses by **Milan** have managed to finish in the first six places on eleven occasions, with six of those eleven runs resulting in a pay-out for each-way backers. At this juncture, the statistic may not be especially mouth-watering to punters, but I consider the 3m chase category is an area which is well worth keeping an eye on for the future. To emphasise my view that **Milan**'s offspring are potentially performing well within this category, it is perhaps informative to advise that of the eight horses by **Milan** that failed to make a top six finish, half of them were sent off as 33/1 outsiders with the other four SPs being 9/1, 14/1, 20/1 and 100/1, so many of the runners were clearly considered to be "also-rans" even before setting off. That is not to say, however, that all eleven horses that finished in the top six in their respective races were all towards the head of the market. Indeed, six of these eleven **Milan** sired runners returned double figure odds or more, specifically 3rd @ 14/1, 4th and 5th @ 16/1, 6th @ 25/1 and 33/1, and 3rd at 100/1.

When the name '**Milan**' is mentioned, many people will talk about the stunning cathedral that has a capacity to hold 40,000 people; or that the city is recognised as one of the world's most influential fashion capitals; or discuss the history of AC Milan and Inter Milan, two of Italy's most famous football clubs. Nothing much has changed. People have been speaking about these attributes of

Milan in the past and they will do so in the future. There is a consistency and reliability about the city of **Milan** and whoever decided to give the name '**Milan**' to a young foal some 20 years ago was probably onto something. As the excitement starts to build for the 2019 Cheltenham Festival and we start to pick out our bets for the festival, we can be sure there will be ups and downs, predictable results and some surprises. There is something, however, which I believe we can all rely upon, which is **Milan**'s 2019 festival representatives rewarding punters with a win or a place for one in every three wagers. Déjà vu. All over again!

Montjeu (IRE)

Quote from the 2018 Cheltenham Festival Stallion Guide - "If one takes out the five heroic performances of **Hurricane Fly**, Montjeu sired runners have recorded two victories and two place dividends from a total of 45 festival races. Moreover, within those 45 events, the progeny have failed to finish in the first eight positions on 29 occasions."

Montjeu (Died as a 16-y-o in 2012)							
Race Format	*Miles*	*Won*	*Placed*	*Unplaced*	*Total*	*Win %*	*Place %*
Hurdles	About 2m	3	3	24	30	10%	20%
	About 2m 4f	0	0	4	4	0%	0%
	About 3m	0	0	2	2	0%	0%
Chases	About 2m	0	0	1	1	0%	0%
	About 2m 4f	1	0	3	4	25%	25%
	About 3m	0	0	2	2	0%	0%
	About 4m	0	0	0	0	-	-
Bumper	About 2m	0	0	1	1	0%	0%
Total	2009-2018	**4**	**3**	**37**	**44**	**9%**	**16%**

There is one horse by **Montjeu** whose festival accomplishments are completely out of line with what has been achieved by the other 31 of the progeny who have been fortunate enough to experience the thrills and spills of racing at Cheltenham in March. That horse is the stupendous **Hurricane Fly** whose name will be mentioned at festival meetings for many years to come. The brilliant **Hurricane Fly** burst onto the festival scene when beating *Peddlers Cross* by just over a length in the 2011 *Stan James Champion Hurdle Challenge Trophy*. Two years later, he won the *Champion Hurdle* again, this time beating *Rock On Ruby*, his conqueror in the 2012 running of the race, when **Hurricane Fly** finished 3rd. In 2014, even though he was 10 years old, he went off as the 11/4 favourite when finishing in 4th place, the one and only time that he failed to place in the event. And in the 2015 renewal of the race, his 8/1 starting price reflected the fact that he was an eleven-year-old veteran competing against youngsters in a two mile hurdle contest where they usually go like the clappers. Despite his age, the *Champion Hurdle* hero ran brilliantly to finish in third place in what was his fifth consecutive run in the race. When he was retired five months later, having amassed £1,861,015 in prize money, his trainer *Willie Mullins* justifiably stated that he was "the horse of a generation".

Whereas **Hurricane Fly**'s Cheltenham record has been phenomenal, with one or two exceptions, the festival performances delivered by the rest of **Montjeu**'s progeny have been, for the most part, absolutely awful. For example, in last year's Stallion Guide, I highlighted that on 29 occasions, **Montjeu** sired runners had failed to finish in the front eight places. If we add to the total, the four also-ran performances from **Montjeu**'s offspring at last year's festival, that number now reads as 33. If we exclude **Hurricane Fly** from the statistics, then the numbers highlight that only once in every three appearances will a **Montjeu** sired festival runner finish within the first eight places.

And don't make the mistake of thinking that a top-8 finish means that a wager on the sire's runners is likely to be a winning bet. The table above provides the festival record of **Montjeu**'s offspring over the past decade of four wins and three places achieved from 44 appearances which equates to strike rates of 9% for winning and 16% for win and place, percentages that don't read too badly. However, if we exclude the out-of-the-ordinary **Hurricane Fly** and include all of **Montjeu**'s festival representatives going back to 2006 and the progeny's first festival runner, **Rosecliff**, then the numbers are far less encouraging and would read as 2 wins, 2 placed and 45 unplaced, providing a 4% win rate and an 8% win & place strike rate. These statistics can be thought of as one win and one place for every 25 times that a horse by **Montjeu** runs at a Cheltenham Festival, which in my view, reflects a much more realistic portrayal of the offspring's festival record.

The vast majority of **Montjeu** bred horses that have raced at the Cheltenham Festival have contested two mile hurdle events. Indeed, out of a total of 54 festival appearances from the offspring, 40 of them have taken place in the two mile hurdle category. Outside of this category, **Montjeu** has been represented in just 14 races, of which just seven have been over fences. **Noble Prince**'s victory in the 2011 *Jewson Novices' Chase* was rather untypical, as on the other six occasions, the offspring have finished well behind. And in the six middle and long distance hurdle events in which the stock have competed, as well as the sole appearance in last year's *Bumper*, performances have been largely uninspiring.

Deeper analysis of how the progeny have performed within the 2m hurdle category reveals a captivating statistic. With the obvious exception of **Hurricane Fly** who achieved two wins and two places in the *Champion Hurdle*, not one horse by **Montjeu** to have raced at an age of five or older has managed to secure a front four placing in a festival two mile hurdle event. Nineteen have tried. All of which means that, within this two mile hurdle category, the sole victory and two places achieved by **Montjeu**'s festival representatives (ignoring **Hurricane Fly**) have occurred in events that are restricted to four year olds, these being the *Triumph Hurdle* and the *Fred Winter Juvenile Handicap Hurdle*. In the 2008 *Triumph Hurdle*, **Won In The Dark** finished 3rd and eight years later, **Ivanovich Gorbatov** won the 2016 renewal. The other place position was secured in the 2009 *Fred Winter Juvenile Novices' Handicap Hurdle*, where **Alexander Severus** secured a place dividend by finishing 4th.

Of the four horses that appeared at last year's festival, one six-year-old (**Ivanovich Gorbatov**) and a couple of seven-year-olds (**John Constable** and **Tigris River**) competed in two mile hurdle events. All three disappointed with **John Constable** (66/1) achieving the highest place position of 9th in the *Champion Hurdle*, but then again there was only 11 in the field and two of them were pulled up!

The chances of seeing another festival winner sired by **Montjeu** is becoming increasingly remote. In National Hunt racing, one is most likely to see younger horses, aged between say 4 and 6 years old, racing in bumpers or shorter distance hurdle events, with a number of the races being for novices only. As these racehorses get older, they tend to go up in distance and many of them will leave the hurdles behind and be campaigned over fences. **Montjeu** died in 2012 which means that his stock will be aged six or older. Even if some of the offspring are high enough in the official ratings to get to a Cheltenham Festival, the current age profile combined with the fact that the progeny rarely race in events other than two mile hurdle contests, suggests that there will be very few festival opportunities where **Montjeu** bred entries are likely to be competitive. **Montjeu**'s progeny are too old to run in events for four-year-olds where they have previously had some success, and **Hurricane Fly** has long since retired, so it is difficult to see where a winner or even a place position will come from. If we take all 54 festival runs by **Montjeu**'s offspring, and exclude four-year-old competitors and **Hurricane Fly** from our analysis, then **Noble Prince**, who won the 2011 *Jewson Novices' Chase*, is the only horse by **Montjeu** to register a top four finish.

The last remaining hope for supporters of **Montjeu** probably rests with the lightly raced **Rhinestone**, owned by *John P McManus* and trained by *Joseph Patrick O'Brien*. As of early January, the six-year-old has raced in four National Hunt Flat Races and two hurdle events. Last year, he finished 9th in the *Weatherbys Champion Bumper*, weakening inside the final furlong to finish 10¾ lengths behind the winner. *Rhinestone* does look to have some class about him and has excellent connections, but I'm sure he isn't a *Hurricane Fly*. So, taking *Hurricane Fly* out of the equation, can *Rhinestone* be the first horse by **Montjeu** aged five or more, since *Noble Prince*, to claim a top four finish at a Cheltenham Festival? Somehow, I doubt it. If you have a different opinion, as of early January, he can be backed at big odds in both the *Sky Bet Supreme Novices' Hurdle* and the *Ballymore Novices' Hurdle*.

Network (GER)

Quote from the 2018 Cheltenham Festival Stallion Guide - "There does appear to be a very clear division in the festival results of those that have lined up at odds of 18/1 plus and those that have competed at odds of 16/1 or shorter. (Ignoring *Sprinter Sacre* from the analysis); of the five runners that were sent off at odds of 16/1 or shorter, four of the finishing positions were 3rd, 4th, 4th and 5th with two of the representatives rewarding each-way bets with a place dividend."

Race Format	Miles	Won	Placed	Unplaced	Total	Win %	Place %
	Network (22-y-o)						
	About 2m	0	1	3	4	0%	25%
Hurdles	About 2m 4f	0	1	2	3	0%	33%
	About 3m	1	0	1	2	50%	50%
	About 2m	3	0	2	5	60%	60%
Chases	About 2m 4f	0	1	2	3	0%	33%
	About 3m	0	0	6	6	0%	0%
	About 4m	0	0	1	1	0%	0%
Bumper	About 2m	0	0	0	0	-	-
Total	2009-2018	**4**	**3**	**17**	**24**	**17%**	**29%**

There were five horses by **Network** that appeared at the 2018 Cheltenham Festival, and the results were 100% in line with last year's analysis as alluded to in the quote at the top of the page. The bit about "ignoring *Sprinter Sacre* from the analysis" probably needs some explanation.

No one will be surprised when I write that *Sprinter Sacre* was one of the best horses ever to be trained by *Nicky Henderson*. And his racing career flows just like most family movies. You know the sort of thing. A gentle introduction followed by great success and the world is your oyster before something goes wrong and the sad music starts playing. Eventually, the hero overcomes adversity to achieve something nigh impossible. Some of us even shed a tear at this point and the film-goers all go home with smiles on their faces.

Sprinter Sacre, sired by **Network**, raced around Prestbury Park in March on five occasions. His festival debut was over hurdles, where he finished 3rd in the 2011 *Stan James Supreme Novices' Hurdle*. Afterwards, he went chasing and won ten consecutive races including two breath-taking performances at the 2012 and 2013 Cheltenham Festivals. In the *Racing Post Arkle Challenge Trophy Chase* on 13th May 2012, *Sprinter Sacre* coasted to victory to win by seven lengths from *Cue Card*. The distance could have been a lot further but for jockey *Barry Geraghty* easing him down in the closing stages. The jockey later described the race as the equivalent of a "schooling session". The following season, *Sprinter Sacre* started as the 1/4 favourite for the *Sportingbet Queen Mother Champion Chase*, the shortest price at a Cheltenham Festival since *Arkle* won his third *Gold Cup* in 1966. He was never off the bridle and recorded another impressive victory this time by 19 lengths from runner-up *Sizing Europe*. After this race, the British Horseracing Authority raised his Official Rating to 188, a mark upon which he won his next two chases.

We now approach the sad part of the movie, as *Sprinter Sacre*'s ten race winning run was halted in dramatic style in the *williamhill.com Desert Orchid Chase* at *Kempton Park*, when the 2/9 favourite was pulled up just after the seventh fence. Post-race tests revealed that he was suffering from an irregular heartbeat and he missed the rest of the season. Over the next eighteen months, *Sprinter Sacre* continued to suffer from a series of injury and health problems and it looked as if he would never again experience his previous triumphs. During this period, one of the most sombre moments was when he was pulled up in the 2015 *Betway Queen Mother Champion Chase*. Retirement of *Nicky Henderson*'s star two-miler was mooted once again.

We need a happy ending and we get one. Somehow, master trainer *Nicky Henderson* is able to get *Sprinter Sacre* back onto a racecourse and he wins a couple of races, albeit not with the same ease with which he beat his rivals a couple of years ago. And then the film's finale as our hero returns to Cheltenham to race in the 2016 *Betway Queen Mother Champion Chase* for the third time. His big rival in the race is the 4/6 favourite, *Un de Sceaux*, the highly impressive 2015 winner of the *Arkle*. What follows is an incredible performance from the ten-year-old *Sprinter Sacre* and he beats the odds-on favourite to regain his *Champion Chase* crown. The noise from the Grandstand is deafening. Roll the Credits!

Sprinter Sacre was such a great racehorse and his achievements are up there with the best of them. However, if you are tasked with providing a commentary on how well **Network**'s offspring perform at Cheltenham Festivals, and the 'wonder horse' is responsible for over 25% of all festival runs from the stallion's stock, then any analysis can be highly misleading. So back to the quote at the top of the page! In order to provide punters with an analysis that better reflects the festival performances of **Network**'s progeny, it makes sense to take out *Sprinter Sacre* from the statistics.

In last year's Guide, I highlighted that if one excluded *Sprinter Sacre*'s festival achievements, then what remained were ten of **Network**'s offspring competing in 14 festival events, of which five races consisted of the **Network** sired runner lining up at odds of 16/1 or shorter. It is an incredibly small sample upon which to pick out any trends, and clearly the betting market should be a reasonably accurate reflection of the runners' finishing positions, but in **Network**'s case, there is a clear 100% link between starting price and finishing position. If we look at the data pre the 2018 Cheltenham Festival, for the five runners that were sent off at odds of 16/1 or shorter, the finishing positions in chronological order were 3 5 4 4 6. For the nine **Network** bred outsiders who lined up in their respective races at 18/1 or greater, their finishing positions (in date order) were 14 12 PU BD 6 8 PU Fell 20.

So, what about the five horses by **Network** that appeared at the 2018 Cheltenham Festival. As insinuated in the very first sentence of this chapter, they performed exactly in line with their predecessors, although the 6/1 chance, *Delta Work* didn't just get placed, he won. *(I will write more about this horse later as, provided connections enter him the race that best suits him, he is my nap of the 2019 Cheltenham Festival).* Below are the results from **Network**'s five representatives at the 2018 Cheltenham Festival:

Dame Rose (40/1) Pulled Up in the *Sky Bet Supreme Novices' Hurdle*
Allysson Monterg (50/1) Pulled Up in the *RSA Insurance Novices' Chase*
Saint Are (33/1) Pulled Up in the *Glenfarclas Cross-Country Chase*
Delta Work (6/1) Won the *Pertemps Network Final Handicap Hurdle*
Le Richebourg (33/1) 15th position in the *Randox Health County Handicap Hurdle*

Based upon these five festival performances and the 14 runs preceding them, the data is clear-cut. To date, horses by **Network** (excluding *Sprinter Sacre*) that line up with a starting price of 16/1 or less have a 100% record of registering a top six finish. On the other hand, if you are one of those punters who like to bet on big priced outsiders, then horses by **Network** are not the place to go searching for them.

Looking at **Network**'s progeny, there are two six year-old novice chasers who, provided they arrive at Cheltenham fit and sound, should also attain a top-six placing. The first of these is **Le Richebourg**, trained by *Joseph Patrick O'Brien* and who runs in the green and gold colours of *John P McManus*. The 33/1 shot finished in 15th place in last year's *Randox Health County Handicap Hurdle* and six months later, he was put over fences. He has won three of his four chases to date, his last victory being the *Racing Post Novice Chase* at *Leopardstown* on Boxing Day. *Footpad* won the previous year's renewal and went on to win the *Arkle* at the 2018 Cheltenham Festival. **Le Richebourg** is currently around 6/1 to win the 2019 *Arkle*.

Le Richebourg's only chase defeat to date was in the *baronracing.com Drinmore Novice Chase* at *Fairyhouse* in early December. He was beaten by another **Network** bred novice chaser, **Delta Work**, who in my view, provided he is entered for the event this March, will win the festival's *JLT Novices' Chase*. At the time of writing, most commentators believe that **Delta Work** will be entered for the *RSA Chase* over 3m½f because he has proven himself to have the necessary stamina. And they may well be right and if he takes the *RSA* option, he may well win. Nevertheless, for a number of reasons, I think he has a much better chance of winning the *JLT Novices Chase* over half a mile less. If he takes up this engagement, then without doubt, he will be my nap of the 2019 Cheltenham Festival.

Delta Work is owned by *Gigginstown House Stud* and trained by *Gordon Elliott*. As already advised, at last year's festival, he won the *Pertemps Network Final Handicap Hurdle*, just edging out his stablemate *Glenloe* by a nose in a highly exciting finish. Beaten by a neck in his last hurdle race at *Punchestown* in April, connections started his chasing career at the start of November. At the time of writing, he has won all three of his starts over the bigger obstacles, the latter two races being Grade 1 events. His last race at the end of December was over three miles in the *Neville Hotels Novice Chase* at *Leopardstown*. He won by 8 lengths going clear on the run-in. **Delta Work** holds an entry for the 2m5f *Flogas Novice Chase* at *Leopardstown* after this Guide goes to print which has been a good pointer in the past for finding the winner of the *RSA Chase*. Four of the past ten winners of the *RSA Chase* had previously contested the *Flogas Novice Chase*.

At the time of writing, **Delta Work** is around 9/2 for the RSA Chase and more than twice that price for the *JLT Novices' Chase*. I'm hoping that the difference in the markets is due to the number of comments about **Delta Work**'s stamina rather than a concrete plan by connections, otherwise it's goodbye to my nap of the festival. There are a number of trends that are in **Delta Work**'s favour for the *JLT* as shown below:

- The last 3 winners of the JLT were rated 152 or more. **Delta Work** currently has an Official Rating of 155.
- Irish Trainers have won 7 of the 8 JLT renewals.
- French Bred contenders have won 3 of the 8 renewals.
- This is a strange statistic and probably has little relevance, but here goes. Only 9 contenders of the *JLT* to date started their racing career on the flat. Three won! (**Delta Work** started life on the flat in France whilst trained by *Emmanuel Clayeux*.)
- Approximately two-thirds of *JLT* runners had contested a Grade 1 over hurdles. Of the 12 who had won a Grade 1 hurdle event, four of them won the *JLT Novices' Chase*. (Note: **Delta Work** has not won a Grade 1 over hurdles, but did come close, beaten by a neck in the *Irish Daily Mirror Novice Hurdle* at *Punchestown* on 25th April 2018)

There are other factors that are positive for **Delta Work**'s chances in the race, but I haven't listed them all, as those trends are typically positive for most of the *JLT* contenders. For example, six of the past 8 winners won last time out; only one of the 8 winners had failed to complete the course in any of their chase starts; and so on. I assume many readers will want to know why I am not so keen on his chances in the *RSA Chase*. Here is another list to look at:

- **Delta Work** is six years old. There have only been three *RSA Chase* winners aged six since 1978.
- **Delta Work** has won all his chase starts. Six of the past 9 *RSA Chase* winners were beaten on their chase debut. Also six winners this century had previously fallen over fences.
- Traditional Irish bred National Hunt horses have won 14 of the past 18 renewals. The remaining 4 winners are split evenly; two French-bred (like **Delta Work**) and two GB-bred.
- In the past 18 years, 29 horses lined up for the *RSA Chase* unbeaten over fences (like **Delta Work**). Only two won and they were very short in the betting (6/5F and 13/8F)

Finally, last year's winner of the *JLT Novices' Chase* had originally been pencilled in for the *RSA*, but was switched in the days leading up the festival. That winner was the mare, *Shattered Love*, whose previous outing before the *JLT* was the *Neville Hotels Novice Chase* at Leopardstown, a race she won at a price of 10/1. There are a number of similarities here. *Shattered Love* is in the same ownership and with the same trainer as **Delta Work**. And **Delta Work** also won the *Neville Hotels Novice Chase*.

My nap of the 2019 Cheltenham Festival is **Delta Work** to win the *JLT Novices' Chase*.

Old Vic (GB)

Quote from the 2018 Cheltenham Festival Stallion Guide - "Due to **Old Vic**'s death in 2011, this stallion's remaining stock are now in their later years and, as a result, those that appear at the 2018 Cheltenham Festival are most likely to appear in the longer distance chase events."

Race Format	Miles	Won	Placed	Unplaced	Total	Win %	Place %

Race Format	*Miles*	*Won*	*Placed*	*Unplaced*	*Total*	*Win %*	*Place %*
	About 2m	0	0	3	3	0%	0%
Hurdles	About 2m 4f	3	1	10	14	21%	29%
	About 3m	0	2	15	17	0%	12%
	About 2m	0	0	1	1	0%	0%
Chases	About 2m 4f	0	3	9	12	0%	25%
	About 3m	2	4	25	31	6%	19%
	About 4m	0	1	4	5	0%	20%
Bumper	About 2m	0	0	5	5	0%	0%
Total	2009-2018	**5**	**11**	**72**	**88**	**6%**	**18%**

Table title: *Old Vic (Died as a 25-y-o in 2011)*

Old Vic's progeny has been around for a very long time. The first horse by **Old Vic** to appear at a Cheltenham Festival was *L'Opera* in 1997, when registering a 4th place in the *Elite Racing Club Triumph Hurdle* at a price of 11/2. Hailing from *David Nicholson*'s yard, one of the top National Hunt trainers within my lifetime, *L'Opera* also competed at the 1998 festival, this time finishing in 7th position in the *Vincent O'Brien County Handicap Hurdle*. Since then, a further sixty-nine **Old Vic** bred horses have turned up at Cheltenham Festivals, of which seven have tasted victory. All seven horses have won just once and to perhaps bring back some warm memories for festival devotees, the winners are **Kicking King, Our Vic, Ninetieth Minute, Andytown, Sunnyhillboy, Spring Heeled** and **Killultagh Vic**. To complete the overall picture, the seventy **Old Vic** sired horses to appear at the festival have registered 124 festival appearances in total, recording not only seven victories, but also eighteen place dividends, equating to a 20% win and place strike rate.

The above paragraph may read a little like a person's obituary and that's because there is a very strong possibility that 2019 may well be **Old Vic**'s final appearance within the Cheltenham Festival Stallion Guide. In short, due to **Old Vic**'s death in 2011, this stallion's remaining stock are now in their later years and connections of the few **Old Vic** sired horses that remain, will need to decide whether or not the veterans under their tutelage can perform effectively in a festival event.

In last year's Guide, I pointed out that we would most likely see the progeny take part in four festival contests where older horses have a better chance of winning, the four races being the *Ultima Handicap Steeple Chase* (3m1f); the *Glenfarclas Cross Country Steeple Chase* (3m6f); the *Fulke Walwyn Kim Muir Challenge Cup Handicap Steeple Chase* (3m2f); and the *St. James's Place Foxhunter Steeple Chase Challenge Cup* (3m2½f). The only one of these four races that isn't a Class 2 race is the *Ultima Handicap Steeple Chase*, which is a Class 1 Grade 3 Handicap. Taking all four events together over the past decade, 32 of the 40 winners have been aged eight or older. Based on the fact that the vast majority of winners in the other 24 festival races, two-thirds of which are Grade 1 and Grade 2 contests, are seven years old or younger, I advised that the chances of seeing **Old Vic**'s offspring record any type of success in these events would be highly improbable.

As it turned out, six **Old Vic** bred horses took their chance at the 2018 Cheltenham Festival. Three of them competed in the four events highlighted above where older horses have a better chance of winning, and the other trio tried their luck in those contests where younger winners are more prevalent. Unsurprisingly, none of them managed to win or place, although the youngest of the sextet, the eight-year-old **Ballyoptic** wasn't too far away, when he finished 4th in the Grade 1 *RSA Insurance Novices' Chase*, albeit over 15 lengths away from the impressive winner, *Presenting Percy*.

Also attempting a Grade 1 event last year was **Killultagh Vic**, who was last seen at a Cheltenham Festival in 2015, when winning the *Martin Pipe Conditional Jockeys' Handicap Hurdle*. On this occasion, **Killultagh Vic** had been entered for the biggest prize of all, the *Timico Cheltenham Gold Cup Chase*, and lined up at a price of 8/1. Although not a novice chaser, having won his first two races over the bigger obstacles over two years earlier, this race was to be only the fourth ever race under rules in which **Killultagh Vic** was to tackle fences. In my view, more experience is needed to win this highly competitive event, as evidenced by the fact that *Coneygree* is the only novice to have won a *Gold Cup* in the past 44 years. Hence, I wasn't in the least bit surprised when the nine-year-old largely struggled at the rear of the field before being pulled up towards the end of the race. Although *Willie Mullins* has six *Gold Cup* runner-up finishes to his name, the trainer of **Killultagh Vic** has never won the Blue Riband event. The wait goes on.

The race that takes place immediately after the *Gold Cup*, and run over the same course and distance, is the *St. James's Place Foxhunter Challenge Cup Open Hunters' Chase*, a race where among the list of entries were two of **Old Vic**'s offspring. Both horses were having their second run in the race, as they both competed in the 2017 renewal. *Grand Vision* finished 14th at 50/1 and *Minella For Value* was only 3½ lengths away from the winner, *Pacha Du Polder*, when securing a very respectable sixth place at the huge odds of 100/1. Both horses were now 12 years old for the 2018 race, so it was a little surprising that their odds were considerably shorter, although *Grand Vision* did improve on his 2017 run, this time finishing in 6th place at a price of 14/1. As for *Minella For Value*, he went off at odds of 25/1, and although prominent for the first two thirds of the race, he weakened four from home and was pulled up. There have been four other **Old Vic** bred contestants that have appeared in the *Foxhunters*, of which all four were pulled up, so *Minella For Value*'s effort was not out of the ordinary.

The *Fulke Walwyn Kim Muir Challenge Cup Handicap Steeple Chase* which takes place on the third day of the Festival, has been a much more rewarding race for supporters of **Old Vic**. If one had backed all nine runners blind to a £1.00 each-way stake, the resultant profit would be a very satisfying £27.88. In chronological order, horses by **Old Vic** have recorded finishing positions of 6th, 1st, 1st, 4th, 3rd, 4th, 2nd, 12th and 15th. **Pendra**, who was last seen in public when finishing a gallant runner-up in the 2017 renewal of this race, was unsuited by the soft ground conditions of the 2018 contest, and he weakened rapidly after making a mistake at the second last.

All six of **Old Vic**'s progeny raced in chase events at the 2018 Cheltenham Festival, of which only one runner, **Village Vic**, competed in a race that did not fall within the 3m chase category. Racing off a top weight of 11-12, as well as being the joint oldest in the race at eleven years old, the *Philip Hobbs* trained **Village Vic** had it all to do in the 2m5f *Brown Advisory & Merriebelle Stable Plate Handicap Chase*. The 33/1 outsider, ridden by *Richard Johnson*, led for the first two thirds of the race until weakening towards the latter stages to finish a remote 15th of 22 runners.

As we approach the 2019 Cheltenham Festival, we won't see many horses entered where **Old Vic** is listed as the sire, and for those that do turn up, my guess is that it will be the same horses that competed at the 2018 festival. The highest rated of **Old Vic**'s offspring that are still racing is **Killultagh Vic** off a mark of 161. He is listed as a possible runner in the *Magners Cheltenham Gold*

Cup Chase, but as a 10-year-old, I think it highly unlikely that he will trouble the judge. The last 10-year-old to win the *Gold Cup* was *Cool Dawn* in 1998. In addition, it is very rare for a horse to win a *Gold Cup*, having been beaten on their first attempt in the race. Before *Native River*'s success last year, 66 runners this century who had failed to win on their *Gold Cup* debut had tried again. All were beaten. *Native River* bucked the trend in 2018, the first time the feat had been achieved since *See More Business* was successful in winning the 1999 *Gold Cup* renewal having been carried out by *Cyborgo* in the early stages of the 1998 running.

There is a possibility, I suppose, that **Grand Vision** and **Minella Value** may attempt the *Foxhunters* for a third time in 2019, even though both horses will be thirteen years old. For anyone out there who may be interested in backing either runner, my advice is to think again. There has only been one thirteen-year-old winner of this race going back to 1956, when *Earthmover*, trained by *Paul Nicholls* took the prize in the 2003 renewal. The only other potential **Old Vic** bred runner for this event may be **Southfield Vic** who is within the team of Hunter Chasers trained by *Paul Nicholls*. The 10-year-old hasn't been seen on a racecourse since May 2017 and has yet to appear at a Cheltenham Festival.

Other potential **Old Vic** sired Cheltenham entries (ages in brackets) are **Ballyoptic** (9), **Folsom Blue** (12), **Knock House** (10) and **Pendra** (11), although none of them especially appeal as potential festival winners, and I'm also inclined to believe that their trainers may well decide to miss the festival and instead take their chance at *Aintree*'s April meeting. Those of you who have read previous editions of this Guide will be well aware that **Old Vic**'s offspring have a very impressive track record in *Aintree*'s *Grand National* race. In brief, there have been seven horses by **Old Vic** that have finished in the first three places in the past eleven renewals of the *Grand National*, which equates to over 20% of the top three positions being reserved for **Old Vic**'s progeny. All seven runners, at an earlier point in their racing career, had previously contested a three mile event at the Cheltenham Festival.

It is very possible that one or more of the four horses highlighted above may be among the 40 runners that line up for the start of the 2019 *Randox Health Grand National*, and it is worth noting that nine-year-olds have won five renewals this century and a further ten winners have been aged ten or older. The **Old Vic** sired entries most likely to take their chance come April are **Ballyoptic** and **Folsom Blue**, who both contested the *Coral Welsh Grand National Handicap Chase* at *Chepstow* on 27th December 2018. **Ballyoptic** ran reasonably well to finish in 6th place and they probably went a little too quick for **Folsom Blue** who finished a couple of places further back in 8th. Trained by the formidable *Gordon Elliott*, **Folsom Blue** ran a couple of cracking races in 2018, both of which were long distance chase events, sponsored by *BoyleSports*. The second of these two contests was the *Irish Grand National Chase* at *Fairyhouse* in April where the veteran ran well to take 4th place. Previous to this race, **Folsom Blue** had been successful in winning the *Grand National Trial Handicap Chase* at *Punchestown*. At the time of writing, **Folsom Blue** is available at around 40/1 for *Aintree*'s showpiece. If he manages to finish in the first 4 places, he will be the first of **Old Vic**'s offspring to achieve the feat without having previously competed in a three mile event at the Cheltenham Festival, unless in March, his connections decide to prepare him for the *Grand National* by entering him in a three mile festival contest beforehand.

In my opinion, the *Nigel Twiston-Davies* trained **Ballyoptic** has better credentials to be successful in *Aintree*'s showpiece event. The nine-year-old has appeared in two festival races within the three mile category, these being the 2017 *Sun Bets Stayers' Hurdle* where he was pulled up, and last year, when he finished 4th in the *RSA Insurance Novices' Chase*, just behind third-placed *Elegant Escape*, who most recently beat both **Ballyoptic** and **Folsom Blue** when victorious as the 3/1 favourite in the 2018 *Coral Welsh Grand National Handicap Chase*. **Ballyoptic** has also been to *Aintree* on three previous occasions, the high point when winning the Grade 1 *Doom Bar Sefton Novices' Hurdle* in

2016 and the low point when falling in the *Becher Handicap Chase* over the *Grand National* Fences in December 2018, a few weeks before his *Welsh National* appearance. As of early January 2019, he can be backed at around 33/1 for the 2019 *Randox Health Grand National*.

To conclude this chapter, I would advise supporters of **Old Vic** to focus their attention on just two races, the *Fulke Walwyn Kim Muir Challenge Cup Handicap Steeple Chase* at Cheltenham and the *Randox House Grand National* at Aintree. As of early January, if I was forced to place an ante-post bet on an **Old Vic** sired horse, it would be an each-way bet on ***Ballyoptic*** for the 2019 *Randox Health Grand National*.

Oscar (IRE)

Quote from the 2018 Cheltenham Festival Stallion Guide - "If an **Oscar** bred is to bag a winner at the 2018 Cheltenham Festival, the trends suggest that the victory will come in one of the festival's non-handicap races. In the past decade, all 46 of **Oscar**'s representatives who lined up in the festival's handicap races have failed to win."

Race Format	Miles	Won	Placed	Unplaced	Total	Win %	Place %
			Oscar (25-y-o)				
Hurdles	About 2m	1	5	8	14	7%	43%
	About 2m 4f	1	2	13	16	6%	19%
	About 3m	2	4	24	30	7%	20%
Chases	About 2m	1	5	6	12	8%	50%
	About 2m 4f	0	3	14	17	0%	18%
	About 3m	3	4	23	30	10%	23%
	About 4m	2	0	5	7	29%	29%
Bumper	About 2m	0	0	7	7	0%	0%
Total	2009-2018	**10**	**23**	**100**	**133**	**8%**	**25%**

The jinx has been broken!

In last year's Guide, I commented that **Oscar**'s offspring had won 12 festival races between 2006 and 2014, but the victories had ground to a halt ever since 2015, the year in which I launched the first of the Cheltenham Festival Stallion Guides. I made the facetious remark that perhaps my writing of this book had put a jinx on the stallion. Thankfully, last season's victory by **Kilbricken Storm** in the *Albert Bartlett Novices' Hurdle*, has put an end to any semblance of witchcraft against **Oscar**!

2018 was indeed a fantastic Cheltenham festival for **Oscar** supporters. Twelve horses by **Oscar** lined up in festival races last year, and as well as **Kilbricken Storm**'s victory, four others were placed. All five runners were priced at 12/1 or bigger, providing punters with a massive pay-out of £45.10 had they backed all 12 horses blind to a £1.00 each-way stake. This huge profit wiped out the £39.05 total losses that would have been incurred by adopting the same staking strategy of backing every **Oscar** bred runner at the previous three Cheltenham Festivals of 2015 through to 2017.

William Blake, the famous English poet, is known to have said that "Hindsight is a wonderful thing but foresight is better, especially when it comes to saving life, or some pain." Clearly, saving lives is far more important than losing money to bookmakers, but perhaps with a small alteration, an appropriate quote for Cheltenham Festival supporters could be "Hindsight is a wonderful thing but foresight is better, especially when it comes to identifying festival winners!" I refer to the above quote, because in hindsight, I am of the view that the turnaround in the performances of **Oscar**'s offspring at the 2018 Festival was aided by last year's soft going.

As advised in the Introduction to this year's Guide, preceding the 2018 Cheltenham Festival, only 24 races this century had taken place on ground officially described as Soft. Hence, I hadn't especially paid attention to the ground conditions. Indeed, in previous Guides, the only stallion where I have mentioned a preference for soft ground is *Beneficial*, and only because on two specific days when there was torrential rain, results from this sire's offspring jumped out of the page and hit me between the eyes! As we all know, the ground conditions at last year's meeting were highly unusual with the first 5 races of the festival run on ground officially described as Heavy and the remainder of the races being run on Soft ground. So, I decided to take a look and see if any horses by **Oscar** had run in any of the 24 soft ground festival races between 2000 and 2017. The results are highly enlightening as can be seen below:

2013 – **Rock On Ruby** (11/2) 2nd in the *Stan James Champion Hurdle Challenge Trophy*
2013 – **At Fishers Cross** (11/8 Favourite) 1st in the *Albert Bartlett Novices' Hurdle*
2013 – **O'Faolains Boy** (16/1) 4th in the *Albert Bartlett Novices' Hurdle*
2013 – **Oscar Delta** (20/1) Unseated Rider in the *CGA Foxhunter Chase Challenge Cup*
2013 – **Tricky Trickster** (10/1) Pulled Up in the *CGA Foxhunter Chase Challenge Cup*
2015 – **Lord Windermere** (20/1) Pulled Up in the *Betfred Cheltenham Gold Cup Chase*

A winner, a runner-up and a 4th placing from just six soft ground festival appearances, preceding last season, arguably supports the belief that **Oscar**'s progeny perform well on soft ground. That conclusion looks rather more concrete when one takes into account the famous incident when *Oscar Delta* was just 150 yards away from winning the 2013 *CGA Foxhunter Chase Challenge Cup*, before suddenly jinking left and unseating the incredibly unfortunate jockey, *Jane Mangan*. As it is, if we add the above six races to the dozen runs from **Oscar**'s offspring last season, we come up with 18 festival appearances this century and a profit of £38.85 to a £1.00 each-way stake, when the ground was officially described as Soft - (Note: none of **Oscar**'s progeny lined up in the first five heavy going festival races in 2018). And if *Jane Mangan* had managed to stay on board *Oscar Delta* for a further 150 yards to claim victory in the 2013 *Foxhunters*, then the profit would read as a rather whopping £64.85 to a £1.00 each-way stake.

If you are a punter who has a tendency to support outsiders rather than short priced favourites, then supporting horses sired by **Oscar** may well bring you some healthy profits. Of the 13 festival victories recorded by the sire's offspring, eight of them have entered the Winners Enclosure at double figure odds, ranging from 10/1 to 33/1. The biggest priced winner of the thirteen victors is last year's champion of the *Albert Bartlett Novices' Hurdle*, **Kilbricken Storm** (33/1), who drew clear at the run-in and stayed on gamely to see off the challenge of *Ok Corral* and favourite *Santini*, who finished third.

The *Colin Tizzard* trained **Kilbricken Storm** wasn't the only big-priced **Oscar** bred runner at the 2018 Cheltenham Festival to provide punters with profits. The shortest priced of the progeny's four placed horses at last year's meeting was **Rather Be**, trained by *Nicky Henderson*. The 12/1 chance had won two of his three novice chases, all of which were at a distance of around two miles, so there was a question mark on how he would cope with the extra half mile to be tackled in the *Close Brothers Novices' Handicap Chase*. As it turned out, despite a blunder at the 7th fence, **Rather Be** finished runner-up in the race, travelling well before being caught in the dying strides by *Mister Whitaker*, who won by a head, and thereby rewarding trainer *Mick Channon* with his first Cheltenham Festival winner. Finishing just over three lengths behind this pair to finish in 3rd place was another **Oscar** sired entry, the 25/1 outsider, **Rocklander**, who was given a front-running ride by jockey, *Adrian Heskin*, but was unable to match the pace of the front two in the final 200 yards.

The trainer of **Rocklander** is *Tom George* and his stable was to register another third place with one of **Oscar**'s more recognisable offspring, **God's Own**, who is often touted as a horse capable of sneaking into a place position in the *Queen Mother Champion Chase*. Primarily a specialist two mile chaser, **God's Own** has visited the Cheltenham Festival on four occasions. He opened his account by finishing runner-up at 33/1 in the 2015 *Racing Post Arkle Challenge Trophy*, and followed up with a 4th place finish, at 20/1, in his first *Betway Queen Mother Champion Chase* run in 2016. Rather surprisingly, in 2017, he went off as the 6/1 second favourite in what was perhaps a weak renewal of the *Champion Chase*, with the exception of the odds-on 2/9 favourite, *Douvan*. The contest became far more competitive than anyone predicted as *Douvan* surprisingly flopped, and the door was left open for another two mile chase stalwart, *Special Tiara*, at odds of 11/1, to take the prize as a veteran ten-year-old. The year younger, **God's Own**, was unable to take advantage of *Douvan*'s washout, when a bad mistake two fences from home, put an end to his impending challenge. He eventually finished in fifth position, 7½ lengths behind the 159 rated winner. 2018 provided a much stronger renewal of the race, with the front three in the market, *Altior*, *Min* and *Douvan* all running off an Official Mark of 167 or more, which no doubt influenced the 40/1 starting price for the **Oscar** sired **God's Own**. *Tom George* was no doubt hoping for another upset in the race, but it wasn't to be as the Evens favourite *Altior* forged clear at the tail end of the race to win by seven lengths from the 5/2 second favourite *Min*. The unfortunate *Douvan*, at 9/2, was travelling strongly until falling four out, which left the way clear for **God's Own** to take 3rd place, albeit some distance behind the impressive *Altior*.

The fifth of **Oscar**'s stock to reward punters with a top three placing at last year's meeting was the veteran, **Splash Of Ginge**, who lined up in the *Brown Advisory & Merriebelle Stable Plate Handicap Chase*. It was somewhat déjà vu for **Splash Of Ginge**, who was sent off at 25/1 on soft going, just as he was four months earlier in the *BetVictor Gold Cup Handicap Chase* at Cheltenham's November Meeting. On that occasion, the **Oscar** bred gelding, came home victorious just seeing off the late challenge of *Starchitect* to win by a neck, and no doubt, trainer *Nigel Twiston-Davies* was dreaming of a repeat win as they set off in the festival's Grade 3 *Stable Plate Handicap Chase*. It was a fantastic effort by the 10 year-old **Splash Of Ginge**, who was two lengths up at the last, but unable to match *The Storyteller*'s strength of stamina after the last. *The Storyteller*, who was the 5/1 favourite for the contest, stayed on well to beat runner-up, **Splash Of Ginge**, by 1¾ lengths.

Last year's 2nd placing by **Splash Of Ginge**, and finishing places of 2nd, 3rd and 8th for **Rather Be**, **Rathvinden** and **Any Second Now**, respectively, in the *Close Brothers Novices' Handicap Chase*, all occurred in the festival's two handicap chases within the 2½m category. The results were a complete turnaround from the previous six runs by **Oscar** bred runners in these two events, where the performances had been dire. Four of the offspring completed their races, but in their own time, hence with finishing positions of between 12th and 19th. Of the other two runners, one was pulled up and the other fell at the 1st fence.

If we expand the analysis of **Oscar**'s stock in all 2m and 2½m festival handicap races (hurdles and chases), preceding the 2018 Cheltenham Festival, the results reinforce just how poor the progeny had been performing. In a total of 21 appearances, nineteen runners had either failed to complete the course or had finished 10th or worse. The two exceptions were **Askthemaster**, who was runner-up in the 2011 running of the *Johnny Henderson Grand Annual Chase Challenge Cup*, and **Ozzie The Oscar**, who secured 3rd place in the 2017 *Randox Health County Handicap Hurdle*. Both runners achieved their place dividends at the rewarding odds of 50/1.

The results for **Oscar**'s stock are only marginally better in the three festival handicaps within the 3m category. Back in 2010, **Offshore Account** registered a place dividend in the then titled William Hill Trophy Handicap Chase, when David Casey rode the *Charlie Swan* trained runner into 4th position at odds of 33/1. Five years later, when the race was sponsored by *Baylis & Harding*, the *Tony Martin* trained, **Gallant Oscar** (9/1), went one better when taking 3rd place, some five lengths behind the clear winner, *The Druids Nephew*. Two place positions from 7 runs in this event can be considered a reasonable return, something which cannot be said for the *Fulke Walwyn Kim Muir Challenge Cup Handicap Chase*, where none of **Oscar**'s five runners have delivered.

In the Cheltenham Festival's only three mile handicap hurdle contest, the *Pertemps Final*, fifteen **Oscar** sired runners have competed of which six have managed to trouble the judge, by finishing in the top six positions. One of that half-dozen, *Oscar Park*, is the only one of **Oscar**'s progeny to be successful in a festival handicap, winning at odds of 14/1 in the 2007 renewal. Six years later, and two more horses by **Oscar** gave punters a run for their money. In the 2013 running of the *Pertemps Final*, *Captain Sunshine* (11/1) and *Jetson* (10/1) finished 2nd and 3rd respectively, behind the clear winner, *Holywell*.

Highlighted at the top of this chapter, the quote taken from last year's Guide concluded that the most likely source of a winner for **Oscar**'s offspring at the 2018 Cheltenham Festival would be in one of the festival's non-handicap races, and so it proved. The victory in the *Albert Bartlett Novices' Hurdle* by *Kilbricken Storm* was the 13th festival win for **Oscar**'s progeny, twelve of which have materialised in non-handicap events. **Oscar** has been represented by his stock at Cheltenham Festivals on 156 occasions, of which 102 runs have taken place in non-handicap events, which calculates to a win percentage strike rate of just below 12%. If one had placed a £1.00 each-way bet on all 102 non-handicap festival appearances from **Oscar**'s offspring, the result would have been a profit of £48.75. This welcome profit is in stark contrast to the losses that would have occurred for anyone who had focused solely on the 54 horses by **Oscar** that have raced in the festival's handicap events, where, as already advised, the one and only **Oscar** bred victory was secured by *Oscar Park* in the *Pertemps Final*. This equates to a 2% win strike rate for **Oscar**'s stock in the meeting's handicap races and a loss of £23.25 had one placed a £1.00 each-way wager on all 54 **Oscar** bred competitors.

If we focus on the non-handicap festival contests, the most impressive set of results for **Oscar**'s offspring are in the two and two and a half mile hurdle contests. Of the £48.75 profit to a £1.00 each-way stake as advised above, 58% of it, or £28.20, has been achieved by **Oscar** sired horses competing in the festival's 2m and 2½m non-handicap hurdle events. In a total of 22 races, **Oscar** bred runners have hit a top six spot on no less than sixteen occasions, recording three victories and nine others who finished 2nd or 3rd. At last year's festival, there were four horses by **Oscar** entered in hurdle events, but all four of them lined up in long distance hurdle contests over three miles.

Oscar's progeny were also unrepresented at the 2018 Cheltenham Festival in the two longest races, these being the *Glenfarclas Cross Country Steeple Chase* (3m6f) and the *National Hunt Challenge Cup Amateur Riders' Novices' Chase* (4m). If you fancy a flutter on an **Oscar** bred runner in either of these events, then my advice is to go ahead and place your bet. **Oscar** bred runners have won twice in their five runs to date in the *National Hunt Challenge Cup*, with victories secured by *Tricky Trickster* at 11/1 in 2009, and *Teaforthree*, the *Rebecca Curtis* trained 5/1 favourite, in 2012. As for the Cross Country event, no conclusions can be drawn from just the two appearances from **Oscar**'s offspring in 2009 and 2011. On each occasion, the two runners were outsiders priced up at 28/1 and 40/1. Both were pulled up.

At the time of writing, there are a number of **Oscar** bred horses with an Official Rating of around 150 that all have the capability to make their presence felt at the 2019 Cheltenham Festival. Amongst the candidates are *Ozzie The Oscar, Beggar's Wishes, Kilbricken Storm, Bags Groove, Rather Be* and *Minella Awards*. *God's Own*, who is rated higher than all of the above, won his opening appearance of the 2018-2019 National Hunt season when winning the Grade 2 *bwin Haldon Gold Cup* at *Exeter* on 6th November 2018. Although he may be entered to make his 4th appearance in the festival's *Queen Mother Champion Chase*, it will be a tremendous achievement if he could register a top three finish as an eleven-year-old, but I wouldn't dismiss him entirely.

Sadly and rather unfortunately, two other highly rated **Oscar** sired horses won't be at the 2019 Cheltenham Festival. On 19th April 2018, *Our Duke*, trained by *Jessica Harrington*, suffered a massive heart attack following his usual morning exercise. The 167 rated gelding was pulled up on his last racecourse appearance which was in the 2018 *Timico Cheltenham Gold Cup*. He was the 9/2 second favourite for the big prize, but never travelled with any fluency and following a couple of mid-race jumping errors, jockey *Robbie Power* pulled him up. **Our Duke** won six of his 13 races and amassed earnings in excess of £300,000.

Less than three months later, and we were mourning the loss of another of **Oscar**'s highly rated offspring. **Finian's Oscar** was only six years old when, in July 2018, he died of organ failure having suffered complications after being treated for colic. Perhaps the number 13 really is unlucky, as just like **Our Duke**, **Finian's Oscar** had also raced 13 times, earning over £200,000 in prize money and winning seven of his 13 races. The *Colin Tizzard* trained gelding had also appeared at last year's festival meeting, when finishing 5th in the *JLT Novices' Chase*. To many, it was a rather disappointing performance at Cheltenham, but he made up for it in two subsequent runs in April when securing victory in the *Big Buck's Celebration Manifesto Novices' Chase* at Aintree, and then being rather unfortunate two weeks later in an eventful race at *Punchestown*, when he was carried out by *Al Boum Photo* when about to make his challenge in the *Growise Champion Novice Chase*.

In summary, supporting **Oscar**'s offspring at Cheltenham has generally been profitable. If you had placed a £1.00 each-way bet on all 156 of **Oscar** sired horses that had competed in festival races, then you would now be £25.50 better off. To increase your profits, the advice would be to focus your bets on the 102 non-handicap races, in which case, the same staking plan would have delivered a profit of £48.75. And if we have a repeat of a wet winter, and the going comes up soft at the 2019 Cheltenham Festival, then as far as supporting horses by **Oscar**, we need not be too concerned. Not that it has to be soft for **Oscar**'s stock to perform. Of the 13 victories to date, two have been won on soft going, 4 have been won on officially good/soft ground, and the remaining 7 wins have occurred on good going.

Oscar's progeny have consistently delivered at the Cheltenham Festival and the positive profit figures prove it. Punters should focus their analysis on the **Oscar** sired entries within the non-handicap races, and take no notice of the odds on offer or the going. This stallion's offspring, inclusive of big priced outsiders, are capable of performing at the festival whatever the ground conditions. Better still, if there ever was a jinx on **Oscar**'s stock over the past few years - it no longer exists! Put your bets on!

Poliglote (GB)

Quote from the 2018 Cheltenham Festival Stallion Guide - "Although it has been a little cumbersome to work out a profitable staking strategy for this stallion's runners, it should not deflect us away from the compelling reality. When it comes to Cheltenham Festivals, **Poliglote**'s progeny deliver high quality performances, consistently, year after year."

Poliglote (Died as a 26-y-o in 2018)							
Race Format	Miles	Won	Placed	Unplaced	Total	Win %	Place %
	About 2m	1	3	4	8	13%	50%
Hurdles	About 2m 4f	2	2	4	8	25%	50%
	About 3m	0	0	3	3	0%	0%
	About 2m	0	0	3	3	0%	0%
	About 2m 4f	0	1	4	5	0%	20%
Chases	About 3m	1	2	4	7	14%	43%
	About 4m	0	0	1	1	0%	0%
Bumper	About 2m	0	0	0	0	-	-
Total	2009-2018	**4**	**8**	**23**	**35**	**11%**	**34%**

Immediately after last year's Cheltenham Festival, on Monday 19th March 2018, the *Haras d'Etreham stud* announced the death of **Poliglote**. Although in National Hunt circles, he will be known for producing horses like **Politologue**, **Don Poli** and **Top Notch**, he is most likely to be remembered for being the sire of **Solemia** who won the 2012 *Prix de l'Arc de Triomphe*. The mare's victory in that race has resulted in **Poliglote** holding the distinction of being the one and only stallion to have been champion sire in France in both Flat and National Hunt codes within the same year. **Poliglote** was 26 years old.

Nineteen horses by **Poliglote** have raced on 37 occasions at Cheltenham Festivals, of which all bar two have taken place within the past decade. Ten of the 19 horses that have experienced the atmosphere of a Cheltenham Festival have rewarded punters with winnings, with four of the progeny registering wins and six more securing a place.

The statistics are highly impressive which is why we should be very interested in **Poliglote**'s stock at Cheltenham Festivals, as no doubt, the offspring will continue to perform. However, from a financial perspective, making a profitable return from such excellent festival results has not been as easy as one would expect. If we take the results overall, then a £1.00 each-way bet on all 37 festival runs from **Poliglote**'s progeny at Cheltenham Festivals, would have resulted in a total profit of £28.45. However, this profit is largely influenced by the three bigger priced winners; **Butler's Cabin** at 33/1 in the 2007 *National Hunt Chase Challenge Cup*; **Spirit River** at 14/1 in the 2010 *Coral Cup*; and **Don Poli** at 14/1 in the 2014 *Martin Pipe Conditional Jockeys' Handicap Hurdle*. In the twelve festivals that have taken place between 2007 and 2018, it is only in the three years when these big priced wins occurred (2007, 2010 and 2014) that backing **Poliglote**'s representatives blind to level stakes would have resulted in making a profit.

The 2018 Cheltenham Festival was below par for **Poliglote**'s progeny, where only one of the five horses that took their chance at the meeting rewarded supporters with a place dividend. The first of the offspring to make an appearance was **Casse Tete** (16/1) who finished 8th in the highly competitive *Ultima Handicap Chase* over a distance of 3m1f. Trained by Gary Moore, **Casse Tete** was held up towards the rear of the field and made some modest headway two-thirds into the race before weakening.

The following day, *Politologue* (12/1) lined up in the *Betway Queen Mother Champion Chase* with the problematic challenge of trying to get the better of three formidable opponents in the shape of *Altior*, *Min* and *Douvan*. Although he perhaps flattered to deceive when leading four out, the Cheltenham Hill soon found him out and he trailed home in 4th place some 23 lengths away from *Altior*, the impressive winner. I quite like *Politologue*, but not when he is racing at Cheltenham. In four races at Prestbury Park, he has never managed to finish in the front three. Since joining *Paul Nicholls* in September 2015, *Politologue*'s record for racing on left-handed tracks is won 2 and lost 8, whilst on right-handed tracks, his record stands as won 7, lost 1. Enough said.

The mare, *Let's Dance*, owned by *Susannah Ricci*, was visiting Cheltenham for the 3rd time when among the runners for Thursday's *Sun Bets Stayers' Hurdle*. She was four years old on her first appearance when finishing fourth in the 2016 *JCB Triumph Hurdle*. In 2017, she was the warm favourite for the second running of the Grade 2 *Trull House Stud Mares' Novices' Hurdle* and rewarded favourite backers when quickening away up the run-in to win by 2¾ lengths from *Barra*. It was a highly contrasting day for her in the 2018 *Stayers' Hurdle*, as she lined up at a price of 33/1 and then fell half way through the race.

As the excitement of Friday's *Gold Cup* was dying down, *Wonderful Charm*, who had been to the festival on four previous occasions, was racing in the *St. James's Place Foxhunter Challenge Cup Open Hunters' Chase*. *Wonderful Charm* (11/2) was attempting to go one better than the runner-up spot that he had secured in the 2017 renewal of the race, but it wasn't to be, and the *Paul Nicholls* trained gelding was eventually pulled up with five still to jump.

The penultimate race of the festival is the *Martin Pipe Conditional Jockeys' Handicap Hurdle*, and lining up in the 2018 renewal was the *Gordon Elliott* trained **Sire Du Berlais**. Poliglote had been represented in this contest twice before - in 2014, when *Don Poli* (12/1) was victorious and in the 2015 renewal, when the 3/1 favourite, **Roi Des Francs**, finished third. Supporters of this stallion were no doubt hoping that *Sire Du Berlais* could match the efforts of his **Poliglote** bred predecessors. As it turned out, not quite, as *Sire Du Berlais* finished in 4th position at 10/1, but nevertheless, being a handicap, fourth place paid out a place dividend.

With *Sire Du Berlais* securing a placing last year, it means that **Poliglote**'s offspring have registered a minimum of at least one place at the past six festivals. Although 2018 was not the best for the progeny, the evidence from the past six meetings clearly implies that **Poliglote** is a stallion to follow at Cheltenham Festivals. Since 2013, 14 of the 27 **Poliglote** bred runners have achieved a top four finishing position, inclusive of 3 winners and 8 place dividends. These figures represent an admirable strike rate.

Poliglote's first two festival representatives were **Liverpool Echo** (unplaced in the 2m5f *Jewsons Novices' Handicap Chase* in 2005) and, as highlighted earlier, **Butler's Cabin** (winner of the *National Hunt Chase Challenge Cup* over a distance of 4m½f in 2007). As these two races took place over ten years ago, they aren't included in the table above which shows **Poliglote**'s festival statistics over the past decade. In looking at the table, it is interesting to see that the best strike rates are within the race categories where the offspring have raced more often. Horses by **Poliglote** have raced on eight occasions apiece in the 2m and 2½m hurdle categories where the win & place strike rate is 50%. Just behind is a 43% win & place strike rate in 3m chases where the progeny have appeared on seven occasions. The numbers aren't big enough to make any firm conclusions but one explanation is that National Hunt racehorse trainers are an astute bunch and know that **Poliglote**'s stock are best suited to these three race categories. Alternatively, one can argue that **Poliglote**'s offspring will probably perform equally as well across the board once there have been enough runs in each category to prove it. Indeed, if the 2007 victory of *Butler's Cabin* was included in the table, it would show a win and a defeat from two runs in the 4m chase category equal to a 50% win and place strike rate. The jury is still out.

The statistics in the table are there for everyone to see. Punters will receive a pay-out for one in every three occasions that a horse by **Poliglote** competes in a festival race. If a 1:3 ratio isn't good enough, then perhaps you may wish to focus on all hurdle races but exclude the long distance three mile events. This strategy provides a win/place ratio of 1:2. Or, for those punters who are ultra-cautious and possess a huge amount of self-control and patience, why not keep your powder dry until the last day of the meeting and wait to see if there are any **Poliglote** bred entries listed in the *JCB Triumph Hurdle* and/or the *Martin Pipe Conditional Jockeys' Handicap Hurdle*? *Let's Dance* (4th) finished just outside the places in the 2016 *Triumph*, but *Far West* in 2013 and *Top Notch* in 2015 were runners-up. In the *Martin Pipe*, *Don Poli* won in 2014, *Roi Des Francs* was 2nd in 2015 and *Sire Du Berlais* was 4th in 2018. Combining the two races, the win/place strike ratio is just off 100% at 5:6.

One unsatisfactory festival hasn't persuaded me to change my view on **Poliglote**. His offspring have consistently performed at the Cheltenham Festival and punters should make a note of all festival entries that show **Poliglote** as the sire.

Presenting (GB)

Quote from the 2018 Cheltenham Festival Stallion Guide - "If you are inclined to bet on outsiders, my strong recommendation is to steer clear of **Presenting**'s offspring at the Cheltenham Festival hurdle events. Over the past decade, 39 of the progeny have lined up in the festival's hurdle races at odds of 10/1 or greater and not one has managed to finish in the first three."

Presenting (Died as a 25-y-o in 2017)

Race Format	Miles	Won	Placed	Unplaced	Total	Win %	Place %
	About 2m	0	3	8	11	0%	27%
Hurdles	About 2m 4f	2	1	23	26	8%	12%
	About 3m	2	2	15	19	11%	21%
	About 2m	0	1	10	11	0%	9%
Chases	About 2m 4f	3	6	18	27	11%	33%
	About 3m	3	9	41	53	6%	23%
	About 4m	0	2	18	20	0%	10%
Bumper	About 2m	1	1	11	13	8%	15%
Total	2009-2018	**11**	**25**	**144**	**180**	**6%**	**20%**

The record of **Presenting**'s offspring at Cheltenham Festivals in the five years between 2013 and 2017 has been a solitary winner at every festival. The winners have been *Rajdhani Express*, *Present View*, *Call The Cops* and *Yorkhill* twice. *Rajdhani Express* (2013) and *Present View* (2014) were both triumphant in the opening day's final race for the two years in which the race was sponsored by *Rewards4Racing*. The race, run over 2m4½m, is now named the *Close Brothers Novices' Handicap Chase*. In the 2015 *Pertemps Network Final*, the *Nicky Henderson* trained, *Call The Cops*, was sent off as the well fancied third favourite at 9/1 and didn't disappoint when staying on strongly to beat *Unique De Cotte* by 1¾ lengths. And in 2016 and 2017, *Yorkhill* became only the third of **Presenting**'s offspring to win two Cheltenham Festival races, a feat also achieved previously by *Denman* and *Weapon's Amnesty*.

In a bid to win at the Festival for three successive years, *Willie Mullins* entered *Yorkhill* in the 2018 *Unibet Champion Hurdle Challenge Trophy*. *Yorkhill* wasn't particularly fancied in the race due to his quirky antics coming to the fore in his previous three runs. In a nutshell, *Yorkhill*'s undoubted talent can be overshadowed by his enormous quirkiness, as demonstrated by his run in the *Ryanair Gold Cup Novice Chase* at *Fairyhouse* in April 2017, just a month after his second Cheltenham Festival victory in the *JLT Novices' Chase*. In the *Fairyhouse* race, he was unhappy being held up, so soon pulled his way to the front after just four fences. Despite jumping violently to his left and hitting a number of fences, remarkably, he was still leading towards the end of the race, when he almost went through the wing of the last fence before coming close to a standstill having cleared it. Having been headed by victor, *Road To Respect*, *Yorkhill* rallied close home and just failed by only a neck to get back up! *Yorkhill*'s next two performances, both at *Leopardstown*, were also desperately erratic, where he finished 8th in the *Leopardstown Christmas Chase* in December 2017 and 6th of 7 in the *Coral Dublin Chase* some five weeks later. In the 2018 *Champion Hurdle*, therefore, at a price of 14/1, it wasn't particularly surprising to see *Yorkhill* being pulled up before the last when well behind.

Yorkhill was one of twenty entries representing **Presenting** at Cheltenham last year, all of whom failed to secure a win, and hence the first time since 2012 that the offspring had failed to register a festival victory. One may question whether last year's soft going had a bearing on this outcome, but I don't believe the ground made any difference. This century, excluding the 2018 Festival, **Presenting**'s stock had achieved one win and two places in the thirteen festival contests in which the progeny had a runner and where the ground was officially described as soft, resulting in strike rates that are very much in line with the statistics shown in the table above. In my view, when looking at the class and quality of the 20 runners last season and the festival races in which the progeny appeared, it was not overly surprising that the results turned out as they did.

In last year's Guide, I remarked that if one is to make a profit at Cheltenham Festivals betting on **Presenting**'s offspring, one needs to be selective. Taking the festival's hurdle events first, I advised of a straightforward betting strategy, this being to support runners sired by **Presenting** provided the betting market has determined they line up at single figure odds. For runners at odds of 10/1 or greater, they should be avoided. At the 2018 Cheltenham Festival, there were seven runners in the festival hurdle events and all of them were priced at double-figure odds, ranging from 12/1 to 40/1. The highest position was achieved by the *Gordon Elliott* trained 25/1 shot, **Brelade**, who finished 7th in the *Randox Health County Handicap Hurdle*. The fact is that over the past decade, 43 of **Presenting**'s stock have lined up in the festival's hurdle races at odds of 10/1 or greater and not one has managed to finish in the first three. In those 43 runs, punters would have been rewarded just twice by virtue of a couple of 4th place finishes in big field handicaps, these being **The Sliotar** in the 2009 *Pertemps Final* and **Cockney Trucker** in the 2011 *Vincent O'Brien County Handicap Hurdle*. If any of **Presenting**'s hurdling representatives at last year's festival had been sent off at single figure odds, it may have been a different story. Of the 13 runners in the past decade that have been sent off at single figure odds, four have won and four have been placed which equates to a 31% win ratio and a 61% win & place ratio. Placing a £1.00 each-way bet on all 13 shorter priced **Presenting** sired hurdle race entries, would have delivered a very welcome profit of £23.59.

In contrast to hurdles, it is rather more convoluted to decide if a runner by **Presenting** is worth backing in the festival's chase events. In last year's Guide, I advised punters that **Presenting**'s progeny have a profitable track record in festival chases within the 2½ and 3 mile categories. In 2½m chases, over the past decade, backing **Presenting**'s progeny blind in 2½ mile chases would have produced a £6.93 profit to a £1.00 each-way stake, with punters being rewarded with at least a place dividend for one in every three runs. However, this small return is very much influenced by one race in particular, the *Close Brothers Novices' Handicap Chase*, a race in which **Presenting**'s offspring have a particularly strong record. In the past 10 years, **Presenting**'s stock has been represented on 12 occasions registering two victories and three place dividends. If one had supported all 12 runners blind to a £1.00 each-way stake, the resulting profit would be £23.00.

As for the 2½m chases at the 2018 Cheltenham Festival, there were just two **Presenting** bred entries, both of whom had an uncanny similarity to each other, over and above just being half-brothers. Both horses, **Movewiththetimes** (8/1) and **Drumcliff** (25/1) took their chance in the *Brown Advisory & Merriebelle Stable Plate Handicap Chase*; both of them were running in their 4th race over fences; both were pulled up 2/3rds into the race; both were 7 years old; both were owned by *John P McManus* and both horses were novices – which means that they could have taken their chance in the opening day's *Close Brothers Novices' Handicap Chase*, which, (as advised above), is a race in which **Presenting**'s offspring have a superb record! Indeed, in the week before the festival kicked off, *Paul Nicholls*, the trainer of **Movewiththetimes** announced on a social media festival preview video that the chestnut gelding would run in the *Close Brothers* sponsored event. I'm not sure who decided that the gelding should switch to the Thursday's Handicap Chase, but perhaps someone should have pointed connections to last year's Stallion Guide which highlighted the performance of **Presenting**'s representatives in Tuesday's Novice Handicap Chase!

In the 3m chase category, **Presenting**'s stock has an excellent Cheltenham Festival record. In total, 64 **Presenting** bred runners have lined up in three mile chases at the festival resulting in 7 winners and 10 places. Backing all 64 runners blind would have provided a profit of £32.84 to a £1.00 each-way stake. That said, a note of caution is needed as all bar 70p of that profit was won over a decade ago between 2005 and 2008, where eleven of **Presenting**'s offspring recorded 4 wins and a 40/1 place position.

Of the five races within the 3m chase category, **Presenting**'s representatives have generally run well in the *Cheltenham Gold Cup Chase* (2 wins and 5 places in 12 appearances) and the *RSA Steeple Chase* (2 wins and 3 places from 12 appearances). Supporting all of the progeny's runners in these two races to a £1.00 each-way stake would have resulted in a profit of £12.54 from the *RSA Chase* runs and £11.70 from the *Gold Cup* runs. Punters may be interested to take note that every **Presenting** bred runner that has lined up in the *Gold Cup* at odds of 16/1 or under, has finished either 1st or 2nd in the race. ***War Of Attrition*** was the offspring's first *Gold Cup* contender in 2006, when victorious at odds of 15/2, which was followed by ***Denman***'s four runs in the *Gold Cup*, the first of which he won at 9/4, before runner-up spots in the following three years at 4/1, 7/1 and 8/1. The closest that *Willie Mullins* has come to winning the *Gold Cup* was in 2014, when ***On His Own*** at 16/1, failed by just a short head to peg back winner, *Lord Windermere*.

Of the other three races in this category, from a total of 40 appearances, **Presenting**'s stock has been victorious on 3 occasions and hit a place position twice. The *Foxhunters* has been very much boom and bust with two big-priced winners, these being ***Drombeag*** (20/1) in 2007 and ***Zemsky*** (33/1) in 2011. Of the other 16 runs in the *Foxhunters*, only ***Balnaslow*** has managed to achieve a top eight finish when 5th in 2017 and 7th last year. Fourteen runners by **Presenting** have lined up in the *Fulke Walwyn Kim Muir Challenge Cup*, but only one of them passed the post in first place, which was ***Ballabriggs***, the *Donald McCain* trained 2011 *Grand National* winner, who beat *Faasel* by a ½ length in 2010. As for Tuesday's *Ultima Handicap Chase*, **Presenting** bred runners have so far drawn a blank from 8 runs.

Despite the positive trends of **Presenting**'s offspring in the 3m chase category, the six runners at the 2018 Cheltenham Festival were all disappointing, although taking into account the races in which the six were entered and their starting prices, perhaps the poor performances were to be largely expected. For starters, none of the six entries appeared in the two races in which **Presenting**'s runners have previously performed well, the *Gold Cup* and *RSA Chase*. Three of the progeny were entered in the *St James's Place Foxhunter Challenge Cup Open Hunters' Chase*, of which two were 100/1 rank outsiders and the 28/1 chance, ***Balnaslow***, as highlighted earlier, finished 7th. Another two of **Presenting**'s stock ran in the *Fulke Walwyn Kim Muir Challenge Cup Amateur Riders' Handicap Chase*. ***Sugar Baron***, trained by *Nicky Henderson* and ridden by *Katie Walsh*, was towards the front of market at 8/1, but was very disappointing, making mistakes throughout the race and finished in 14th position. At 100/1, ***Marinero***, the other **Presenting** bred was pulled up. The sixth 3m chase entry sired by **Presenting** appeared in the *Ultima Handicap Chase*. ***Gold Present*** (10/1) had it all to do, being top weight in the opening day's heavy ground, and so it proved when he was pulled up towards the end of race by jockey *Nico de Boinville*.

In the shortest and longest chase events at the Cheltenham Festival, **Presenting**'s progeny have a particularly poor record. Indeed, in 25 runs in the two 4m category chases, the *Glenfarclas Handicap Chase Cross Country Handicap Chase* over 3m6f and the 4m *National Hunt Challenge Cup Amateur Riders' Novices' Chase*, the best that runners by **Presenting** have achieved is three 3rd place positions.

Haymount (33/1) finished 3rd in the 2017 *JT McNamara National Hunt Challenge Cup Amateur Riders' Novices' Chase*, and the other 3rd placings were courtesy of *Drombeag*, who was a one-paced 3rd in the *134th Year of National Hunt Chase Challenge Cup* in 2004 and then filled the same position five years later in the 2009 *Glenfarclas Handicap Chase Cross Country Chase*. Last season, *Duel at Dawn* (16/1) and *Reigning Supreme* (33/1) were the only two horses by **Presenting** that tackled four miles at the festival and both were pulled up four from home in the *National Hunt Challenge Cup Amateur Riders' Novices' Chase*.

Other than in 2003, where there weren't any **Presenting** bred festival entries, the only year in which the progeny failed to achieve at least a place position occurred at the 2002 Cheltenham Festival, where the very first festival runner by **Presenting** would appear as the offspring's sole representative at the meeting. At a price of 66/1, *Special Present* finished 11th in that year's *Weatherbys Champion Bumper*. The second festival runner by **Presenting** was *War Of Attrition*, who took the runner-up spot in the 2004 *Letheby & Christopher Supreme Novices' Hurdle* at a price of 33/1, the start of a 15 year run in which **Presenting**'s offspring have secured at least a place or a win at every Cheltenham festival meeting. That said, after 27 races had been run at the 2018 meeting, it looked highly probable that the run would end at 14 successive years.

After 27 races last season, not one of 18 runners sired by **Presenting** had managed to finish in the top six positions in their respective races, let alone secure a win or place. And the signs were ominous for the two **Presenting** bred representatives, *Top Gamble* (8/1) and *Bright New Dawn* (66/1), who lined up at the start of the 28th and very last race at the Cheltenham Festival, the *Johnny Henderson Grand Annual Challenge Cup Handicap Chase*. This event is run over a distance of 2m62yds, and preceding the race, in a total of eleven attempts, **Presenting**'s stock had failed to win or place in the festival's two mile chase category. Therefore, a great deal of credit is deserved for *Kerry Lee*, trainer of *Top Gamble*, who was the first to achieve the feat when her 8/1 chance secured 3rd place. It was a welcome reward for the Herefordshire based trainer, as *Top Gamble* was just a head away from a third place in the 2017 *Betway Queen Mother Champion Chase*, running on strongly after the last but failing to catch *Sir Valentino*, who just held on for 3rd place.

As we approach the 2019 Cheltenham Festival, the advice given to punters in last year's Guide remains. Over hurdles, support runners sired by **Presenting** provided the betting market has determined they should line up at single figure odds. If the odds are 10/1 or greater, the progeny can be safely ignored. As for **Presenting**'s offspring over fences, the best chance of making a profit would appear to be in the 2½m and 3m chase categories, and special focus should be paid to three races in particular, these being the *Close Brothers Novices' Handicap Chase* (2m4½f); the *RSA Steeple Chase* (3m½f); and the *Magners Cheltenham Gold Cup Steeple* Chase (3m2½f).

Robin Des Champs (FR)

Quote from the 2018 Cheltenham Festival Stallion Guide - "Will there be a **Robin Des Champs** bred victor at the 2018 meeting, making it 10 years on the trot for the progeny to register a Cheltenham Festival winner? I wouldn't bet against it."

Robin Des Champs (22-y-o)							
Race Format	*Miles*	*Won*	*Placed*	*Unplaced*	*Total*	*Win %*	*Place %*
Hurdles	About 2m	1	1	6	8	13%	25%
	About 2m 4f	8	0	6	14	57%	57%
	About 3m	0	1	3	4	0%	25%
Chases	About 2m	0	0	2	2	0%	0%
	About 2m 4f	3	0	2	5	60%	60%
	About 3m	2	1	3	6	33%	50%
	About 4m	0	1	1	2	0%	50%
Bumper	About 2m	0	0	5	5	0%	0%
Total	2009-2018	**14**	**4**	**28**	**46**	**30%**	**39%**

With just two races left to run on the last day of last year's meeting, it was something of a surprise to realise that of the 418 horses that had so far competed in the previous 26 races of the 2018 Cheltenham Festival, only three of them had been sired by **Robin Des Champs**. None of the three had won, but two of them had been placed, which was a rather good result considering that the three runners lined up at 66/1, 8/1 and 80/1. A £1.00 each-way stake on all three horses would have resulted in a profit of £13.60.

In last year's Guide, I had closed off the chapter on **Robin Des Champs** with the advice that I wouldn't bet against the offspring registering a winner at the 2018 Cheltenham Festival, and that should it happen then the progeny would have registered a festival victory for ten successive seasons. And with just two races to go, only one of the 45 runners who were scheduled to appear in the festival's last two races was by **Robin Des Champs**. Appearing in the famous maroon and white colours of *Gigginstown Stud*, **Blow By Blow** was an 11/1 shot to win the *Martin Pipe Conditional Jockey's Handicap Hurdle*, and he duly obliged, beating *Discorama* by five lengths and ensuring that **Robin Des Champs'** offspring had recorded a festival winner for every year going back to 2009.

It was a comfortable victory for **Blow By Blow** who dictated the pace and appeared to be in command throughout the entire race. Horses by **Robin Des Champs** have a 100% win record in this event, as seven years earlier, the same trainer (*Gordon Elliott*) and owners (*Gigginstown Stud*), won the 2011 renewal with **Sir Des Champs**, who went on to claim victory in the *Jewson Novices' Chase* in 2012. **Blow By Blow** hasn't set the world alight in his races following last year's festival success, and so would appear to have a more challenging task than his predecessor of securing a second victory at the 2019 Cheltenham Festival. As of early January, he is possible entry in the *RSA Chase* and can be backed at anything up to 50/1.

Adding **Blow by Blow'**s *Martin Pipe* victory to the two place positions that had been achieved in the earlier festival races ensured that it was a very successful meeting for supporters of **Robin Des Champs**. Had one backed all four runners by this stallion blind to level stakes, the outcome to a £1.00 each-way stake would have been a very healthy £27.35.

The second race of the meeting, the *Racing Post Arkle Challenge Trophy Novices' Chase*, attracted a field of just five with starting prices of 5/6, 11/4, 4/1, 14/1 and 66/1. The horse representing **Robin Des Champs** was the 66/1 outsider, *Robinshill*, so it wasn't surprising to see the *Nigel Twiston-Davies* runner trail home in last place. The 5/6 favourite, *Footpad*, was the highly impressive winner. Later in the day, over a distance of four miles, a couple of ten-year-old novice chasers would line up in the *National Hunt Challenge Cup Amateur Rider's Novices' Chase*, one of whom was the *Colin Tizzard* trained, **Sizing Tennessee**. The 8/1 chance was prominent throughout the race but the soft ground didn't help him as he weakened up the run-in to finish in 3rd place and more than 20 lengths behind the front two, one of which was the other 10-year-old in the race, *Rathvinden*, who found extra at the finish to win at a price of 9/2, from runner-up *Ms Parfois*. At the time of writing, **Sizing Tennessee** has been in the form of his life, and on 1st December at *Newbury* in the *Ladbrokes Trophy Chase*, he beat his stablemate, *Elegant Escape*, who at the end of December went one better to win the *Coral Welsh Grand National Handicap Chase*. I anticipate that both of the *Tizzard* horses will go for the *Grand National* at *Aintree*, for which *Elegant Escape* is around the 20/1 mark and **Sizing Tennessee** can be backed at 33/1.

The *Trull House Stud Mares' Novices' Hurdle* resulted in a facile victory for the odds-on favourite and *Willie Mullins* trained *Laurina*, who, to my eyes, may be even better than *Annie Power*. Although she has several options for the 2019 Cheltenham Festival, if she lines up for the *Unibet Champion Hurdle Challenge Trophy*, I think she will have a great chance of winning, especially with her sex allowance. Following *Laurina* home, in 3rd place and just a short head away from claiming the runner-up spot was the *Alan Fleming* trained, **Champayne Lady**, at the huge price of 80/1. By a weird coincidence, the 4:50pm races at the 2018 Cheltenham Festival proved to be highly rewarding for the offspring of **Robin Des Champs**. On day 1, the race resulted in a 3rd place at 8/1; On Thursday, a 3rd place at 80/1; and on Friday, an 11/1 winner!

Twenty-seven horses by **Robin Des Champs** have raced on 47 occasions at Cheltenham Festivals, of which all bar one has taken place within the past decade. Eight of the 27 horses that have experienced the atmosphere of a Cheltenham Festival have rewarded punters with winnings, with five of the progeny having registered victories and three others securing a place. As of today, **Blow By Blow** stands alone as the only horse by **Robin Des Champs** to have won a single festival race, the other four of the offspring all being multiple winners. **Sir Des Champs** and **Un Temps Pour Tout** have two successes to their name, whilst **Vautour** was hugely impressive in all three of his victories and may well have secured further wins if he had not been so tragically taken from us when breaking a foreleg in late 2016 whilst out in a paddock. The one other winner sired by **Robin Des Champs** will be remembered forever, the amazingly talented **Quevega**, who won the *David Nicholson Mares' Hurdle* a record six times.

The progeny of **Robin Des Champs** show highly impressive festival statistics of 14 wins and 4 places having been delivered by eight of the 27 of the offspring who have competed at Cheltenham Festivals. And a profit of £23.20 would have resulted, had one staked a £1.00 each-way bet on all 47 of this sire's festival runners. One can't take the following information too seriously as the number of **Robin Des Champs** bred runners to have competed in the races listed below are so low. Nevertheless, to amaze (or bore) your friends with festival trivia, you may be interested to learn that horses by **Robin Des Champs** have a 100% win record in the *Martin Pipe Conditional Jockey's Handicap Hurdle* (2 from 2); the *Golden Miller Novices' Chase* (2 from 2); and the *David Nicholson Mares Hurdle* (6 out of 6 and all courtesy of **Quevega**).

Looking at the current group of National Hunt horses sired by **Robin Des Champs**, I am optimistic that at the 2019 Cheltenham Festival, we are likely to see more appearances from the progeny than just the four that competed at last year's meeting. With that in mind, I very much anticipate that we will witness at least one of the 28 festival races being won by a runner whose sire is listed as **Robin Des Champs**. Who knows? A *Gordon Elliott* trained **Robin Des Champs** bred horse, owned by *Gigginstown Stud*, may be among the list of runners for the 2019 *Martin Pipe Conditional Jockey's Handicap Hurdle*? If so, punters may wish to consider backing it!

Saddler Maker (IRE)

Quote from the 2018 Cheltenham Festival Stallion Guide - "**Saddler Maker**'s progeny have so far managed to achieve five top three finishes in six festival events over a distance of 2½ miles, making the middle distance by far the most profitable for punters to follow."

Saddler Maker (Died as an 18-y-o in 2016)							
Race Format	*Miles*	*Won*	*Placed*	*Unplaced*	*Total*	*Win %*	*Place %*
Hurdles	About 2m	0	2	3	5	0%	40%
	About 2m 4f	1	3	1	5	20%	80%
	About 3m	0	1	1	2	0%	50%
Chases	About 2m	0	0	1	1	0%	0%
	About 2m 4f	0	3	0	3	0%	100%
	About 3m	0	0	3	3	0%	0%
	About 4m	0	0	0	0	-	-
Bumper	About 2m	0	0	0	0	-	-
Total	2009-2018	**1**	**9**	**9**	**19**	5%	53%

Having read through this chapter in last year's Stallion Guide, there were a number of quotes that I could have used in this year's Guide. I eventually used the one that you can see at the top of the page which advises that **Saddler Maker**'s offspring have finished in the first three positions five times out of six in festival races run over a distance of 2½m. That is some statistic. Data like this provides compelling evidence that a horse's breeding is highly influential when it comes to a horse's performance when competing at the pinnacle of jump racing which is the Cheltenham Festival.

Non-believers may say this is a coincidence. And that's fine. Thankfully, everyone is entitled to their own opinion, which is why it is so enthralling discussing with friends and colleagues the reasons why your selection is going to win a race. Imagine if we couldn't do that. How dull life would become! To the non-believers, I point to last year's results from the five horses by **Saddler Maker** that made the trip to the 2018 Cheltenham Festival. Of the five competitors, two of them ran in festival races over a distance of 2½m. Both horses secured a top three finish. So, the coincidence continues. In festival events over a distance of 2½m, horses by **Saddler Maker** have finished in the first three positions seven times out of eight attempts.

"But they must have all been favourites!" I hear someone shout. So to close off that argument, here are the returned prices, starting with the shortest price, of the seven that hit a top three spot: 1/2F, 7/2, 4/1CF, 8/1, 10/1, 14/1, 33/1. To complete the picture, the one horse that missed out lined up with odds of 25/1.

Without doubt, **Saddler Maker** is a punter's friend when it comes to the Cheltenham Festival. He is the only stallion within this Guide where the statistics show that his offspring has a better record of finishing in the first three at Cheltenham Festivals than not doing so. The win and place strike rate currently stands at 53%. The situation, however, isn't all rosy in the garden. The win rate is just 5%. What is remarkable about **Saddler Maker** is that his progeny have finished in 2nd or 3rd position nine times from nineteen festival runs, or close to one in every two festival appearances. In some ways this is hugely frustrating and reminds me of a period in time when the football team I support went through a run of matches when they kept drawing. They were playing fantastically well, had all the possession, created loads of chances but missed most of them. Invariably, with a few minutes of the match remaining, the opposition who had been under the cosh for most of the match would score an equaliser with their one chance in the game. When I looked at our league position, I would look at all those draws and think about how much further up the table we would be if those draws had been wins instead.

I have that same frustrated feeling with this stallion in calculating the profit return had one placed a £1.00 each-way bet on all nineteen festival runners sired by **Saddler Maker**. The profit would be a pitiful £1.45. If only 2 or 3 of those nine placed positions had resulted in victories instead?

One result from the 2018 Cheltenham Festival that wouldn't have made much difference to that £1.45 profit, win or place, was the 3rd place position registered by **Apple's Jade** in the 2018 *OLBG Mares' Hurdle*. The result was a surprise as **Apple's Jade** was expected to win and started as the odds-on 1/2 favourite, but today wasn't one of her best days and she lacked pace as they approached the Cheltenham Hill, finishing behind 9/2 winner *Benie Des Dieux* and runner-up, *Midnight Tour* (33/1).

The other horse by **Saddler Maker** to secure a place at last year's meeting was **Discorama**, who I had backed each way on the Tote, in the festival's penultimate event, the *Martin Pipe Conditional Jockey's Handicap Hurdle*. Detached from the rest of field at the beginning of the race and still at the back two hurdles from the finish, I was convinced that **Discorama** would be the second horse by **Saddler Maker** not to secure a top three finish. But I was certainly not the only one who got it wrong. **Discorama** started to make rapid headway turning in and by the time he had reached the final hurdle, he had made it to 4th place. He kept on well from the last and picked off two of the three in front of him to finish in second place at 33/1. He never threatened the winner, *Blow By Blow*, who was away and gone, and finished 5 lengths behind him.

At the meeting last year, another **Saddler Maker** bred mare and hot favourite, who was expected to win her race, failed to live up to expectations. Lining up in a field of just nine runners for the *JCB Triumph Hurdle*, **Apple's Shakira**, trained by *Nicky Henderson*, was the warm 6/5 favourite, courtesy of having already won three *JCB Triumph Hurdle* trials at Cheltenham, the latter two of which were over course and distance. Although the mare travelled strongly throughout the race, she was outpaced approaching the last hurdle and despite trying her best to stay on, she couldn't catch the leaders and finished in 4th place, over six lengths behind the winner.

It obviously wasn't a good year for Apples at the 2018 Cheltenham Festival, and going off at a tangent for a moment, if **Apple's Jade** and/or **Apple's Shakira** win at the 2019 Cheltenham Festival, they will have me to thank. In mid-January, a close friend of mine who rents out a most beautiful 3-bedroom cottage in the Devon countryside about 30 minutes from Exeter, invited me down for the village Wassail, which is an ancient tradition dating back to pagan times. In short, Wassail ceremonies take place in villages around the South of England to bless the orchards so the forthcoming crop of apples will be plentiful. Whilst there, we were also told to make a huge amount of noise to drive away evil spirits. The evening was fantastic fun with lots of singing, shouting, dancing from Morris Men, and a colossal volume of cider to drink. At one point, the master of ceremonies announced, *"Anyone who mentions Dry January will be banished!"* I drank enough cider to make sure that the **Saddler Maker** sired 'Apple Mares' will have a much better festival in 2019!

The other two horses by **Saddler Maker** from last year's festival failed to complete the course. **Chef Des Obeaux** was disappointing in the *Albert Bartlett Novices' Hurdle*. He had won his three previous races, hence his starting price of 6/1, but he weakened towards the end of the race and was pulled up before the final hurdle. As for *Bouvreuil*, he was plain unlucky being brought down at the second fence in the festival's final race, the *Johnny Henderson Grand Annual Challenge Cup Handicap Chase*.

Bouvreuil, incidentally, was the very first **Saddler Maker** bred runner to appear at a Cheltenham Festival, when at the 2015 meeting, he finished runner-up in the *Fred Winter Juvenile Handicap Hurdle*, at a starting price of 14/1. The following year, *Bouvreuil* was runner-up for the second year in a row and once again returning a price of 14/1 in the *Close Brothers Novices' Handicap Chase*, losing out to *Ballyalton* by half a length in what was a neck to neck battle for the line. *Bouvreuil* made his third festival appearance in the 2017 *Brown Advisory & Merriebelle Stable Plate Handicap Chase*. Although he didn't win, it was another sound performance and he came home in 3rd place at a price of 10/1. At seven years old, *Bouvreuil* had already achieved three Cheltenham Festival top three finishes, but having been brought down in his race at last year's meeting, the chance to make it four festival placings in a row was taken from him.

There is plenty of fire-power in **Saddler Maker**'s stock for the 2019 Cheltenham Festival, including amongst others *Bristol De Mai, Janika, Chef Des Obeaux, Cepage, Bouvreuil* and *Discorama*. As far as the two 'Apple Mares' are concerned, I expect them to be racing against each other in the *OLBG Mares' Hurdle*. As we approach this year's meeting, in terms of form, the mares appear to have gone in opposite directions. At the time of writing, *Apple's Shakira* appears to have gone backwards and was pulled up in her last appearance at *Sandown* on 8th December. The five year-old's trainer, *Nicky Henderson*, has the task of getting her back to her best. She can currently be backed at around 25/1 for the *OLBG hurdle*.

Whilst *Apple's Shakira* has gone backwards, *Apple's Jade* seems to be in impervious form and right back to her best. She clearly a major disappointment being beaten at odds-on at last year's festival and similarly when she lost, also at odds-on, in the *Irish Stallion Farms EBF Annie Power Mares Champion Hurdle* at *Punchestown* in late April. One would imagine that there would be some explanation for these defeats and in November last year, her trainer, *Gordon Elliott* advised, "We had an awful problem with her last year as she kept coming in season every day she went racing at the end of the season. She did it at *Punchestown* and at Cheltenham. We're just trying to sort that out and hopefully it's all behind her now."

Apple's Jade is 11/10 favourite for the festival's forthcoming *OLBG Mares' Hurdle* and provided she takes part in the race, I think it will be very difficult for any of her rivals to beat her. Especially now that I have banished away the evil spirits!

Saint Des Saints (FR)

Quote from the 2018 Cheltenham Festival Stallion Guide - "I am a huge fan of **Saint Des Saints'** offspring. Sixteen top six finishes inclusive of two wins and eight place dividends from just 27 festival appearances says everything."

Saint Des Saints (21-y-o)							
Race Format	*Miles*	*Won*	*Placed*	*Unplaced*	*Total*	*Win %*	*Place %*
	About 2m	0	4	2	6	0%	67%
Hurdles	About 2m 4f	1	0	5	6	17%	17%
	About 3m	0	1	4	5	0%	20%
	About 2m	0	0	2	2	0%	0%
Chases	About 2m 4f	1	0	4	5	20%	20%
	About 3m	0	3	7	10	0%	30%
	About 4m	0	0	0	0	-	-
Bumper	About 2m	0	1	1	2	0%	50%
Total	2009-2018	**2**	**9**	**25**	**36**	**6%**	**31%**

Following the 2018 Cheltenham Festival, where only one of nine racehorses by **Saint Des Saints** secured a place position, my enthusiasm for this stallion has somewhat waned. When I wrote the first of these Cheltenham Festival Stallion Guides in 2015, I was quite upbeat about the eleven festival appearances that had been made by the progeny of **Saint Des Saints**. Up to and including the 2014 festival, eight of the offspring had finished in the first eight places, including two place dividends and a first victory. The other three pre-2015 festival runners of the eleven had all been running well in their races before falling and the trio would no doubt have secured a top eight finish had they managed to complete the course. Having expressed a bullish commentary about the progeny's chances preceding the 2015 festival, I felt especially smug when the five horses by **Saint Des Saints** that lined up that year, recorded finishing positions of 1st, 2nd, 3rd, 3rd and 4th.

The following year, there was no way that the progeny were going to match the festival achievements of 2015, but nevertheless, the eight **Saint Des Saints** bred 2016 festival entrants produced a solid set of results, earning three place dividends. Surprisingly, at the 2017 Cheltenham Festival, only three horses by **Saint Des Saints** would make it to Cheltenham. All three failed to register a place, with **Djakadam**, who started as the 3/1 favourite for the *Timico Cheltenham Gold Cup Chase*, coming closest when he finished just outside the places in 4th.

The sole place dividend for the offspring at last year's festival was recorded by **Connetable** in the *Pertemps Network Final Handicap Hurdle*, who was accompanied in the race by another **Saint Des Saints** sired runner, **Wait For Me**. The *Philip Hobbs* trained **Wait For Me** was appearing at the Cheltenham Festival for the 4th year in a row, and had secured place dividends on his first two visits, taking 3rd place in the 2015 *Weatherbys Champion Bumper* and 4th position in the 2016 *Vincent O'Brien County Handicap Hurdle*. **Wait For Me** has never won beyond 2m4f, so the soft ground in the 2018 *Pertemps Final* would not have helped him in the stamina department and he weakened towards the end of the race to finish in 10th place at 25/1. **Connetable**, meanwhile, had every chance as they raced up the Cheltenham Hill, but he was unable to go the pace of the front two, and he eventually finished in 3rd place at 33/1.

Connetable, incidentally, was having his second festival appearance, as he also raced at Cheltenham two years previously, in the 2016 *JCB Triumph Hurdle*, when he finished 11th at a price of 14/1. The *Triumph* and the *Boodles Fred Winter Juvenile Handicap Hurdle* are confined to four year olds, and *Connetable* is the only one of four **Saint Des Saints'** sired racehorses to have appeared in these events, who was unable to secure a top three finish. The three runners that did achieve a placing rewarded backers with big priced returns. In the 2013 running of the *Triumph Hurdle*, **Sametegal** returned a starting price of 33/1 when he finished third and some seventeen lengths behind the runaway winner, *Our Conor*. The other two place positions occurred in the *Fred Winter Juvenile Handicap Hurdle*. In the 2015 running of the contest, it was another 33/1 outsider for 4-year-old horses by **Saint Des Saints**, as *The Saint James* finished in 3rd place behind the *Paul Nicholls* trained duo of *Qualando* and *Bouvreuil* who finished 1st and 2nd respectively. *Paul Nicholls* was at it again in the 2016 *Fred Winter*, securing a 1-2 for the second year in a row when stablemates *Diego Du Charmil* and **Romain De Senam** fought out a tight finish. It was so very close to being a winner for the **Saint Des Saints** bred **Romain De Senam** (20/1), who ran on really strongly in the last 100 yards, just failing to catch *Diego Du Charmil* by a head. One or two more yards and **Romain De Senam** would have won.

As of mid-January, there are three **Saint Des Saints** bred four year olds who could potentially make it to the 2019 Cheltenham Festival, these being **Fructine, Fusil Raffles** and the wonderfully named, **Please God**. The last of this trio won his first two hurdle races in *Auteuil* and is currently with *Guillaume Macaire*, 13-time champion jumps trainer in France. The former two horses also hail from France, but have since been moved to *Nicky Henderson*'s yard in *Upper Lambourn*. Based on the knowledge that the **Saint Des Saints** duo of **Fusil Raffles** and **Fructine** are now in the hands of *Nicky Henderson*, punters may wish to think about placing some ante-post bets on them for the *JCB Triumph Hurdle*. As advised earlier, three of the four **Saint Des Saints** bred four year olds to have raced in the festival's juvenile races have finished in the first three places, and *Nicky Henderson* has trained the winner of the *Triumph Hurdle* on six occasions, the victors being *First Bout* (1985), *Alone Success* (1987), *Katarino* (1999), *Zaynar* (2009), *Soldatino* (2010) and *Peace and Co* (2015).

Nicky Henderson's record in the *Fred Winter* is not as impressive, but then again, the race wasn't introduced to the Cheltenham Festival until 2005. He has just missed out with his entries in the past two years, with *Divin Bere* (2017) and *Style De Garde* (2018) both recording runner-up spots. His one victory in this contest occurred in 2012 with the mare, *Une Artiste*, who won at a price of 40/1. The owner of *Une Artiste* is *Simon Munir*, who also owns **Fusil Raffles**.

If this stallion's progeny are to make a comeback at the 2019 Cheltenham Festival, in addition to making a note of any **Saint Des Saints** sired runner that is amongst the entries for the festival's two hurdle races confined to four year-olds, punters may also wish to favour the sire's entries in the 2½m and 3m chase categories. Analysis of the results show that in a combined total of fifteen appearances by **Saint Des Saints'** offspring in 2½m and 3m chase events, on six occasions, the progeny finished in the first 4 places. Four more runners finished between 5th and 8th and there were two fallers who would have been up with those who finished to the fore if they had stayed on their feet. Some caution is required with these statistics, however, as it should be noted that of the 12 runs where the horse by **Saint Des Saints** finished in the first 8 positions or fell, *Djakadam* is responsible for five of those results, including his two *Gold Cup* runner-up achievements in 2015 and 2016.

Although results of the last two meetings have been disheartening and one can perhaps imagine another year of disappointment for this stallion at the 2019 Cheltenham Festival, neither would it be a major surprise to see a rapid turnaround in results. As advised earlier, if results are to improve, punters may wish to focus upon chases within the 2½m and 3m categories, as well as paying extra special attention to any **Saint Des Saints** bred runner who lines up in the *JCB Triumph Hurdle* or the *Boodles Fred Winter Juvenile Handicap Hurdle*.

Will the 2019 Cheltenham Festival rekindle my enthusiasm for **Saint Des Saints**? Perhaps *Guillaume Macaire* can help? ***Please God***!

Shantou (USA)

Quote from the 2018 Cheltenham Festival Stallion Guide - "In this Guide's Introduction, I write *"There is compelling evidence that a horse's breeding is a critical factor when it comes to picking winners. The progeny of some stallions perform creditably at the festival time and time again, whereas others consistently struggle"*. **Shantou** is a classic example of a stallion whose offspring perform at Cheltenham Festivals year after year."

Race Format	Miles	Won	Placed	Unplaced	Total	Win %	Place %
	Shantou (26-y-o)						
Hurdles	About 2m	0	0	5	5	0%	0%
	About 2m 4f	0	2	2	4	0%	50%
	About 3m	0	3	8	11	0%	27%
Chases	About 2m	0	0	0	0	-	-
	About 2m 4f	3	0	4	7	43%	43%
	About 3m	0	6	3	9	0%	67%
	About 4m	0	1	2	3	0%	33%
Bumper	About 2m	1	0	0	1	100%	100%
Total	2009-2018	**4**	**12**	**24**	**40**	**10%**	**40%**

Twenty-seven horses by **Shantou** have raced on 41 occasions at Cheltenham Festivals, and only one run took place over a decade ago, the very first appearance from a **Shantou** sired horse, when *De Valira* finished 10th in the 2007 *Anglo Irish Bank Supreme Novices' Hurdle*. Five years would pass before the next festival appearance from the offspring, which also occurred in the *Supreme*. *Dylan Ross* fared no better than *De Valira* and trailed home in 16th place. At that same 2012 festival, the **Shantou** bred *Our Father* lined up as the 11/2 favourite for the *Pertemps Handicap Final*, but he also disappointed finishing back in 15th. So, not a great start with finishing places of 10th, 16th and 15th. But come the spring of 2013, everything started to get better, much better. Thirteen of the next 24 horses by **Shantou** that would race at the festival would secure a top four placing on no less than sixteen occasions.

Considering that there are 28 races at a Cheltenham festival on which to gamble, a punter would need to possess a huge amount of self-control to decide upon a strategy of placing very few bets over the course of four days of racing heaven. As everyone knows, hindsight is a wonderful thing, but bear with my racing fantasy for a moment and imagine that a person born in the city of Shantou, on the eastern coast of Guangdong, China, had in older life become a Cheltenham Festival devotee. This person, as well as being extremely fond of his birthplace, was also a well-disciplined chap and following the Chinese New Year of 2013, he had decided to only place bets on festival runners that were sired by **Shantou**. To make the numbers bigger and emphasise the point, let us assume that he had placed £1,000 each way on every single **Shantou** sired festival runner. The outcome of such a strategy would have been a total profit of £ 67,925 and an annual festival return on his investment as follows:

2013 – Profit of £ 28,375
2014 – Profit of £ 7,800
2015 – Profit of £ 2,200
2016 – Profit of £ 3,800

2017 – Profit of £ 11,500
2018 – Profit of £ 14,250

Adopting a strategy of blindly backing every **Shantou** bred runner at level stakes has been rewarded with a profit at the past six Cheltenham Festivals. At some point, this lucrative run will surely come to an end, so if you are thinking of following the same strategy as our imaginary Chinese punter, then beware of the Chinese proverb, "Of all the stratagems, to know when to quit is the best".

2018 brought about another successful Cheltenham Festival for **Shantou**'s stock, and the offspring got off to a flyer in the opening day's first handicap, the *Ultima Handicap Chase* with the appropriately named ***Shantou Flyer***. Trained by *Richard Hobson* in *Stow-On-The-Wold*, ***Shantou Flyer***, who fell on his one previous appearance at the Cheltenham festival, ran really well, at a price of 14/1, to finish a neck second to the favourite *Coo Star Sivola*. Nine lengths behind him to pick up a 4th place dividend, was ***Beware The Bear,*** also by **Shantou**.

The next three runners by **Shantou** competed in two of Thursday's events, these being the *Pertemps Network Final Handicap Hurdle* and the *Brown Advisory & Merriebelle Stable Plate Handicap Chase*. In the former race, ***Taj Badalandabad*** rewarded each-way backers by making late headway and keeping on up the Cheltenham Hill to secure 4th at 40/1. Not too far behind him, finishing in 9th place, was ***The Mighty Don*** (33/1), who also made late headway before making a mistake at the last.

Later in the day, the *Gordon Elliott* trained ***The Storyteller*** became the third horse by **Shantou** to win one of the festival's 2½m handicap chases, when taking the *Brown Advisory & Merriebelle Stable Plate Handicap Chase*. The ***Storyteller*** was sent off the 5/1 favourite and duly obliged under a canny ride by jockey *Davy Russell*. ***Ballynagour*** by **Shantou** also won this event back in 2014 at a price of 12/1.

With a victory and three place dividends from five runners, it was asking too much to wish for further success on *Gold Cup* day and so it proved as both the mare ***Smaoineamh Alainn*** (16/1) in the *Randox Health County Handicap Hurdle* and the 100/1 outsider, ***Shantou Magic***, in the *St. James's Place Foxhunter Challenge Cup Open Hunters' Chase*, were both pulled up. ***Smaoineamh Alainn*** was the sixth of **Shantou**'s progeny, attempting to achieve a placing in one of the festival's two mile hurdle events. In fact, none of the representatives have yet to finish in the first six positions, so there is a slight suspicion that horses by **Shantou** may not be suited to National Hunt's minimum race distance. Also, it hasn't gone unnoticed that, as yet, no trainer has yet entered **Shantou** in a two mile chase. Perhaps they know something I don't. That said, based on the fact that the one appearance from a **Shantou** sired runner in the 2m½f *Weatherbys Champion Bumper*, resulted in a 25/1 victory for the *Willie Mullins* trained ***Briar Hill***, there may well be a flaw in my thinking.

Although **Shantou**'s representatives have yet to taste victory in a festival hurdle race, the progeny have achieved five place dividends in the middle and longer distance hurdle events. In brief, four appearances in the 2½m hurdle category have produced two places, and three place positions have been recorded over three miles, all of them from six runs in the *Pertemps Network Final Handicap Hurdle*. Based upon a 50% place strike rate in the *Pertemps*, it would appear to be a race in which punters should take note, especially at the prices returned of 20/1, 66/1 and 40/1.

Where National Hunt horses by **Shantou** excel, is in the festival's chases, where the progeny has registered three wins and seven place dividends from just 19 appearances within just 15 races. Within the 2½m category, all three victories have been achieved in just five races. In four renewals in what is now called the *Brown Advisory & Merriebelle Stable Plate Handicap Chase*, the finishing positions of **Shantou** sired runners have been 8th, 1st, 7th and 1st. The other three horses sired by

Shantou all lined up in the 2017 *Close Brothers Novices' Handicap Chase*. ***All Hell Let Loose*** was pulled up, ***Bun Doran*** was placed 6th and ***Tully East***, trained by *Alan Fleming*, ran on well up the Cheltenham Hill to win relatively comfortably at a price of 8/1.

In the 3m chase category, a festival victory for **Shantou**'s representatives has so far been elusive, but by golly, the progeny have been knocking on the door. How is this for a statistic? For every three **Shantou** sired runners that line up in a three mile chase at a Cheltenham Festival, two of them will be placed. To date, the offspring have recorded two 4th places, two 3rd places and two runner-up spots. Prices have ranged from 11/2 through to 14/1, with the three who failed to place returning prices of 11/1, 25/1 and 100/1.

Shantou is, without question, one of my favourite Cheltenham Festival stallions. How can one not be a fan of this sire whose offspring have achieved a profitable return at every meeting between 2013 and 2018? I sincerely hope that at the 2019 festival meeting, **Shantou**'s progeny will once again deliver profits for what will be seven years in a row. I can't wait to write about his continued success in the 2020 Cheltenham Festival Stallion Guide. Fingers crossed!

Stowaway (GB)

Quote from the 2018 Cheltenham Festival Stallion Guide - "I was a little concerned that **Stowaway** may turn out to be a stallion that produced a Cheltenham "one-hit wonder", as the impressive statistics, albeit from very few festival runs, was dominated by the now retired **Champagne Fever**. But the 2017 festival performances from **Champagne Classic**, **Runfordave** and **The Worlds End** in addition to **Hidden Cyclone**'s 2nd place finish in the 2014 **Ryanair Chase**, has eliminated my doubts."

Stowaway (Died as a 21-y-o in 2015)							
Race Format	*Miles*	*Won*	*Placed*	*Unplaced*	*Total*	*Win %*	*Place %*
	About 2m	1	0	2	3	33%	33%
Hurdles	About 2m 4f	1	1	3	5	20%	40%
	About 3m	0	0	3	3	0%	0%
	About 2m	0	1	0	1	0%	100%
Chases	About 2m 4f	0	1	2	3	0%	33%
	About 3m	0	0	3	3	0%	0%
	About 4m	0	0	0	0	-	-
Bumper	About 2m	1	0	2	3	33%	33%
Total	2009-2018	**3**	**3**	**15**	**21**	**14%**	**29%**

For anyone who follows **Stowaway**'s stock at Cheltenham Festivals, it is a roller-coaster ride. One year, everything looks rosy. The next year, we get depressed. The next year, we are happy again and so on. In last year's Guide, I sarcastically advised that 2017 had been a bumper year for **Stowaway** as a record number (and that is 4) of his offspring had attended the festival. Well, that record was broken at the 2018 Cheltenham Festival as eight **Stowaway** bred runners showed up.

The 2018 Festival was a "down-year". Of the eight horses by **Stowaway** that raced, none of them returned with a win or a place. I'm convinced the same thing won't happen in 2019. As I said, **Stowaway** has good years and bad years and I believe that the 'squad' that will represent the progeny in 2019 have a far greater chance of success than those **Stowaway** bred runners that competed at the 2018 Cheltenham Festival.

Before delving into the 2018 performances, let's have a quick recap on **Stowaway**'s offspring that appeared at earlier festivals. In the three festivals between 2012 and 2014, the Cheltenham Festival statistics for this stallion read as 2 wins and 2 runners-up from a total of 4 runs, hence a 50% win strike rate and a 100% win and place strike rate! These superb statistics were courtesy of the *Susannah Ricci* owned **Champagne Fever**, who had run in all three festivals, winning the 2012 *Weatherbys Champion Bumper*, followed by victory in the *William Hill Supreme Novices' Hurdle*, before being narrowly beaten by a head by *Western Warhorse* in the 2014 *Racing Post Arkle Challenge Trophy Chase*. The *John Joseph Hanlon* trained **Hidden Cyclone** ensured that **Stowaway**'s stock maintained a 100% festival record of finishing within the first two places when taking the runner-up spot in the 2014 *Ryanair Chase*.

Five horses by **Stowaway** would make their way to Cheltenham over the next 24 months and the 1st or 2nd one hundred percent record disappeared as all five competitors failed to place. Just nine runs by **Stowaway**'s stock at Cheltenham and a rather inconclusive set of results made it rather difficult to give any advice in the 2017 Stallion Guide. In the end, I wrote, *"I am rather undecided on the likely* *success or otherwise of* **Stowaway** *sired runners at the 2017 Cheltenham Festival. My hunch is that, over time, the progeny will provide us with further festival successes, but at this juncture, I will maintain a watching brief and see what the position is when* **Stowaway**'s *stock have had a few more festival runs under their belt."*

I wish I hadn't maintained a 'watching brief' at the 2017 Cheltenham Festival. Four horses by **Stowaway** went to the festival and registered a 12/1 win, a 9/1 place and another runner who looked likely to be in the shake up towards the end of his race before falling. Results had resumed to 2012-2014 levels, or so I had thought. Eight runs without even a place from the offspring at the 2018 Cheltenham Festival bring to mind the saying "one step forward, two steps back".

So what went wrong for **Stowaway**'s offspring at the 2018 Cheltenham Festival? In short, in looking at the eight participants by **Stowaway**, I think one could argue that results weren't too far off what one might expect. Only two runners of the eight runners lined up at a price shorter than 20/1, and both of them finished just outside the places. *Willie Mullins* saddled five runners in Wednesday's last race, the *Weatherbys Champion Bumper* and all five finished in the first 7 places. The **Stowaway** bred **Blackbow** (5/1) was the most fancied of the five contenders but could only manage 5th place some six lengths away from the winner, *Relegate*.

The next most fancied of **Stowaway**'s contingent at the 2018 Festival was *Paloma Blue*, trained by *Henry de Bromhead*. He was one of 19 runners in the *Sky Bet Supreme Novices' Hurdle* and at a price of 14/1, he ran well, finishing in 4th position and just three lengths away from the winner, *Summerville Boy*. Before his defeat to *Summerville Boy*, *Paloma Blue* had finished 3rd to *Samcro*, winner of the 2018 *Ballymore Novices' Hurdle*, and earlier in his career, had been beaten into 2nd place by *Fayonagh* who won the 2017 *Weatherbys Champion Bumper*. So, he hasn't finished too far away from at least three festival winners. At the time of writing, *Paloma Blue* has run in a couple of low key novice chases, winning one of them, and will hope to make his way to Cheltenham for the *Racing Post Arkle Challenge Trophy Novices' Chase* or the *JLT Novices' Chase*.

The six remaining **Stowaway** sired runners at last year's festival were all priced up at 20/1 plus, and more or less performed in accordance with what the market would have us believe: PU @ 20/1, 12th @ 28/1, 7th @ 33/1, 8th @ 33/1, 12th @ 33/1, and 10th @ 66/1.

In looking at the current crop of horses by **Stowaway**, I anticipate that another eight or more of the offspring will make it to the 2019 Cheltenham Festival, but I believe there is quite a difference in the quality of runners who will take their chance compared to those who competed in 2018. Punters may want to study the form of **Stowaway** sired possible festival runners such as *The Worlds End*, *On the Blind Side*, *Pym*, *Posh Trish* and *Paloma Blue*.

Finally, my top two **Stowaway** fancies for the 2019 Cheltenham Festival are both 'champagne' contenders, *Champagne Platinum* and *Champagne Classic*. The former horse is trained by *Nicky Henderson* and owned by *John P McManus*, and has had two novice hurdle outings in December, winning them both. He looks impressive and could be the real deal. *Champagne Classic* has already won at Cheltenham back in 2017 when he won the *Martin Pipe Conditional Jockeys' Handicap Hurdle*. The following month at *Punchestown*, he took on *Penhill* who had also won at the 2017 Cheltenham Festival when victorious in the *Albert Bartlett Novices' Hurdle*. Despite the difference in odds for *Punchestown*'s *Irish Daily Mirror Novice Hurdle*, with *Champagne Classic* at 14/1 and *Penhill* the 2/1 favourite, *Champagne Classic* prevailed and won by over two lengths. Whilst *Penhill* returned to Cheltenham in 2018 to win the *Sunbets Stayers' Hurdle*, *Champagne Classic* suffered a leg injury which kept him away from a racecourse for 641 days. He returned only recently, on 27th January 2019, at *Naas* and ran a fine race considering he had been off the course for so long. He finished in 3rd place in his first race over the bigger obstacles and hopefully will make it to the festival in one of the novice chases. He has class and quality. It's just a question of whether or not he will be back to his best by March.

Vinnie Roe (IRE)

Quote from the 2018 Cheltenham Festival Stallion Guide - "With just seventeen festival runs to go on, there is nowhere near enough data on which to make foolhardy conclusions, but on the basis that 50% of **Vinnie Roe** sired runners that had an SP of less than 20/1, delivered a top 4 finish, an each-way bet on those towards the front of the market may well produce a pay-out. As for the outsiders, ignore them."

Vinnie Roe (21-y-o)							
Race Format	*Miles*	*Won*	*Placed*	*Unplaced*	*Total*	*Win %*	*Place %*
	About 2m	0	0	2	2	0%	0%
Hurdles	About 2m 4f	0	1	3	4	0%	25%
	About 3m	0	1	3	4	0%	25%
	About 2m	0	1	1	2	0%	50%
Chases	About 2m 4f	0	1	0	1	0%	100%
	About 3m	0	0	1	1	0%	0%
	About 4m	0	0	3	3	0%	0%
Bumper	About 2m	0	0	1	1	0%	0%
Total	2009-2018	**0**	**4**	**14**	**18**	**0%**	**22%**

Vinnie Roe entered the Cheltenham Festival Stallion Guide in 2018 on the back of eight of his progeny having made the trip to Prestbury Park in the spring of 2017. With just 17 horses to consider on which to make a judgement, I advised punters last year that they may get a reward if they placed each-way bets on those to the fore of the betting market.

Having had eight participants in 2017, it was quite a surprise that for the 2018 Cheltenham Festival, the offspring would be represented by just one solitary runner. Nevertheless, **Barney Dwan** was reasonably short in the betting at 15/2 for the *Close Brothers Novices' Handicap Chase*, and duly confirmed my judgement about each-way bets being rewarded on **Vinnie Roe** bred horses towards the front of the market. In a field of 19, **Barney Dwan** ran well for most of this *Novices' Handicap Chase* and had every chance as they came into the straight, but he was soon ridden and had no more to give towards the finish, eventually taking the last of the place dividends when finishing in 4th position.

Barney Dwan was one of the eight **Vinnie Roe** sired horses that competed at the 2017 meeting and one of two that recorded runner-up places. He put in an excellent effort in the *Pertemps Network Final Handicap Hurdle* to finish behind the progressive *Presenting Percy* who stayed on very strongly after the last to go clear and win by 3¾ lengths. At a price of 16/1, that was an excellent performance considering that *Presenting Percy*, the current favourite for this year's *Magners Cheltenham Gold Cup*, went on to win the 2018 renewal of the *RSA Insurance Novices' Chase*. So **Barney Dwan** is responsible for two of the four place positions attained by **Vinnie Roe**'s progeny. To advise on the other two place positions, **Claret Cloak** took 3rd place in the 2014 *Johnny Henderson Grand Annual Chase Challenge Cup Handicap*, and **Neon Wolf** finished runner-up to *Willoughby Court* in the 2017 *Neptune Investment Management Novices' Hurdle*.

Going back to this chapter's opening paragraph, further explanation is required as to why I considered that supporting **Vinnie Roe**'s offspring that were more fancied in the market, may provide some reward on each-way bets. Adding **Barney Dwan**'s run of last year into the calculations, exactly half of **Vinnie Roe**'s progeny have returned starting prices of less than 20/1, which equates to nine festival outings. Although three horses by **Vinnie Roe** with SPs of 12/1, 14/1 and 14/1 again didn't run especially well, as already advised, four of the nine appearances resulted in a place dividend being collected, courtesy of **Claret Cloak**, **Neon Wolf** and **Barney Dwan** twice. With regard to the remaining two horses, they set off in their races at 6/1 and 7/1. **Royal Caviar** (6/1) finished 4th in the 2017 *Racing Post Arkle Challenge Trophy Novices' Chase* and **Our Vinnie** (7/1) was brought down at half-way in the 2013 *Albert Bartlett Novices' Hurdle*.

As for the nine festival runners by **Vinnie Roe** that lined up at odds of 20/1 or greater, two finished 9th, five were pulled up and the other two were placed 16th and 18th. At the 2019 Cheltenham Festival, punters should forget all about **Vinnie Roe** bred outsiders.

There are a couple of horses by **Vinnie Roe** that I consider are worth considering at the meeting this forthcoming March. One of these is the *Kim Bailey* trained **Vinndication** who, at the time of writing, is unbeaten in six races, the last two of which have been chase events. I'm not convinced he has the quality of some of the other novice chasers that are around right now, so the 12/1 at which he can be backed for either the *RSA Novices'* or *JLT Novices'* chases would appear about right. He is officially rated above 150, but a few pounds lower and I'm not sure if he would perhaps be better suited to one of the festival's handicap races.

The **Vinnie Roe** bred horse for which I have a preference is **First Assignment**, trained by *Ian Williams*. At the time of writing, this six year-old has had eight career starts over hurdles, and has only once finished outside of the first three places. He has never been to a festival before, but has won two handicap hurdle events at Cheltenham in the late autumn of last year. If he goes to Cheltenham, he will almost certainly be entered for the 3m *Pertemps Network Final Handicap* on the basis that his last three runs have all been over three miles. As of mid-January, his odds for this contest are 20/1.

Voix Du Nord (FR)

Quote from the 2018 Cheltenham Festival Stallion Guide - "The three festival wins represent a 12% win strike rate which is better than the majority of stallions featured in this Guide, and the win and place hit rate is a reassuring 27%."

Voix Du Nord (Died as a 12-y-o in 2013)

Race Format	Miles	Won	Placed	Unplaced	Total	Win %	Place %
Hurdles	About 2m	1	1	5	7	14%	29%
	About 2m 4f	1	2	4	7	14%	43%
	About 3m	0	1	2	3	0%	33%
Chases	About 2m	0	0	3	3	0%	0%
	About 2m 4f	1	0	9	10	10%	10%
	About 3m	0	0	1	1	0%	0%
	About 4m	0	0	0	0	-	-
Bumper	About 2m	0	0	0	0	-	-
Total	2009-2018	**3**	**4**	**24**	**31**	**10%**	**23%**

Fifteen horses by **Voix Du Nord** have raced on 31 occasions at Cheltenham Festivals, of which three have won and two have hit a place. Two of the three winners have also recorded runner-up positions, hence the table above showing three wins and four places from the total of 31 festival appearances.

The 2018 Cheltenham Festival turned out to be a damp squib for the progeny of **Voix Du Nord**. Five runners for the sire lined up in their respective races and four of the five disappointed. The only one of the offspring that put in a reasonable effort was *Kemboy*, who finished 4th in the *JLT Novices' Chase*. It was *Kemboy*'s second run at Cheltenham, his first appearance being at the 2017 festival where he finished 5th in the *Neptune Investment Management Novices' Hurdle*. In the *JLT*, he probably ran as well as he could, but never looked as if he would trouble the leaders. A bad mistake at the 9th fence wouldn't have helped.

Barring an unforeseen setback, *Kemboy* is on course to travel over to Cheltenham for the 3rd year in succession, and may well line up in the *Magners Cheltenham Gold Cup*, attempting to give trainer *Willie Mullins* his first success in the race. *Kemboy* is seven years old but certainly seems to be an improving horse. Following his trip over from Ireland last March, a few weeks later, he was entered for the *Boylesports Irish Grand National Chase*. The race didn't last long for him as he fell at the very first fence. Since that fall, he has gone on to win his next four races, the last of which was hugely significant, when he won the Grade 1 *Savills Chase* at Leopardstown on 28th December by seven lengths. *Kemboy* was the youngest horse in the field and yet saw off more experienced rivals such as *Monalee, Road to Respect* and *Bellshill* with relative ease, going clear on the run-in and staying on strongly. As a result of that success, his Official Rating has jumped from 157 to 167 making him the highest rated of all **Voix Du Nord**'s progeny. This century, three winners of the *Savills Chase* have gone on to win the *Gold Cup*, hence *Kemboy*'s odds (as of mid-January) of around the 10/1 mark. For those who like kicking themselves, *Kemboy* was freely available at 50/1 before his success at Leopardstown.

Kemboy also holds an entry in the *Ryanair*, but I really hope that connections decide to enter him for the *Gold Cup* as he does appear to have the necessary stamina, otherwise why would he have been entered for the *Irish Grand National* over 3m5f? If punters would like to know the record of **Voix Du Nord**'s results in the *Ryanair* and *Gold Cup*, then here goes: For the *Ryanair Steeple Chase*: 2015 - **Taquin Du Seuil** (9th); 2016 - **Taquin Du Seuil** (6th) and **Vibrato Valtat** (Fell); 2017 – **Vaniteux** (8th). For the *Cheltenham Gold Cup*: 2018 – **Bachasson** (Fell 2nd fence).

Going back to last year's festival, only one of the quintet was making their Cheltenham Festival debut, the *Gordon Elliott* trained **Duca De Thaix**, who travelled across the Irish Sea for his first appearance in Britain. Due to the *Gigginstown House Stud* ownership and his prolific trainer, **Duca De Thaix** lined up at a relatively short 10/1, but he didn't live up to his price, trailing home in 19th place. He looks on course to make another appearance at the festival in 2019 as he currently holds entries in the *Arkle* and *JLT Novices'* Chases. He has won two of his six chase starts so far but hasn't exactly set the world alight, hence his current odds of around 33/1 for either race.

Of the other three **Voix Du Nord** runners that raced at the festival twelve months ago, **Bachasson** fell at the 2nd in the *Gold Cup*, and **Voix Du Reve** (*Coral Cup Handicap Hurdle*) and **Vaniteux** (*Grand Annual Handicap Chase*) both faded in the latter stages of their respective races to finish in 14th.

It is interesting to note that **Voix Du Nord**'s offspring have only managed one top three finish in the festival's chase events, this being **Taquin Du Seuil**'s victory in the 2014 *JLT Novices'* Chase. I'm not convinced that this state of affairs will continue as it isn't as if the other 13 chase runs have been dire. Five appearances, for example, have resulted in finishing positions between 4th and 8th. Nevertheless, as it stands today, the festival results for **Voix Du Nord**'s progeny are definitely better over hurdles with a 35% win and place strike rate compared to just 7% over fences.

For the four festivals preceding 2018, **Voix Du Nord**'s offspring succeeded in securing at least one place dividend at every meeting, registering three festival wins over that period with **Taquin Du Seuil** in 2014, **Vroum Vroum Mag** in 2016 and **Defi Du Seuil** in 2017. So last year's meeting was clearly a disappointment for the progeny and out of kilter with previous festivals and hence I would advise punters to focus upon the results over the past five years rather than 2018 alone.

For the 2019 Cheltenham Festival, I recommend that punters should clearly look out for horses by **Voix Du Nord** that are entered in the festival's hurdle races. Historically, the offspring have registered a win or a place for one in every three appearances in a festival hurdle event. Also, I wouldn't be surprised if the progeny achieve a win or a place in a chase event for the first time since **Taquin Du Seuil** in 2014, and it may well be **Kemboy** that delivers it. I have been impressed by the seven-year-old's performances since last year's festival and if *Willie Mullins* enters him for the *Gold Cup*, I will certainly have a small each-way bet on him.

Westerner (GB)

Quote from the 2018 Cheltenham Festival Stallion Guide - "I guess we are all pondering as to whether last year was genuinely a one-off "annus horribilis" for **Westerner**'s progeny or conceivably the start of a trend of dismal festival results."

Race Format	Miles	Won	Placed	Unplaced	Total	Win %	Place %
Westerner (20-y-o)							
	About 2m	0	1	3	4	0%	25%
Hurdles	About 2m 4f	0	1	9	10	0%	10%
	About 3m	1	1	14	16	6%	13%
	About 2m	2	0	3	5	40%	40%
	About 2m 4f	1	0	8	9	11%	11%
Chases	About 3m	0	0	10	10	0%	0%
	About 4m	0	0	3	3	0%	0%
Bumper	About 2m	0	0	4	4	0%	0%
Total	2009-2018	**4**	**3**	**54**	**61**	**7%**	**11%**

Oh dear! **Westerner** was represented on 17 occasions at the 2018 Cheltenham Festival and every single wager on his offspring turned out to be a loser. So, as to the question at the top of the page, I think we are starting to err on the side of believing that we are indeed seeing the start of a trend of dismal results.

There have been 56 Cheltenham Festival races since the **Westerner** sired *Solar Impulse* won the very last race of the 2016 meeting, the *Johnny Henderson Grand Annual Chase Challenge Cup*. At that festival, only two of the festival winners returned odds of 16/1 or more. Both were sired by **Westerner**. *Solar Impulse* won at a price of 28/1 and *Empire Of Dirt* returned odds of 16/1 when victorious in the *Brown & Merriebelle Stable Plate*. After *Solar Impulse*'s success, in the 2017 Cheltenham Festival Stallion Guide, I advised punters that **Westerner** had a win strike rate of 13% and that had one placed a £1.00 win bet on all 30 of **Westerner** sired festival runners to date, a huge profit of £65.00 would have been the result.

It's all gone a bit pear-shaped since! In the 56 festival races since *Solar Impulse*'s win, 31 **Westerner** bred horses have lined-up in 25 of those races, and not one runner has paid out on any bets placed on them. The outcome, had one placed a £1.00 each-way bet on all 30 of **Westerner**'s festival representatives pre the 2017 meeting, would have been a profit of £71.65. The mathematics is quite straightforward to calculate the position as of today. It is still a profit, but the £71.65 has been eaten away to just £9.65.

For **Westerner**'s stock to still be showing a festival profit following 31 consecutive races of making a loss is rather remarkable and highlights the big prices that were returned for the four horses by **Westerner** that have been winners. The first **Westerner** sired festival winner was *Western Warhorse* (33/1) who sprang a major surprise when he managed to get up on the line to beat the *Willie Mullins* trained favourite *Champagne Fever* by a head in the 2014 *Racing Post Arkle Challenge Trophy Chase*. The second festival victory for the progeny occurred in the following year with *Cole Harden*'s 14/1 victory in the 2015 *Ladbrokes World Hurdle* at odds of 14/1. It was the first ever Cheltenham Festival victory for both the trainer, *Warren Greatrex*, and jockey, *Gavin Sheehan*. The two other victors have already been highlighted above - **Empire Of Dirt** (16/1) and **Solar Impulse** (28/1).

The evidence from the past two years of festival results suggests that we should hold off placing any bets on **Westerner**'s offspring at the 2019 Cheltenham Festival and watch and learn instead. That said, Murphy's Law will probably strike and in one festival race at least, a big priced **Westerner** outsider will romp home! Should that happen, I decided to spend some time analysing the offspring's performances to see if I could figure out within which race category the win would most likely come from.

The trends are hardly compelling, but it does appear to me that **Westerner**'s progeny have performed best at the minimum distance. The obvious place to start is the 2m chase category, where horses by **Westerner** have already registered two Cheltenham Festival victories, which represents a 40% win strike rate. Last year, **Westerner** was represented by *Three Stars* in the *Johnny Henderson Grand Annual Challenge Cup Handicap Chase* running a very reasonable race to finish in 5th position and just outside the places. The previous season, **Three Stars** was the 66/1 outsider of nine runners in the *Racing Post Arkle Challenge Trophy Novices' Chase*. He ran as one may expect, well behind before being pulled up.

Although **Westerner**'s stock has had just four appearances in 2m hurdle races, one could definitely argue that performances have been encouraging. Back in 2013, the *Paul Nicholls* trained **Caid Du Berlais** made his festival debut in the *Fred Winter Juvenile Handicap Hurdle*, and ran a fine race to finish runner-up at a price of 20/1. Incidentally, **Caid Du Berlais** made his 6th festival appearance at last year's festival, performing best of **Westerner**'s 17 runners when finishing fifth and less than 4 lengths behind the winner in last year's *St. James's Place Foxhunter Challenge Cup Open Hunters' Chase* over a distance of 3m2½ furlongs.

Albeit that the other three **Westerner** sired horses to compete in two mile festival hurdle events have failed to secure a place position, they have all performed credibly. In 2014, following the effort of **Caid Du Berlais**, *Paul Nicholls* entered another **Westerner** bred 4-year-old in the *Fred Winter Juvenile Hurdle*, in the shape of the previously mentioned **Solar Impulse**. Although he could only finish in seventh place, he was only 5½ lengths off the winner. In the same year, **Gilgamboa** (9/1) was well fancied to do well in the festival's opening race, the *Sky Bet Supreme Novices' Hurdle*, but having been tracking the leaders and about two lengths off the pace, he blundered two hurdles from home after which he weakened to finish 13th. In last year's renewal of the *Supreme*, **Westerner** was to be represented in the race for a second time, courtesy of **Western Ryder**, trained by *Warren Greatrex*. The horse very much looked like he would be involved in the finish before he was badly hampered two from home, losing all chance before staying on to finish in 6th place and 7½ lengths behind the winner, *Summerville Boy*, the same horse that he had beaten in a Novices' Hurdle Qualifier at Cheltenham three months earlier.

To complete the picture of the progeny's performances over a distance of two miles, I should also mention the *Weatherbys Champion Bumper*, where in four appearances to date, **Westerner** bred runners have had two of its representatives finish in 5th position. In 2016, **Westend Story** (20/1) was beaten by 3¼ lengths by **Ballyandy** and in the 2017 contest, the previously mentioned **Western Ryder** (7/1) was beaten by exactly the same distance when defeated by *Fayonagh*, the *Kalanisi* bred mare that graced the front cover of the 2018 Cheltenham Festival Stallion Guide.

In summary, I fear that the run of 31 consecutive losses for **Westerner** bred horses that has built up over the past two festivals will continue into 2019. In looking at **Westerner**'s progeny that currently have official ratings above 140, none especially appeal to me with the possible exception of **Rocky's**

Treasure, trained by *Kim Bailey*, who had a wonderful Cheltenham Festival in 1995, when he saddled the winners of both the *Champion Hurdle* (*Alderbrook*) and the *Gold Cup* (*Master Oats*). At the time of writing, **Rocky's Treasure**, an eight-year-old, has won 4 out of 5 small field novice chases, with arguably his best performances being the race in which he failed to win. The race in question was the *Ladbrokes John Francome Novices' Chase* at *Newbury*, where *Santini*, trained by *Nicky Henderson* won the race, beating **Rocky's Treasure** by 4 lengths. As of early January, *Santini* is the favourite for the festival's *RSA Insurance Novices' Chase* at a price of around 7/2. **Rocky's Treasure** is also available to be backed at odds of around 25/1.

I may change my mind for future Cheltenham Festivals, but for 2019, for betting purposes, my advice to punters is to leave **Westerner** sired entries alone, even though I have a niggling uneasiness that just one of the offspring may pop up to win a race at huge odds. Should that happen, then the trends suggest that it is most likely to occur in a two mile distance contest.

Winged Love (IRE)

Quote from the 2018 Cheltenham Festival Stallion Guide - "With regard to recommendations for the 2018 Cheltenham Festival, it is interesting to note that the four horses sired by **Winged Love** that have tasted festival success have all registered a top official rating of between 152 and 162."

Race Format	Miles	Won	Placed	Unplaced	Total	Win %	Place %
Winged Love (Died as a 23-y-o in 2015)							
Hurdles	About 2m	0	1	3	4	0%	25%
	About 2m 4f	0	0	0	0	-	-
	About 3m	0	0	6	6	0%	0%
Chases	About 2m	0	1	4	5	0%	20%
	About 2m 4f	1	1	9	11	9%	18%
	About 3m	1	1	9	11	9%	18%
	About 4m	0	3	6	9	0%	33%
Bumper	About 2m	0	0	1	1	0%	0%
Total	2009-2018	**2**	**7**	**38**	**47**	**4%**	**19%**

Twenty-four horses by **Winged Love** have raced on 52 occasions at Cheltenham Festivals, of which 47 have taken place in the past decade. The two festival victories and the seven place dividends have been achieved by just four of the progeny, all of whom have managed to record a win or place more than once. The four horses in question are *Bostons Angel*, *Hunt Ball*, *Josses Hill* and *Bless The Wings*.

Bless The Wings has probably been to the Cheltenham Festival on more occasions than most of the crowd who have come to watch him! He made three rather disappointing appearances between 2012 and 2014 when at *Alan King*'s yard at *Barbury Castle*, finishing down the field on every occasion, so it wasn't surprising that *Bless The Wings* was rather unfancied for his 4th appearance in the 2015 *Fulke Walwyn Kim Muir Challenge Cup Handicap Chase*. However, the switch to *Gordon Elliott*'s yard in the summer of 2014 had clearly had some effect, as *Nina Carberry* rode *Bless The Wings* into the runner-up spot. For the next two seasons, *Bless The Wings* was to complete a hat-trick of runner-up performances when finishing 2nd in the 2016 and 2017 renewals of the cross country *Glenfarclas Chase*.

At the 2018 Cheltenham Festival, at the grand age of 13, *Bless The Wings* was entered in the *Glenfarclas Chase* for the third year in a row, but a fourth successive runner-up finish wasn't to be as the horse fell for the first time in his career. The fall didn't seem to cause him any damage as one month later, *Bless The Wings* was to make his *Grand National* debut at *Aintree*, and at a price of 40/1, jockey *Jack Kennedy* negotiated all 29 fences (one was omitted) to finish in 3rd place behind the winner and stablemate, *Tiger Roll*, who had also won the 2018 *Glenfarclas Chase*, the race in which *Bless The Wings* had fallen. There appears to be no stopping *Bless The Wings*. At the time of writing, he has already raced at Cheltenham twice in the November and December 2018 renewals of the *Glenfarclas Cross Country Handicap Chase*. Don't be surprised, therefore, to see in March, the familiar sight of this wonderful horse, negotiating the obstacles of Cheltenham's cross country fences once again, as a veteran 14-year-old, in the *Glenfarclas Chase*.

Bless The Wings was one of four horses sired by **Winged Love** that competed at the 2018 Cheltenham Festival, and only one of them, the *Warren Greatrex* trained **Lovenormoney**, managed to finish a race. Ridden by *Andrew Tinkler*, **Lovenormoney** was tracking the leaders before weakening at the business end of the race in the *Pertemps Network Final Handicap Hurdle*. Registering a 16^(th) place finish, **Lovernormoney** was the second horse by **Winged Love** to compete in this Grade 3 hurdle race, as three years previously, the *Michael Blake* trained **Knight Of Noir** did slightly better in the 2015 renewal, when he was beaten by some 16 lengths to finish 9^(th). **Knight Of Noir**'s second appearance at the festival occurred last year in the opening day's first handicap race, the *Ultima Handicap Chase*. It was a poor performance from the 33/1 chance as he struggled at the rear of the field before being pulled up before two out.

The last race of the 2018 Cheltenham Festival, the highly competitive *Johnny Henderson Grand Annual Challenge Cup Handicap Chase*, turned out to be a bruising and buffeting affair in which three horses lost their lives, of which one was the **Winged Love** sired, *Some Plan*. The fatalities in the race quite rightly created a huge amount of media attention and so immediately after the festival, the BHA announced a Safety Review. On 12^(th) December 2018, the BHA unveiled 17 recommendations, among which was the reducing of the field in two mile chases to 20 runners, which in my view was a very sensible decision.

As advised in the quote at the top of the page, horses by **Winged Love** that have won or been placed at a festival have all recorded a top official rating of between 152 and 162. Based upon this, I believe it is unlikely that any of this stallion's offspring will trouble the judge at Cheltenham unless they are of (a) an age which means they can be competitive and (b) that they hold a current official rating above the mid-140s. All of this means that, in my opinion, there is only one horse by **Winged Love** that may register a win or place at the 2019 Cheltenham Festival. The horse in question is *Thomas Patrick*, seven years old, who as of early January, holds an official rating of 147. *Thomas Patrick* won three of his first four chase events, but since November 2018, he has failed to win. The failure to beat *Elegant Escape* by a ½ length at *Sandown* on 11^(th) November 2018 could hardly be seen as a worrying failure but since that race, *Thomas Patrick* has failed to impress, being pulled up in the *Ladbroke Trophy Chase* at *Newbury* on 1^(st) December, before finishing well down the field in the *Gerrard Silver Cup Handicap Chase* at *Ascot* some three weeks later. To win or be placed at the Cheltenham Festival, he needs to improve significantly on his last two racecourse appearances.

In summary, I believe it is unlikely that any horse by **Winged Love** will trouble the judge at the 2019 Cheltenham Festival and so, for betting purposes, I would recommend that come the spring, we should give **Winged Love**'s offspring the cold shoulder, and wait to see if the progeny has more to offer in 2020.

Yeats (IRE)

Yeats was not featured in the 2018 Cheltenham Festival Stallion Guide.

Race Format	Miles	Won	Placed	Unplaced	Total	Win %	Place %
	Yeats (18-y-o)						
Hurdles	About 2m	0	0	2	2	0%	0%
	About 2m 4f	0	0	5	5	0%	0%
	About 3m	0	0	3	3	0%	0%
Chases	About 2m	0	0	0	0	-	-
	About 2m 4f	1	0	0	1	100%	100%
	About 3m	0	0	1	1	0%	0%
	About 4m	0	0	1	1	0%	0%
Bumper	About 2m	0	0	2	2	0%	0%
Total	2009-2018	**1**	**0**	**14**	**15**	**7%**	**7%**

Yeats earns his place in the 2019 Cheltenham Festival Stallion Guide as a result of having seven of his progeny compete at last year's meeting. I also anticipate that a similar number of the offspring will appear at Cheltenham this coming March, which will help to provide further information upon which some more meaningful trends on the success or otherwise of Yeats' sired horses can be developed.

As it stands today, ten horses sired by Yeats have appeared at the Cheltenham festival on fifteen occasions and at last year's meeting, a debut festival victory for the progeny was attained by the mare *Shattered Love*, who became the first of her sex to win a novice chase at the festival since 1995.

Her second trip to the Cheltenham Festival had been far more successful than on the first occasion, where she disappointed in the *Neptune Investment Management Novices' Hurdle*, being the last of the twelve runners that completed the race to finish. At a price of 8/1, she wasn't unfancied before the contest either, having competed in five hurdle events previously and recording a top two placing on every occasion. One month later and she was one of seven entries for the Grade 1 *Irish Stallion Farms European Breeders Fund Mares Novice Hurdle Championship Final at Fairyhouse*. Amongst her rivals was *Augusta Kate*, another Yeats sired mare, who just got up in the closing stages to beat the odds-on favourite, *Let's Dance*. As for *Shattered Love*, she finished last again. It was time to go chasing.

By the time, the *Gigginstown House Stud* owned mare reached Cheltenham last season, her career over fences read as four wins and one second placing in five starts. The race preceding her second appearance at the festival was the Grade 1 *Neville Hotels Novice Chase* at *Leopardstown* which takes place just after Christmas. In the race, she stayed on well to win at 10/1 and delivered a performance that made her one of the leading fancies for one of the novice chases at the festival.

At the 2018 Cheltenham Festival, it had been anticipated that *Shattered Love* would race in the 3m *RSA Insurance Novices' Chase*, but in the days leading up to the meeting, she was switched to the 2m4f *JLT Novices' Chase*. It was clearly a good decision, as once they had gone around the final bend with *Shattered Love* travelling supremely well, barring a fall, it was clear that she was going to win.

And she did, by 7 lengths and at a price of 4/1. The mare provided trainer *Gordon Elliott* with his fourth win of the festival.

It is interesting to note that of the 10 of **Yeats'** progeny to appear at the Cheltenham Festival, eight of them have failed to win in graded company. And they are all boys. The two Graded race winners are the two mares of *Shattered Love* and *Augusta Kate*, both of whom have won Grade 1 events. Barring any unforeseen circumstances, *Shattered Love* will arrive at the festival for a third time to race in either the *Ryanair Chase*, for which as of mid-January, she can be backed at 12/1, or the *Magners Cheltenham Gold Cup Chase* where she is priced up at 25/1. *Shattered Love* hasn't won in five appearances since last year's *JLT* success, although she has managed a trio of runner-up performances. Her most recent run in the Grade 1 *Savills Chase* at *Leopardstown* was very disappointing, where believe it or not, she finished last again!

As for *Augusta Kate*, she has been retired, purchased in November of last year for 85,000 Euros by *Kevin Doyle* to expand the number of broodmares within his set-up at *County Wexford*. She put together some very reasonable performances in her three trips to the Cheltenham Festival. In 2016, she was the 7/2 favourite for the *Weatherbys Champion Bumper* when taking seventh place in what was a bunched finish, beaten by five lengths. The following season, she was placed 6th in the *Albert Bartlett Novices' Hurdle* before signing off her Cheltenham Festival career last season when finishing in mid-field in the *Sun Bets Stayers' Hurdle*.

The eight geldings by **Yeats** that have competed at the festivals have been less convincing. In the ten outings by the boys, only on three occasions has the run delivered a top ten placing, and interestingly every time in a 2½m hurdle event. At the 2017 Cheltenham Festival, *Thomas Campbell* finished just one place off a place dividend when at a price of 20/1, he attained 5th place in the *Martin Pipe Conditional Jockeys' Handicap Hurdle*. He has been the closest of the eight geldings by **Yeats** to deliver a festival placing, being just a neck away from the 4th placed *Coo Star Sivola*, who returned to the festival last season to win the *Ultima Handicap Chase*.

The other horse by **Yeats** to run in a 2½m hurdle at that 2017 Cheltenham Festival also finished just one position outside of the places. Unlike *Thomas Campbell*, however, *Burbank* was a long way from attaining a place position, as he finished four lengths away from the runner that finished third. The race in question was the Grade 1 *Neptune Investment Management Novices' Hurdle* and *Burbank* put in a mighty performance considering he was a 50/1 chance. Trainer *Nicky Henderson* decided to enter *Burbank* in another 2½m festival event at last year's meeting, but this time in a handicap and the ultra-competitive *Coral Cup*. *Burbank* finished in 7th place at a price of 18/1.

To complete the statistics of geldings by **Yeats** to have competed in 2½m festival hurdle events, the one horse not to achieve a top ten finish is *Brave Eagle*, who made his festival debut in the 2018 renewal of the *Martin Pipe Handicap Hurdle*. He finished down the field in thirteenth.

Fifteen festival appearances is rather limited information on which to ascertain any concrete guidance as to how we should approach **Yeats'** offspring that take up engagements at the 2019 Cheltenham Festival. The sage advice is to see what further information is forthcoming following what should be more than half a dozen runs from the progeny at this year's meeting. Nevertheless, for those who are impatient and would like to hear my views despite the lack of data available, then here are some thoughts that punters may wish to consider.

The results to date are signalling that **Yeats'** stock have performed best in races that fall within the 2½m categories. In the five hurdle appearances, the finishing positions have been 4th, 5th, 7th, 12th and 13th. The one occasion when a horse by **Yeats** has appeared in a 2½m festival chase, the result was a victory, secured by **Shattered Love** in the JLT Novices' Chase. In all other race categories, the only horse by **Yeats** that has attained a top ten finish is the mare, **Augusta Kate**, and she managed it three times, in the 2m *Bumper* and twice in 3m hurdle contests. The six finishing positions of the **Yeats** bred geldings in race distances other than 2½m is 11th, 12th, 14th, 17th, 18th and one faller.

I have looked at the potential 2019 festival entries from **Yeats**' progeny and am largely unconvinced by the geldings, which is much in line with what we have seen in previous festivals. Even if any of the boys turn up in 2½m events, I would be inclined to ignore them. I am more attracted to **Yeats**' mares of which three deserve a mention.

All the festival noise surrounding the trainer, *Ruth Jefferson*, revolves around her talented chaser, *Waiting Patiently*, who is around 7/1 for the *Ryanair Chase*. But I like a mare in her yard by the name of **Mega Yeats**, currently available at around 50/1 for the *OLBG Mares' Hurdle*. This race often throws up a big priced placed outsider and I was impressed with how **Mega Yeats** ran when runner-up in the listed *Karndean Mares' Standard Open National Hunt Flat Race* at Cheltenham at the November meeting. The mare made her hurdles debut on Boxing Day in the *Yorkshire Christmas Meeting Mares' Novices' Hurdle* at *Wetherby*, winning comfortably as the 2/5 odds-on favourite. There aren't too many trainers from the North of England that are successful at Prestbury Park in March, but it is worth noting that before he sadly passed away in early 2018, *Malcolm Jefferson*, *Ruth Jefferson*'s father, had trained four Cheltenham Festival winners.

The other two mares to note hail from *Gordon Elliott*'s yard in *County Meath*, and are both owned by *Gigginstown House Stud*, one by the name of **Shattered Love** of whom we already know and the second, a less well-known **Tintangle**.

At the time of writing, **Tintangle** is a 50/1 chance for the *OLBG Mares' Hurdle* and 33/1 for the *Trull House Stud Mares' Novices' Hurdle*. I consider **Tintangle** to be a little behind **Mega Yeats**, and if she is to be involved in the shake-up of either mares race, she will need to improve. She has won once in her four outings to date, but then again, has contested some high quality races, such as the Grade 3 *BetVictor Solerina Mares Novice Hurdle* at *Fairyhouse*, where she finished 3rd at 3/1 and the *Paddy Power Future Champions Novice Hurdle* at *Leopardstown*. This Grade 1 event at *Leopardstown* was **Tintangle**'s first chance to pit her talents against the boys, and she ran well to secure 3rd place at a price of 16/1.

And finally, we come to the only horse by **Yeats** to be a Cheltenham Festival winner, **Shattered Love**. As highlighted earlier, **Shattered Love** hasn't won in five appearances since last year's *JLT* success and appears to be a little behind some of her rivals for either the *Ryanair* or Gold Cup. She is in the very capable hands of Gordon Elliott who knows how to get a horse just right for Cheltenham and it is also a positive, in my view, to be a previous festival winner. Nevertheless, I would have liked to have seen more from the 8-year-old in her races so far this season and so I'm far from convinced that she will be able to add a second festival win to her name; at least for this forthcoming 2019 festival.

Index Table by Stallion

This table shows the British Horseracing Association (BHA) and Irish Horseracing Regulatory Board (I.H.R.B) Official Ratings (as of January 2019) for National Hunt horses. Only horses that were showing an official rating of 135 or greater in January 2019 are listed. Index is in alphabetical order and only for stallions listed within this Guide. In order to distinguish between BHA and I.H.R.B Official Ratings, the I.H.R.B entries are shown in *italics*.

| | | | | Official Ratings as of Jan 2019 | |
Sire	Horse	Age	Sex	Hurdles	Chase
Al Namix	Al Dancer	6	g	141	
Al Namix	Alsa Mix	7	m	137	
Al Namix	Ballyhill	8	g		143
Al Namix	Dear Sire	7	g		142
Al Namix	Elixir De Nutz	5	g	145	
Al Namix	Mr Mix	8	g		136
Al Namix	Pacific De Baune	6	g	139	139
Al Namix	*Petit Mouchoir*	*8*	*g*	*158*	*157*
Authorized	Black Key	7	g	137	
Authorized	Boite	9	g	138	
Authorized	Ennistown	9	g	143	143
Authorized	Sternrubin	8	g		138
Authorized	*Tiger Roll*	*9*	*g*		*159*
Ballingarry	Aubusson	10	g	136	130
Ballingarry	Ballywood	5	g		140
Ballingarry	Diego Du Charmil	7	g		155
Ballingarry	Kauto Riko	8	g		145
Beneficial	*Abbey Magic*	*8*	*m*		*135*
Beneficial	*Ben Dundee*	*7*	*g*		*138*
Beneficial	Benatar	7	g		149
Beneficial	Benbens	14	g		136
Beneficial	Bennys King	8	g		135
Beneficial	*De Plotting Shed*	*9*	*g*	*141*	*140*
Beneficial	Forever Field	9	g	137	137
Beneficial	*Forge Meadow*	*7*	*m*	*144*	
Beneficial	Kilcrea Vale	9	g		137
Beneficial	Kilfilum Cross	8	g	137	132
Beneficial	Knocknanuss	9	g		148
Beneficial	Lady Buttons	9	m	145	149
Beneficial	*Livelovelaugh*	*9*	*g*		*136*
Beneficial	*Mala Beach*	*11*	*g*	*143*	*155*
Beneficial	Maria's Benefit	7	m	143	143
Beneficial	*Monksland*	*12*	*g*	*136*	*138*
Beneficial	Mr Whipped	6	g	145	145
Beneficial	Pawn Star	9	g		136
Beneficial	*Snugsborough Benny*	*9*	*g*	*121*	*136*
Beneficial	Thomas Darby	6	g	140	
Beneficial	Top Ville Ben	7	g		150
Beneficial	Wenyerreadyfreddie	8	g		148
Definite Article	*Articulum*	*9*	*g*		*138*

Sire	Horse	Age	Sex	Hurdles	Chase
				Official Ratings as of Jan 2019	
Definite Article	Definitly Red	10	g	159	164
Definite Article	Pingshou	9	g	142	137
Definite Article	Shanroe Santos	10	g		137
Definite Article	Sizing Platinum	11	g		145
Dubai Destination	Coole Cody	8	g	137	137
Dubai Destination	Elegant Escape	7	g		162
Dubai Destination	Kildisart	7	g		147
Dubai Destination	Knight In Dubai	6	g	139	139
Dubai Destination	Roksana	7	m	142	
Flemensfirth	A Rated	8	g		142
Flemensfirth	Abolitionist	11	g	134	145
Flemensfirth	Ballymoy	6	g	152	
Flemensfirth	Castlegrace Paddy	8	g		155
Flemensfirth	Coney Island	8	g	145	157
Flemensfirth	Conrad Hastings	8	g		140
Flemensfirth	Coolanly	7	g	142	
Flemensfirth	Coole Hall	7	g		137
Flemensfirth	Fitzhenry	7	g	122	135
Flemensfirth	Good Boy Bobby	6	g	135	
Flemensfirth	Highland Lodge	13	g		135
Flemensfirth	Invitation Only	8	g		162
Flemensfirth	Isleofhopendreams	12	g		142
Flemensfirth	Jett	8	g	132	145
Flemensfirth	Jetz	7	g		144
Flemensfirth	Kimberlite Candy	7	g		137
Flemensfirth	Knockgraffon	9	g		142
Flemensfirth	Lostintranslation	7	g	149	149
Flemensfirth	Magic Of Light	8	m		149
Flemensfirth	Molly The Dolly	8	m		139
Flemensfirth	Mr Big Shot	8	g		147
Flemensfirth	Noble Endeavor	10	g	144	151
Flemensfirth	O O Seven	9	g		152
Flemensfirth	Poetic Rhythm	8	g	145	142
Flemensfirth	Red Rising	8	g		135
Flemensfirth	Robinsfirth	10	g		148
Flemensfirth	Sizing Codelco	10	g		154
Flemensfirth	Sumos Novios	11	g		146
Flemensfirth	The Last Samuri	11	g		151
Flemensfirth	Three Musketeers	9	g	132	138
Flemensfirth	Topofthegame	7	g		155
Flemensfirth	Waiting Patiently	8	g		170
Flemensfirth	Wandrin Star	8	g		136
Galileo	Housesofparliament	6	g	138	
Galileo	Monarch	6	g	138	
Galileo	Supasundae	9	g	163	
Galileo	Triplicate	6	g	142	
Germany	Faugheen	11	g	169	
Germany	Kaiser Black	8	g		147
Germany	Moon Over Germany	8	g		135
Germany	Samcro	7	g	162	

Sire	Horse	Age	Sex	Hurdles	Chase
				Official Ratings as of Jan 2019	
Gold Well	Ballyboker Breeze	11	g	132	139
Gold Well	Better Getalong	8	g	135	135
Gold Well	Daklondike	7	g		148
Gold Well	Forever Gold	12	g	124	137
Gold Well	Galvin	5	g	138	
Gold Well	General Principle	10	g	132	142
Gold Well	Good Man Pat	6	g	135	135
Gold Well	Palmers Hill	6	g	136	
Gold Well	The Unit	8	g		140
Great Pretender	Benie Des Dieux	8	m	151	147
Great Pretender	Claimantakinforgan	7	g		148
Great Pretender	Cobra De Mai	7	g		141
Great Pretender	Cracking Smart	7	g	150	
Great Pretender	Dortmund Park	6	g	147	
Great Pretender	Great Field	8	g		163
High Chaparral	Altior	9	g		175
High Chaparral	Cartwright	6	g	135	
High Chaparral	High Jinx	11	g	135	
High Chaparral	High Secret	8	g	139	
Kalanisi	Brain Power	8	g	158	153
Kalanisi	Kalashnikov	6	g	152	152
Kalanisi	Templehills	8	g		140
Kapgarde	A Plus Tard	5	g		140
Kapgarde	Beau Du Brizais	7	g		135
Kapgarde	Clan Des Obeaux	7	g		173
Kapgarde	Dolos	6	g		149
Kapgarde	Fixe Le Kap	7	g	137	
Kapgarde	French Crusader	6	g	135	
Kapgarde	Garde La Victoire	10	g		147
Kapgarde	Hammersly Lake	11	g		152
Kapgarde	Kapcorse	6	g	136	141
Kapgarde	Speredek	8	g		154
Kapgarde	Style De Garde	5	g	140	140
Kapgarde	Ultragold	11	g	137	147
Kayf Tara	A Great View	8	g	137	121
Kayf Tara	Atlanta Ablaze	8	m		143
Kayf Tara	Ballyandy	8	g	148	142
Kayf Tara	Ballyarthur	9	g		140
Kayf Tara	Ballybolley	10	g		136
Kayf Tara	Blaklion	10	g	147	156
Kayf Tara	Blu Cavalier	9	g	140	140
Kayf Tara	Carole's Destrier	11	g		138
Kayf Tara	Champagne At Tara	10	g		143
Kayf Tara	Debece	8	g	141	141
Kayf Tara	Edwulf	10	g		157
Kayf Tara	Final Nudge	10	g		135
Kayf Tara	Good Thyne Tara	9	m	147	
Kayf Tara	Javert	10	g		149
Kayf Tara	Just Cameron	12	g		139
Kayf Tara	Kayf Adventure	8	g		136

Sire	Horse	Age	Sex	Hurdles	Chase
				Official Ratings as of Jan 2019	
Kayf Tara	Master Tommytucker	8	g	143	143
Kayf Tara	Militarian	9	g		135
Kayf Tara	No Comment	8	g		138
Kayf Tara	Relentless Dreamer	10	g		139
Kayf Tara	Rons Dream	9	m	137	139
Kayf Tara	Secret Investor	7	g	145	145
Kayf Tara	*Special Tiara*	*12*	*g*		*152*
Kayf Tara	Tea For Two	10	g		149
Kayf Tara	Thistlecrack	11	g		170
Kayf Tara	War Sound	10	g		143
Kayf Tara	Yalltari	8	g		147
King's Theatre	*Bellshill*	*9*	*g*		*168*
King's Theatre	Born Survivor	8	g		142
King's Theatre	Caius Marcius	8	g	140	
King's Theatre	Champ	7	g	150	
King's Theatre	Cogry	10	g		141
King's Theatre	Diamond King	11	g	143	
King's Theatre	Double Treasure	8	g	140	
King's Theatre	Drinks Interval	7	m		145
King's Theatre	Happy Diva	8	m		142
King's Theatre	Jacks Last Hope	10	g	135	135
King's Theatre	King Of Realms	7	g		138
King's Theatre	Kings Lad	12	g	125	135
King's Theatre	King's Odyssey	10	g		137
King's Theatre	L'Ami Serge	9	g	159	154
King's Theatre	Master Dee	10	g		151
King's Theatre	Minellacelebration	9	g		139
King's Theatre	Monbeg Theatre	10	g	148	
King's Theatre	*Mortal*	*7*	*g*		*148*
King's Theatre	*Peregrine Run*	*9*	*g*		*151*
King's Theatre	Regal Encore	11	g	143	152
King's Theatre	Royal Regatta	11	g		140
King's Theatre	Royal Vacation	9	g		152
King's Theatre	Sumkindofking	8	g		137
King's Theatre	The Druids Nephew	12	g		137
King's Theatre	The New One	11	g	155	
King's Theatre	Theatre Guide	12	g		137
King's Theatre	William Henry	9	g	151	
Martaline	Agrapart	8	g	153	
Martaline	*Judgement Day*	*7*	*g*	*118*	*139*
Martaline	Malaya	5	m	137	
Martaline	Marracudja	8	g		139
Martaline	Ramses De Teillee	7	g	144	149
Martaline	Soul Emotion	6	g	152	
Martaline	Squouateur	8	g	135	138
Martaline	Terrefort	6	g		159
Martaline	Viconte Du Noyer	10	g		140
Martaline	Warthog	7	g	132	137
Martaline	We Have A Dream	5	g	152	
Midnight Legend	Aye Aye Charlie	7	g	140	

Sire	Horse	Age	Sex	Hurdles	Chase
				Official Ratings as of Jan 2019	
Midnight Legend	Crosspark	9	g	135	135
Midnight Legend	Dandy Dan	6	g		140
Midnight Legend	Larry	6	g		136
Midnight Legend	Mercian Prince	8	g		149
Midnight Legend	Midnight Shadow	6	g	158	
Midnight Legend	Midnight Shot	9	g		135
Midnight Legend	*Midnight Stroll*	*7*	*g*	*137*	
Midnight Legend	Midnight Tour	9	m	148	
Midnight Legend	Monbeg Legend	9	g		145
Midnight Legend	One For Billy	7	g		144
Midnight Legend	Shades Of Midnight	9	g	141	135
Midnight Legend	*Sizing John*	*9*	*g*		*168*
Midnight Legend	The Two Amigos	7	g		142
Midnight Legend	Uncle Alastair	7	g	135	135
Midnight Legend	Warriors Tale	10	g		153
Midnight Legend	Whataknight	10	g	139	
Milan	Barel Of Laughs	13	g		136
Milan	Beat That	11	g		141
Milan	Big River	9	g	140	140
Milan	Brewin'upastorm	6	g	146	
Milan	Brillare Momento	8	m	135	132
Milan	*Davids Charm*	*8*	*g*	*143*	
Milan	Double Shuffle	9	g		154
Milan	El Bandit	8	g		137
Milan	Hazel Hill	11	g		139
Milan	If The Cap Fits	7	g	155	
Milan	*Jezki*	*11*	*g*	*145*	
Milan	*Josies Orders*	*11*	*g*	*115*	*135*
Milan	*Mall Dini*	*9*	*g*	*139*	*148*
Milan	Max Ward	10	g		140
Milan	Milansbar	12	g		138
Milan	*Monalee*	*8*	*g*		*161*
Milan	*Monbeg Notorious*	*8*	*g*		*152*
Milan	*Moonshine Bay*	*6*	*g*	*129*	*138*
Milan	One For Arthur	10	g		154
Milan	*Ordinary World*	*9*	*g*		*152*
Milan	Polydora	7	g		140
Milan	Santini	7	g		153
Milan	Singlefarmpayment	9	g		147
Milan	Sizing Granite	11	g	129	146
Milan	Tommy Rapper	8	g	138	138
Montjeu	Eminent Poet	8	g	143	
Montjeu	*Tigris River*	*8*	*g*	*139*	
Network	Allysson Monterg	9	g		142
Network	*Ball D'Arc*	*8*	*g*	*140*	*155*
Network	*Blazer*	*8*	*g*	*143*	*141*
Network	*Bon Papa*	*8*	*g*		*144*
Network	*Borice*	*8*	*g*		*136*
Network	Catamaran Du Seuil	7	g		141
Network	*Delta Work*	*6*	*g*		*155*

				Official Ratings as of Jan 2019	
Sire	Horse	Age	Sex	Hurdles	Chase
Network	Le Richebourg	6	g	140	154
Old Vic	Ballyoptic	9	g		155
Old Vic	Folsom Blue	12	g	128	144
Old Vic	Grand Vision	13	g		136
Old Vic	Killultagh Vic	10	g	150	161
Old Vic	Knock House	10	g	136	136
Old Vic	Pendra	11	g		137
Old Vic	Southfield Vic	10	g		140
Oscar	Any Second Now	7	g		142
Oscar	Bags Groove	8	g		153
Oscar	Beggar's Wishes	8	g		142
Oscar	Boyhood	8	g	143	
Oscar	Buachaill Alainn	12	g		137
Oscar	Divine Spear	8	g		139
Oscar	Drovers Lane	7	g		150
Oscar	Enniscoffey Oscar	7	g	135	133
Oscar	God's Own	11	g		159
Oscar	Gunfleet	7	g	138	138
Oscar	Hearts Are Trumps	6	g	138	
Oscar	Kilbricken Storm	8	g	152	152
Oscar	Lake View Lad	9	g	150	155
Oscar	Louis' Vac Pouch	7	g	141	
Oscar	Minella Awards	8	g	149	149
Oscar	Not Many Left	6	g	140	
Oscar	Oscar Knight	10	g	130	135
Oscar	Ozzie The Oscar	8	g		156
Oscar	Paisley Park	7	g	168	
Oscar	Quick Grabim	7	g	148	
Oscar	Rather Be	8	g		148
Oscar	River Wylde	8	g		150
Oscar	Rocklander	10	g		140
Oscar	Rolling Maul	11	g	137	
Oscar	Sharp Response	8	g		140
Oscar	Splash Of Ginge	11	g	132	137
Poliglote	Capeland	7	g		143
Poliglote	Didero Vallis	6	g		136
Poliglote	Don Poli	10	g	145	157
Poliglote	Le Patriote	7	g	142	
Poliglote	Politologue	8	g		168
Poliglote	Sire Du Berlais	7	g	142	
Poliglote	Top Notch	8	g	154	162
Presenting	Ballycasey	12	g		147
Presenting	Ballyoisin	8	g	142	162
Presenting	Chef D'Equipe	7	g	129	135
Presenting	Childrens List	9	g		141
Presenting	Commodore Barry	6	g	138	
Presenting	Didtheyleaveuoutto	6	g	139	
Presenting	Drumcliff	8	g	139	144
Presenting	Duel At Dawn	9	g		135
Presenting	Duke Of Navan	11	g		144

Sire	Horse	Age	Sex	Hurdles	Chase
				Official Ratings as of Jan 2019	
Presenting	Festive Affair	11	g		139
Presenting	Give Me A Copper	9	g		145
Presenting	Gold Present	9	g		152
Presenting	Haymount	10	g		142
Presenting	Imperial Presence	8	g		150
Presenting	Joe Farrell	10	g		142
Presenting	More Buck's	9	g		139
Presenting	Mount Mews	8	g		137
Presenting	Movewiththetimes	8	g		140
Presenting	Mr Diablo	10	g	123	136
Presenting	Off You Go	6	g	143	
Presenting	Pleasant Company	11	g	128	152
Presenting	Present Man	9	g		150
Presenting	Rene's Girl	9	m		144
Presenting	Rogue Angel	11	g		136
Presenting	Slate House	7	g		139
Presenting	Snow Falcon	9	g		157
Presenting	Spider Web	8	g		135
Presenting	Stellar Notion	11	g		142
Presenting	Sugar Baron	9	g		135
Presenting	Top Gamble	11	g		143
Presenting	Up For Review	10	g		146
Presenting	Whatduhavtoget	7	m	127	135
Robin Des Champs	Blow By Blow	8	g		142
Robin Des Champs	Finawn Bawn	6	g	135	
Robin Des Champs	Geordie Des Champs	8	g		137
Robin Des Champs	Hell's Kitchen	8	g		155
Robin Des Champs	Listen Dear	9	m		143
Robin Des Champs	Pearl Royale	7	m		141
Robin Des Champs	Sizing Tennessee	11	g		164
Robin Des Champs	Tombstone	9	g	146	144
Robin Des Champs	Un Temps Pour Tout	10	g	148	155
Robin Des Champs	Way Back Then	8	g		135
Robin Des Champs	Woodland Opera	9	g	140	154
Saddler Maker	Alpha Des Obeaux	9	g		159
Saddler Maker	Apple's Jade	7	m	162	
Saddler Maker	Apple's Shakira	5	m	140	
Saddler Maker	Bouvreuil	8	g	138	142
Saddler Maker	Bristol De Mai	8	g		173
Saddler Maker	Cepage	7	g		147
Saddler Maker	Chef Des Obeaux	7	g	149	149
Saddler Maker	Defi Bleu	6	g	136	
Saddler Maker	Dinaria Des Obeaux	6	m	131	142
Saddler Maker	Janika	6	g		156
Saddler Maker	Label Des Obeaux	8	g	138	144
Saint Des Saints	Aux Ptits Soins	9	g	149	
Saint Des Saints	Connetable	7	g	135	129
Saint Des Saints	Kobrouk	8	g	143	148
Saint Des Saints	Le Rocher	9	g	141	142
Saint Des Saints	Magic Saint	5	g		142

122

				Official Ratings as of Jan 2019	
Sire	Horse	Age	Sex	Hurdles	Chase
Saint Des Saints	Protektorat	4	g	136	
Saint Des Saints	Romain De Senam	7	g		137
Saint Des Saints	Saint Calvados	6	g		158
Saint Des Saints	Wait For Me	9	g	136	
Shantou	Beware The Bear	9	g		152
Shantou	Bun Doran	8	g		148
Shantou	Measureofmydreams	11	g		137
Shantou	Sevarano	6	g	135	
Shantou	Shantou Flyer	9	g		151
Shantou	Shantou Village	9	g		142
Shantou	The Mighty Don	7	g	150	
Shantou	The Storyteller	8	g		158
Shantou	The Tourard Man	13	g	144	
Shantou	Tully East	9	g	136	146
Stowaway	Another Stowaway	7	g		136
Stowaway	Ballydine	9	g		140
Stowaway	Beakstown	6	g	142	
Stowaway	Champagne Classic	8	g	150	
Stowaway	Champagne Platinum	5	g	140	
Stowaway	Go Another One	7	g	135	
Stowaway	Gun Digger	7	g		139
Stowaway	Haul Away	6	g	135	
Stowaway	Highway One O One	7	g		145
Stowaway	Mind's Eye	7	g		138
Stowaway	Now Mcginty	8	g		142
Stowaway	On The Blind Side	7	g	149	149
Stowaway	Outlander	11	g		159
Stowaway	Paloma Blue	7	g		146
Stowaway	Posh Trish	6	m	145	
Stowaway	Pym	6	g	138	
Stowaway	Seddon	6	g	138	
Stowaway	The Worlds End	8	g		155
Stowaway	Tree Of Liberty	7	g		147
Stowaway	Us And Them	6	g		148
Vinnie Roe	Barney Dwan	9	g		140
Vinnie Roe	Bigbadjohn	10	g		137
Vinnie Roe	Cut The Corner	11	g	125	138
Vinnie Roe	De Dollar Man	8	g	137	137
Vinnie Roe	De Name Escapes Me	9	g	143	132
Vinnie Roe	First Assignment	6	g	142	
Vinnie Roe	Irish Roe	8	m	138	
Vinnie Roe	Vinndication	6	g		151
Voix Du Nord	Azzerti	7	g		137
Voix Du Nord	Bachasson	8	g	147	159
Voix Du Nord	Defi Du Seuil	6	g		151
Voix Du Nord	Destrier	6	g	134	142
Voix Du Nord	Djingle	6	g	140	135
Voix Du Nord	Duca De Thaix	6	g		151
Voix Du Nord	Espoir D'Allen	5	g	159	
Voix Du Nord	Kemboy	7	g		167

Sire	Horse	Age	Sex	Hurdles	Chase
				Official Ratings as of Jan 2019	
Voix Du Nord	Vibrato Valtat	10	g		137
Voix Du Nord	*Vieux Morvan*	*10*	*g*	*128*	*141*
Voix Du Nord	Voix D'Eau	9	g		139
Voix Du Nord	*Voix Du Reve*	*7*	*g*	*145*	*151*
Westerner	*Champagne West*	*11*	*g*		*147*
Westerner	Crucial Role	7	g		145
Westerner	Keeper Hill	8	g	144	
Westerner	Lough Derg Spirit	7	g		135
Westerner	*Magnium*	*6*	*g*	*135*	
Westerner	Rocky's Treasure	8	g		149
Westerner	Skipthecuddles	8	g		139
Westerner	*Solomn Grundy*	*9*	*g*		*136*
Westerner	The Linksman	7	g	135	135
Westerner	Theo	9	g		139
Westerner	*Three Stars*	*9*	*g*		*138*
Westerner	*Total Recall*	*10*	*g*	*146*	*155*
Westerner	Truckers Lodge	7	g	142	
Westerner	Wakanda	10	g	134	150
Westerner	West Approach	9	g	154	138
Westerner	Westend Story	8	g	135	135
Westerner	Western Ryder	7	g	150	
Westerner	*Westerner Point*	*10*	*g*	*116*	*140*
Westerner	Wild West Wind	10	g		138
Winged Love	Baywing	10	g		147
Winged Love	*Bless The Wings*	*14*	*g*		*137*
Winged Love	*Joey Sasa*	*10*	*g*	*145*	
Winged Love	Josses Hill	11	g		148
Winged Love	Knight Of Noir	10	g	135	
Winged Love	Lovenormoney	8	g	140	135
Winged Love	Perfect Candidate	12	g		140
Winged Love	Rock Gone	11	g		135
Winged Love	Thomas Patrick	7	g		145
Yeats	Brave Eagle	7	g	144	144
Yeats	Burbank	7	g		139
Yeats	De Rasher Counter	7	g		139
Yeats	Psychedelic Rock	8	g	137	137
Yeats	Reikers Island	6	g		140
Yeats	*Shattered Love*	*8*	*m*		*155*
Yeats	*Some Neck*	*8*	*g*		*145*
Yeats	*The West's Awake*	*8*	*g*		*141*
Yeats	Thomas Campbell	7	g	147	147
Yeats	Who's My Jockey	6	g	136	
Yeats	Younevercall	8	g	155	